Security Cyberspace: International and Asian Perspectives

Security Cyberspace
International and Asian Perspectives

S.K. Singh

PRASHANT PUBLISHING HOUSE
DELHI-110094

Published by :
Prashant Publishing House
C-34, 28 Foota Road, Gali-3,
West Karwal Nagar, Delhi-110094
Phone : 011-22963970, Mob. : 9810396373
e-mail.: prashantpublishinghouse@gmail.com

Security Cyberspace: International and Asian Perspectives

First Published 2017

ISBN 978-93-80565-8-66

PRINTED IN INDIA
Published by Mr. R.K. Jha M/s Prashant Publishing House and Published at H.S. Offset House Press, Delhi.

Contents

Preface

Cyberspace is a domain characterized by the use of electronics and the electromagnetic spectrum to store, modify, and exchange data via networked systems and associated physical infrastructures. In effect, cyberspace can be thought of as the interconnection of human beings through computers and telecommunication, without regard to physical geography.

The cyber and space domains have been growing in significance in recent decades, with space now regarded as the fourth domain of warfare and cyber as the fifth. Initially conceived for research collaboration between universities and government think tanks in the 1960s before undergoing explosive growth for mainstream commerce from the 1990s onwards, the internet has come to pervade nearly all aspects of modern society. This has made it an increasingly attractive target for cyber attack, with more than a dozen states thought to possess advanced cyberwarfare capabilities at present.

Preparing against the threat of cyber-terrorism requires the same level of planning and preparation to survive an economic or financial crisis. One of the biggest concerns that organizations have when protecting against an emerging threat is the cost associated with it. In fact, the costs associated with countering cyber-terrorism are not new costs at all. Your existing information security strategy need only be tweaked and adapted to be well-prepared.

Although many of the intelligence methodologies and principles remain the same, new ways of thinking appropriate to the cyber-domain are essential. The lack of borders in cyber-space is a critical difference from the more familiar domains of intelligence. Indeed, geography and political borders often aided traditional military intelligence analysis-it is a simple thing to develop threat scenarios if the potential enemy can only use certain terrain or sea lines of communication and then, only at certain times of the year-while simple factors of physics such as time and distance also provided opportunities for warning. Within the Internet, however, these limiting factors are absent, (although other limiting factors, such as geometry of network connectivity, might exist in a form useful to be incorporated into intelligence analysis), contributing to what can appear to be "instantaneous threats".

Terrorists have moved into cyberspace to facilitate traditional forms of terrorism such as bombings. They use the Internet to communicate, coordinate events, and advance their agenda. While such activity does not constitute cyberterrorism in the strict sense, it does show that terrorists have some competency using the new information technologies. All the matter is just compiled and edited in nature. Taken from the various sources which are in public domain.

This book fulfills the long felt necessity of a text dealing with concepts of this subject. It can also prove to be a worthy companion and guide for the students, users and researchers.

—*Editor*

1

An Introduction to Cyberspace

The Internet is a cheap, fast means of international communication of text, sound or image. In other words, an information resource without political or content boundaries; limited only by the extent to which the information providers are willing to disclose their materials and the fruits of their own writing and research. In the present day, web sites displaying information of all kinds are proliferating. These sites are established and controlled by Internet Service Providers (ISPs) or, sometimes, by the company's information technology department.

These sites can be accessed through suitable search engines, which will trace and display information to suit the requirements of the searcher. However, not many of the companies are aware of the risks attached with the hosting of a Web site. Who would be held liable, for instance, if an employee clandestinely posts racist, sexist, or defamatory allegations about a competitor on the company's official web site?

It is to be remembered that a number of features unique to the internet distinguishes it from any other medium. These features have led to the current re-examination of existing laws relating to defamation, to allow for their possible evolution and ultimately their application in cyberspace. A key feature of the internet is its highly interactive nature. The ease with which users of the internet can access information and communicate with each other has engendered in its users a false sense of freedom in their communications. Accessibility is another feature of the internet, which distinguishes it from traditional print or broadcast media. The relatively low cost of connecting to the internet and even of establishing one's own website means that the opportunity for defamation has increased exponentially. Now, on the internet everyone can be a publisher and can be sued as a publisher.

Another key feature of the internet is that users do not have to reveal their true identity in order to send e-mail or post messages on bulletin boards.

Users are able to communicate and make such postings anonymously or under assumed names. This feature, coupled with the ability to access the internet in privacy and seclusion of one's own home or office and the interactive, responsive nature of communications on the internet, has resulted in users being far less inhibited about the contents of their messages resulting in cyber space becoming excessively prone to defamation.

Defamation can be understood as the intentional infringement of another person's right to his good name. It is the wrongful and intentional publication of words or behaviour concerning another person, which has the effect of injuring that person's status, good name, or reputation in society. Libel is written defamation and slander is oral defamation. The primary difference is that in libel, damages are presumed, whereas in slander actions, unless the slander falls into a certain category, called slander per se, the plaintiff must prove actual or quantifiable damages.

A person's good name can only be damaged if maligning statements are made to someone other than that person; that is, the defamatory statement must be disclosed to a third person, thereby satisfying the requirement of publication. When determining whether or not defamation has taken place, the only issue to consider is whether a person of ordinary intelligence in society would believe that the words would indeed injure the person's reputation.

Thus the law of defamation places a heavy burden on the defendant. All that a plaintiff has to prove, in a defamation action, is the publication of defamatory matter. The onus then lies on the defendant to prove innocence. Once again, most people are unaware of this burden.

In essence, the law on defamation attempts to create a workable balance between two equally important human rights: The right to an unimpaired reputation and the right to freedom of expression. In a cyber society, both these interests are increasingly important. Protection of reputation is arguably even more important in a highly technological society, since one may not even encounter an individual or organization other than through the medium of the internet.

The elements of a defamation action can be summarized as follows:

- # The plaintiff must prove publication of the defamatory statement;
- # The plaintiff must prove that the defamation refers to the plaintiff; and
- # The plaintiff must prove that the statement is defamatory.

Upon proof of publication, the law makes several presumptions in favour of the plaintiff:

- # That the statement is false;
- # That it was published with malice; and
- # That in the case of libel or slander per se, the plaintiff has suffered damage.

Defences that can be raised against such a defamation action are as follows:

- # Truth.
- # Fair comment: The defendant is allowed to comment on facts truly stated, as long as the comment is fair and the defendant is not motivated by actual malice.
- # Privilege: On certain occasions, the courts have held that policy and convenience require that a person should be free from responsibility for the publication of

defamatory words. These occasions constitute privileges. Privilege may be absolute, such as statements in the House of Commons or the Courts. It may be qualified, in that it may be lost if the publication is unnecessarily wide or made with malice.

Innocent dissemination: This last defence is potentially very important in cyber libel.

If a defendant proves that his statements were true and in public interest, then his conduct is regarded as lawful. In addition, if the defendant can show that he had no intention to defame (the plaintiff), then he could avoid liability.

This paper seeks to throw light on the law relating to cyber defamation and to suggest a legal framework to handle such situations, which is inevitable, especially in the light of the present IT boom in India.

CYBER DEFAMATION: A SOCIO-ECONOMIC OFFENCE

Cyber law encompasses cyber crimes, electronic commerce, freedom of expression, intellectual property rights, jurisdiction issues and choice of law, and privacy rights. Cyber crimes involve activities like credit card fraud, unauthorized access to computer systems, child pornography, software piracy and cyber stalking. Freedom of expression includes defamation, obscenity issues and censorship. Jurisdiction issues focuses on who makes and enforces the rules governing cyber space.

The definition of what constitutes a crime in cyber space is still being developed. In the past, the states and federal government defined cyber crime activities to include the destruction or theft of computer data and programs. More recently the definition has expanded to include activities such as forgery, illegal gambling, cyber stalking, cyber defamation etc.

There are several areas on the internet where there is a real risk of liability for defamation. The fact that a user is "alone" with his computer and distanced from other users creates a sense of intimacy. There is no spoken/telephonic conversation or dictated correspondence that would normally instill some caution. In addition, the notion that the internet is a "free-for-all" cyberspace where there are no limits or boundaries results in a user's sense of social norms and propriety generally getting blurred.

The Web results in an instant global publication of information at a very low cost. Information, which would not normally have been revealed prior to the dawning of the internet, can now be unearthed by practically anyone. Intranets are intended to be exclusively used by a company. However, information from an intranet can be easily downloaded and forwarded by e-mail or otherwise to third parties. Information posted to a bulletin board can be accessed by anyone. This means that anyone can place defamatory allegations on the bulletin board. E-mail users generally tend to treat their correspondence as a kind of conversation rather than a written interaction. Users forget that e-mails are stored and can be retrieved as hard copies and that their contents then cannot be disputed. One message can be circulated to literally hundreds of people. As a defamatory allegation need only be disclosed to one person for publication to be proved, every time e-mail is forwarded to another person, it is published again and an additional cause of action for defamation arises.

The scope of every firm having a cyber presence to liability for defamation is global. Internet sites can be accessed in most countries throughout the world; huge amounts of data can be transmitted simultaneously to several different destinations; and e-mail can be forwarded to an indefinite number of recipients without the original author having any control over the transmission.

While a legal action based on defamation is usually aimed at stopping the defamatory allegations, the harm in most cases has already been done. Consequently, the most important relief claimed in a defamatory action is damages. The amount of damages granted will depend on the nature of the defamation sought and the extent of publication.

Furthermore, a defamation claim can be instituted in any jurisdiction in which a cause of action arises. In theory then, a potential defendant to a defamation suit could be sued in respect of a particular defamatory statement in a number of different countries with which it has no connection under any number of different laws with which it is totally unfamiliar. Indeed, a potential plaintiff can choose to litigate in whichever country has the most favourable laws. Theoretically, every time a third party accesses a defamatory posting on the Internet, publication has occurred.

The global nature of the Internet also raises some interesting procedural questions for the libel lawyer. In traditional libel law there are three different types of defamatory statements:

(i) The first is a statement that is defamatory on its face and which is obviously defamatory.

(ii) The second is a statement, which contains false innuendo. False innuendo is a defamatory statement that has an inferential meaning, therefore only persons with the necessary contextual knowledge appreciate that the statement is defamatory. Since statements on the internet are published globally, their inferential meanings may vary depending on the geographic or cultural location of the reader or the newsgroups or the Usenet group involved.

(iii) The third category is legal innuendo. While not defamatory on their face, these statements are defamatory when viewed together with extrinsic circumstances. Once again, contextual knowledge may render a statement defamatory in one jurisdiction but not in another.

Cyber defamation need not necessarily be directed against an individual victim, but it could be harmful to the whole society. No doubt, at times, it could be directed against an individual ('victim'), but the criminal act is potentially capable of harming a large number of persons and that is the principal object behind punishing it.

In short it is an offence, which affects the health or material welfare of the community as a whole and not merely of the individual victim. Similarly it is also an offence, which affects the country's economy and not merely the wealth of an individual victim, since defamation of a corporate house could even adversely affect its share value.

Two very significant aspects of such a social and economic offence are:

(i) the gravity of the harm caused to society; and

(ii) the nature of the offence.

The gravity of the harm is not easily apparent, but is nevertheless, undeniable. The nature of the offence is peculiar, in the sense that they are planned and executed in secrecy by shrewd and dexterous persons with sophisticated means. The public welfare is gravity affected; but detection is unusually difficult.

Cases of cyber defamation do not fit neatly in the accepted categories of crimes. They represent harm of greater magnitude than the traditional crimes and of a nature different from them. Unlike the traditional crimes, they are not in the shape of positive aggressions or invasions. They may not result in direct or immediate injury; nevertheless, they create a danger, which the law must seek to minimise. Hence if legislation applicable to such offences, as a matter of policy, departs from legislation applicable to ordinary crimes in respect of the traditional requirements as to mens rea and the other substantive matters as well as on points of procedure, the departure would be justified.

Position in Other Countries

Defamation laws vary from country to country and in countries such as the Canada, Australia and the United States, it can vary from province to province and state to state. Therefore, plaintiffs may have the luxury of "forum shopping" or choosing the jurisdiction with the laws most favourable to him/her.

Position in US

In the United States, about 75% of defamation lawsuits are filed in state courts, and the remaining 25% in federal courts. A comprehensive discussion of what is and is not libel or slander is difficult, because each state's definition differs. Some states lump slander and libel together into the same set of laws. Some states have criminal libel laws on the books, though these are old laws, which are infrequently prosecuted. Most defendants in libel lawsuits are newspapers, which are involved in about twice as many lawsuits as are TV stations. Most plaintiffs are corporations, business people, entertainers and other public figures, and inmates. Most states do not allow defamation lawsuits to be filed if the allegedly defamed person is already deceased. None of the states allow the plaintiff to be a group of people.

In the various states, whether by case law or actual legislation, there are generally several "privileges" that can get a libel case dismissed without proceeding to trial. These include the allegedly defamatory statement being one of opinion rather than fact; or being "fair comment and criticism", as it is important to society that everyone be able to comment on matters of public interest. If a defamation lawsuit actually gets to trial, truth is an affirmative defense. Further, if the allegedly defamatory statement is not actually capable of being defamatory, i.e., an insulting statement that does not harm someone's reputation is prima facie not libelous.

New York Times Company v. Sullivan was a U.S. Supreme Court case which established the actual malice standard before press reports could be considered to be defamation and libel; and hence allowed free reporting of the civil rights campaigns in the southern United States. It is one of the key decisions supporting the freedom of the press. The actual malice standard requires that the publisher knows the statement is false or acts in reckless disregard of the truth.

The decision established that for a plaintiff to win a libel ruling against a newspaper, "actual malice" or "reckless negligence" must be proved on the part of the paper if the statement in question is about a public official or public figure. In the case of a private figure, the plaintiff must merely prove negligence.

Prior to the enactment of the Telecommunications Act of 1996, the position in US with regard to cyber defamation was such that the Courts applied the common law definition of "publisher," which held liable anyone who exercised a substantial degree of editorial control over the distributed product. This definition distinguished between a distributor, such as a newsstand or a library, and a publisher, such as a newspaper or book author. Distributors were not to be held liable for the information they disseminated, while those who reviewed content before publication would be held liable. Courts generally analyzed ISP liability under the same standards applied to newspapers and other media.

Data Security

Data security is the means of ensuring that data is kept safe from corruption and that access to it is suitably controlled. Thus data security helps to ensure privacy. It also helps in protecting personal data.

CYBERSPACE AT A GLANCE

For the most part, the Internet is built upon national and international telecommunications infrastructures, including the landlines of most public phone systems and wireless, and satellite communications. Beyond the Internet, these telecommunications infrastructures tend to be highly dependent on computing technology. Thus, by our definition, they are part of cyberspace. There are currently about 1.3 billion Internet users worldwide. The Internet now comes to ground in over 200 "countries" (Top-Level Domains, i.e. the letters which follow the dot after the domain name).

This enormous growth has been achieved since the early 90s. The only thing growing faster than the Internet is cellular telephony, with about three billion phones in use, to which 1.6 million users are added every day. The fact that soon cellular telephones will be a platform for the Internet means that at least a billion new users will have access to this resource, and this expansion will mostly be in developing countries.

(In)Security (Internet Security) at a Glance

The architecture, design, and practice of the Internet emphasize *access* (ease of use, low cost, universality). It has almost never considered security as a primary or important factor. It is an unfortunate result of the history of the way the Internet was developed that the protocols used by the Internet today are derived from those that were established in the early days of the ARPANet, where there were only a few wellrespected researchers using the infrastructure, and they were trusted to do no harm. Consequently, security considerations were not built in to the Internet. All cybersecurity measures taken today to protect the Internet are add-on measures that do not remedy the underlying security deficiencies.

The situation we have as a result is that current technology asymmetrically favors the attackers; it provides them great "nonlinear leverage", and attackers get their innovations into practice more quickly and effectively than defenders. If we make a comparison between cyber attacks and modern warfare, we would say that it is an asymmetrical conflict. While the state, because of its capacity, has a huge technological advantage over terrorists, the problem is that the kinds of nonlinearities associated with what terrorists do in cyberspace give leverage to those with relatively little technical capability. What has always been thought of as one of the great advantages of the networks can also threaten them: They give a small number of relatively weak people extensive access to a lot of information, each other, potential recruits and sympathizers, and prospective targets. There is also a negative aspect of tightening access against terrorists or other malicious users more generally because it would compromise access and privacy for many, many more "good" users.

The functionality of the Internet ranges greatly. Of particular concern for those aware of the threat of terrorism is the fact that SCADA (Supervisory Control and Data Acquisition) systems now more commonly use the Internet to transmit data and control instructions, rather than the dedicated networks that had been used before. Additionally, very few of the "cyber" parts of the critical infrastructures were designed or implemented with security as much of a consideration, if it was considered at all. Most are riddled with vulnerabilities, which are defined as weaknesses that can be exploited through either hostile attacks or accidents. It would be almost impossible to create "patches" to protect programs from malicious people who seek to find and exploit these vulnerabilities. Another problem to recognize is that Internet defense pushes the burden outward to the end user organizations; most of these find it difficult, and often increasingly difficult, to defend themselves.

In particular, most of the over two hundred connected countries have little or no national cybersecurity capabilities.

International Threats Arising from Globalization

One area of concern that extends broadly across all of the stages of defense is that globalization creates new populations of "insiders"—people who have authorized access with the potential for abuse that can cause great harm. Insiders still probably account for a majority of successful penetrations for criminal purposes. The problem is complicated by changes in organizational relations and technical architectures that make "inside" and "outside" more difficult even to define. The possibility that a terrorist or a terrorist sympathizer might gain employment that would enable him or her to conduct a devastating attack or to provide critical information or access to others cannot be discounted or ignored.

The two most general ways of dealing with infiltration are through deep preemployment investigations, something that most non-government entities are neither capable of doing nor permitted to do in many countries, and through stronger forms of containment and compartmentalization of access within an organization. Globalization has meant that the Internet is now less secure, with vulnerabilities resulting from new systems "intimacies". Transfer of information now takes place in unprecedented transnational contexts.

A particular problem for those who want to control or police the Internet is the spread and ownership of, and access to, transnational transportation infrastructures. Much of the day to day running is outsourced, and offshoring (outsourcing to foreign entities) means that any attempts to control the Internet require international cooperation.

Terrorists in Cyberspace

What do we know or anticipate that terrorists want to do in cyberspace? I believe the answers to this question fall into three categories:

1. Terrorists want to support their activities and infrastructure, but not directly through an attack, using the Internet.
2. They may want explicitly to attack parts of the cyber infrastructure.
3. They may use cyberspace as a means of attacking other targets. These might include compromising transportation or other supervisory control systems to cause disasters resulting in extensive consternation and costing many lives.

It is certain that terrorists and their supporters have been engaging in extensive activities under category 1, and that they will continue to do so. This would cover communications, including encrypted communications with each other; recruiting and "advertising" (for example, via Web sites); and financial transactions such as money transfers and laundering. Training manuals for terrorists, including information about bomb-making and avoiding detection, are freely available. Terrorists are also likely to be scouring cyberspace for information on potential targets and on weapons of mass destruction.

As far as we can tell, terrorists have not been responsible for any of the major attacks or accidents that have occurred in recent years under categories 2 or 3. So much has been written about such possibilities—and they have had some prominence in the media—that it is inconceivable that terrorists are not aware of them. So far, for reasons we can only speculate about, they do not seem to have chosen to pursue these possibilities with vigor and effect, or perhaps they have tried and failed.

Systems and Networks at Risk

Should an attack be launched against systems and networks, the following would be at risk:

1. The Internet.
2. Embedded/real-time computing (e.g. avionics systems for air traffic control, SCADA systems used by the amenities, routing for shipping containers, and process control for toxic chemical production, switching of telecommunications, bank teller machines, floodgates).
3. Dedicated computing devices (e.g. desktop computers).

Each has a different role, and may be the subject of different kinds of attack. Terrorists might attack the Internet physically or "through the wires", the latter being potentially more destructive. One type of attack that we see is directed against Internet operations. Such attacks are often based on self-replicating programs (worms and viruses) that are transmitted from system to system, consuming prodigious amounts of router processing time and network channel bandwidth. In recent years, some of these worms and viruses have been transmitted without explicitly destructive payloads and yet have been able to disrupt key Internet backbone subnetworks for several days.

Another kind of attack on Internet operations seeks to corrupt the routing tables that determine how a packet should travel through the Internet. In both cases, the intent of the attack is to reduce the normally expected functionality of the Internet for some significant portion of its users—that is, a denial-of-service attack in intent, although not one necessarily based on flooding traffic.

An attacker might also target the Internet's Domain Name System (DNS), which translates domain names (e.g. "example.com") to specific Internet Protocol (IP) addresses (e.g.

123.231.0.67) denoting specific Internet nodes. A relatively small number of "root name servers" underpins the DNS. Although the DNS is designed to provide redundancy in case of accidental failure, it has some vulnerability to an attack that might target all name servers simultaneously. Although Internet operations would not halt instantly, an increasing number of sites would, over a period of time measured in hours to days, become inaccessible without root name servers to provide authoritative translation information. Physical replacement of damaged servers would be achievable in a matter of days, but changing the IP addresses of the root name servers would be more complicated.

Recommendations: Focus on Terrorists

It is only a matter of time before cyber terror attacks, at present largely a threat, become a reality. Both government and private sector need to focus on preparations. There are a number of measures that must be taken. Build Much Stronger Defenses, More Integrated Emergency Preparedness and Response Systems, and Improve the Processes for Their Use.

The first order of business is to provide indications and warnings that an attack is taking place. This is a difficult area, and intrusion detection has become a particularly active area in research and development. Not surprisingly, detection and notification are more difficult and prone to false positives during the early stages of an attack, before significant damage has been done.

To prevent penetration of the system at risk from the outside, we try to erect barriers and otherwise harden it. Both cyber and physical approaches are necessary. Passwords are the oldest, and still most widely used, cybertechnique. More recent and somewhat widely used techniques are firewalls and proxy servers. Like all forms of cyberdefense, these can be defeated, although it is possible to make them real barriers against many attempted attacks. Physical protection needs to consider several forms of penetration or attempts to isolate the system. These include attacks on electronics using electromagnetic pulses, and attempts to cut cable endings. A wide variety of forms of physical protection are possible, ranging from fences to biometrics.

In the event of an attack there needs to be a system for incident management, mitigating an attack, and damage limitation. A next line of defense is internal compartmentalization and containment. In this instance, the goals are to limit penetration and damage, protect surviving assets, and protect and gather information to help with recovery and response after the attack. Approaches include creating internal physical barriers and cyberbarriers through compartmentalization and need-to-know access controls, intrusion tolerance schemes, setting up decoys, maintaining protected redundancies, and hiding assets. All have both static (pre-positioned and unchanging during the attack) and dynamic variants.

Another approach is automatic or partial shutdown and reallocation. A system that senses it is under attack would start erecting internal barriers that would not be tolerable during normal operations, in an attempt to isolate those parts of the system that had been compromised. It would also involve load-shedding strategies to reallocate surviving capabilities to the most important functions required by the organization. All of this amounts to various forms of real-time reassignment and reconfiguration under rapid degradation. Particular attention needs to be given to preserving and collecting information during an attack.

This is done most easily if the attack has a clear and precise starting time and backups are made regularly, or if the organization maintains a redundant "shadow" system. More insidious attacks that build up slowly present a much more difficult problem in identifying a state where the system is free from inserted malicious code. It is also important to have strong audit functions to identify when an attack starts and to collect information that might assist in the identification and apprehension of the attacker and help the organization better defend itself against similar attacks in the future.

Organizations should establish security policies and plans for defending against attacks. Special attention should be given to preventing and dealing with insider attacks. Staff should know who to call for help. It might be a good idea to test the plan through the use of exercises. However, most organizations avoid live "fire drills" because they can be expensive, disruptive, and risky in their own right. Many information systems are delicate and their owners are afraid something will go wrong, resulting in the selfinflicted equivalent of a serious attack.

Improve the security of systems that control physical processes (e.g., SCADA). From the standpoint of counter terrorism, we would imagine that attacking physical targets via control and management systems would result in the kind of mass casualties, damage, fear, and loss of confidence that terrorists favor. Many of these systems are vulnerable to tampering with control signals, especially by insiders.

Increasing the security for DC/SCADA systems poses particularly difficult problems. These systems are often small and self-contained, and have constrained power needs (including backup). Security may not readily fit with the space, real-time, or power requirements. Security measures could also reduce performance or be problematic in the synchronization of other more extensive processes. Additionally, most of these systems are in the private or mixed sectors (for example, airports). Their owners and operators may not have sufficient resources to secure them more effectively. National governments that are in positions to do so should give priority to protecting the small percentage of cyberspace users who are private owners and operators of digital control and management systems. This would include providing them with various forms of assistance and technology. Particular attention should be given to transportation systems because for decades they have been highly favored by terrorists both as targets and as the means of delivering an attack.

This kind of defensive work is essentially "target hardening". This can be defined as the use of various technologies and products and procedures (for example, those governing outside dial-in or reconstitution and recovery) to protect the information technology (IT) assets owned or operated by an individual or organization.

It is important to notice that many of these recommendations would have more general value than just vs. terrorists (e.g., they would help against accidents, natural disasters, serious crime, and non-terrorist forms of conflict). However, as defense does not involve serious risk or impose a penalty on the attacker, there is also the need to develop deterrents. For this we need laws:

Design and Implement a Stronger "System of Justice", Especially Its International Dimensions

International cooperation should concentrate on effective intelligence operations. This is an area where a considerable amount of success could be expected, which would create the atmosphere for a long-term international legal framework.

The problems of jurisdiction are greatly compounded by the easy transnational access provided by many components of cyberspace, most notably the Internet. What may be perceived as serious in one country whose cyberinfrastructure may be used as part of a terrorist action may not even make the legal radar screen of others that are part of an attack that crosses multiple sovereign physical jurisdictions. Most countries have given little or no thought to making serious crimes of the various forms of cyberattack, and "without law there is no sin". Seeking widely adopted national laws at least criminalizing attacks against or using the networks is an important objective. Legislating against the support functions to which terrorists put the Internet would be a more distant prospect. The enforcement and prosecution of these laws are also critical elements of cybersecurity.

Given the many technical and evidentiary problems of identifying cybercriminals and prosecuting them, nobody has any delusion that such laws would end criminal or terrorist activities in cyberspace. Nonetheless, they might reduce the enormous amount of malicious "noise" in cyberspace, and this would help make it easier to more readily identify more serious activities. They would also provide a necessary basis for encouraging people to report malicious cyberactivities, and for international cooperation in dealing with several kinds of problem.

Recommendations: CIIP at Every Stage

Security must become a criterion for any system used for CII from the design stage onwards. The priorities in design have been access and throughput. Added security is not just costly; it may also result in reduced efficiency and functionality. Furthermore, so far there does not seem to be much incentive for people to design or redesign systems to be much more secure. There has been much speculation that the design or redesign of systems will occur only in the aftermath of a "digital Pearl Harbor" or in response to the forces of legal liability or insurance necessities and standards. Even better, security should be a factor to be considered over the entire life cycle of such systems. Organizations should build cadres of capable defenders, and contingency plans (including internationally) for crisis and emergency conditions need to be in place. There could be national-level CERTs or CSIRTs (Cybersecurity Incident Response Teams).

A postdesign and implementation variant is to try to prevent attacks by finding and fixing vulnerabilities before an attacker can try to exploit them. Red teams, test beds, or simulations may be used to do this. Another approach, at least to the often-serious threat of possible insider attacks, is to more thoroughly screen employees with potentially sensitive access. It is clear that for a number of these measures operational contingencies among owners and operators and their governments need to be established.

PATROLLING NATIONAL BORDERS IN CYBER SPACE

Online, volunteer cyber-surveillance efforts have also been used to aid in the production of more traditional forms of security, such as defending territorial integrity by patrolling national borders. Since, 9/11, the debate over immigration from the global South has been increasingly linked to the "War on Terror." Part of this linkage can be found in the actions and discourse of what are collectively called "Minutemen" groups. Minutemen groups are most known for their use of physical presence on the U.S.-Mexico border, especially in 2005, a presence spurred by organisers who wanted to draw attention to what they perceived to be the government's lack of intervention in illegal immigration.

Although the Minutemen are not a government agency, their border-watching efforts were meant to supplement—and not replace —the physical intervention of the U.S., Border Patrol; thus the Minutemen appropriated part of the state's power of surveillance without impinging on the state's monopoly on the use of force. In addition, Minutemen groups have also deployed "Cyber Minutemen," extending surveillance onto the Web. Using a mix of fibre-optic fencing, Web cameras, motion detectors, infrared sensors, and even aircraft, various Minutemen groups have posted images and live streams to a variety of Web sites.

This use of relatively inexpensive surveillance and Web technology is touted by Cyber Minutemen as a viable, high-tech, modern way for citizens to succeed where the state has ostensibly failed in stemming the flow of immigrants across the Mexican border. Jim Wood, founder of the nowdefunct Border Fence Project, argues that citizen groups are more efficient and cost-effective than state efforts to secure the border. "The bottom line is this," he argues in a letter to supporters, "Despite bureaucratic refusals, delays and boondoggles, we civilians on the border can build a national Border Fence without them, repairing the old and erecting the new... Therefore, we as American citizens and patriots must stand up and do this ourselves."

Part of the efficiency arises from the use of distributed volunteers across the Web; volunteers from as far away as Australia have reportedly spotted illegal border crossings. In this case, the convergence of state aims and privately deployed technologies echoes previous, new media "crowdsourcing" efforts such as Wikipedia and the NASA Clickworkers project. As in the other convergence security cases, Cyber Minutemen have enjoyed some support from the state, as well as from Internet entrepreneurs. Texas governor Rick Perry, the Texas Border Sheriff's Coalition, and private landowners joined Internet company BlueServo in a "publicprivate partnership" to distribute live feeds of the border to Web volunteers.

This public-private partnership is a for-profit endeavor. BlueServo claims, "Because www.BlueServo.net is an internet social network, in the future, BlueServo anticipates that high volume of traffic to its web site will generate advertising revenue to defray the operations cost of the Virtual Community Watch to the Texas Border Sheriff's Coalition." Thus, in keeping with convergence media business practices, BlueServo intends to meld the Cyber Minutemen desire to secure the border with the political economy of attention found in other Web 2.0 sites such as Facebook and YouTube. This entrepreneurial form of convergence border security has also been proposed by the Heritage Foundation.

However, as with other convergence security groups, the Minutemen have had ambivalent, ambiguous, and tense relationships with the state. Although Texas Governor Perry and California Governor Arnold Schwarzenegger publicly endorsed the movement, George W. Bush referred to them as "vigilantes". The Department of Homeland Security rejected a proposal to formally integrate volunteer citizen patrols into the Border Patrol.

For their part, the Minutemen groups have not sought integration with the state. Rather, they have largely called for an increased police or military presence at the border; they tend to frame their activity as drawing attention to the perceived problem of illegal immigration, drug trafficking, and terrorism. In the main, the Minuteman movement has been strict with members about the use of violence; thus the Minutemen have been careful not to infringe on the state's monopoly on violence for fear of political and legal repercussions.

A large Minuteman group, the Minutemen Civil Defence Corps (MCDC), disbanded in 2010 not long after a leader in that organisation called for a "locked and loaded"—i.e., publicly armed—patrol of the border. The "locked and loaded" muster was intended as a show of arms rather than an explicit call to violence. However, the proposed muster led to an enthusiastic response among members that the MCDC leadership interpreted as potentially violent, stoking fears within the organisation that the MCDC would not be able to prevent members from using weapons on alleged illegal border crossers, thus echoing Bush's earlier fears of vigilantism. The leaders of the MCDC did not want to cross the border between civil society groups and state-sponsored military groups.

Ultimately, in the case of the Minutemen, their proposed virtual surveillance of the border was accepted by the state far easier than their proposed, *embodied* patrol of the border. While the MCDC disbanded in light of the potential use of force by members, BlueServo and its Web camera network remains active to this day. State officials who decry potential vigilantism at the border tend to ignore or tolerate the use of Web-based surveillance. Most state officials who want increased border security eschew Minutemen-style groups and opt instead for state-sanctioned groups such as the U.S., Border Patrol, the National Guard, or new bureaucratic formations such as the Department of Homeland Security.

ASYMMETRIC THREATS IN THE CYBER AND SPACE DOMAINS

The cyber and space fields are both faced with asymmetric threats. This contributes to the increasingly blurred line between 'offensive' and 'defensive' activities in cyber and space. The EU submission describes how cyber and space have 'asymmetric vulnerabilities', from both technological and geopolitical standpoints. Technologically, offence is easier and more cost-effective than defence.

Geopolitically, the consequence is that highly advanced countries are particularly vulnerable to attack from less developed states (as well as from terrorist groups and other actors). Since states are faced with growing threats, and with the cost of defence increasingly elevated, many have chosen to ramp up their offensive activities instead in an effort at deterrence. Once again, this contributes to the ambiguity of intent and perceived threat that prompts other states to militarize in the escalatory cycle.

Cyber domain. In cyberspace, from a technological perspective, it is easier and cheaper to attack a country's networks than it is to defend against such an attack. In order to launch a cyber attack, a malicious actor needs to exploit just one vulnerability in a network. To mount an effective defence against cyber attacks, however, a country would need to identify and 'patch' all potential vulnerabilities, which is much more costly – and likely to be impossible.

This has implications at the geopolitical level, with countries that are highly reliant on the internet– such as the United States, the United Kingdom and other advanced economies – being highly vulnerable to cyber attacks. Since launching an effective cyber attack can be done with only a basic internet connection, countries with lower levels of internet dependency can thus inflict proportionally greater damage at lower cost to countries that are highly internet-reliant. (By contrast, if a highly internet-reliant country wanted to launch a retaliatory cyber attack against a country with a lower level of internet dependency, it would not be able to cause as much damage since there is less to attack.)

Space domain. The situation with regard to space is similar. The US contribution best expresses this by commenting that 'offence is easier and cheaper than defence', citing the challenges involved in missile defence as an example. At the technological level, it is much easier and cheaper to attack a satellite than it is to block an attack. In order to destroy a satellite, an attacker would only need to launch an ASAT, which is relatively easy to obtain and can be adapted from existing technology. (Many types of rocket design can be modified in order to create an ASAT.) However, to defend a satellite against such an attack would require a highly sophisticated and costly missile defence system.

At the geopolitical level, this means that the leading space powers are highly vulnerable to asymmetric attacks. The US submission comments that the country's heavy reliance on satellite technology makes it particularly susceptible in this regard. It notes that while space assets are a valuable enabler of the information age, and a powerful force enhancement tool, US dependence on these assets has also created a potential 'Achilles heel' in terms of vulnerability to asymmetric attacks. While only space powers possess satellites and other space assets that can be attacked, a country does not need to be a space power in order to take down another country's satellite.

This can be accomplished with an ASAT or – in what is becoming an increasingly plausible scenario – by waging a cyber attack (e.g. causing a satellite to spin out of orbit and self-destruct). If attacked by a non-space power, a space power would be unable to respond in kind, since its adversary would not have space assets to counterattack.

Conclusions

In identifying and analysing some of the common challenges in the cyber and space domains, the submissions to this paper point to the existence of an escalatory cycle of militarization in both domains, apparently driven by a set of common factors. The paper examines the interactions of these factors, and offers a visual representation of their interrelation in the form of a flowchart.

At present, only states are believed to have the capability to launch sophisticated cyber attacks, but in the coming years non-state actors (e.g. terrorist groups) are likely to acquire these capabilities as well. In such cases, the asymmetric threat to internet-reliant countries will be even greater, since they will have to contend not only with states but also with non-state foes – which themselves have fewer targets to counterattack.

Given that each factor, in contributing to the cycle, has a magnifying impact on militarization, tackling any of these factors at any point in the chain could help break or dampen the escalatory effect. The flowchart can therefore serve as a foundation for future research aimed at identifying joint solutions to these common challenges. For example, as outlined above, the lack or inadequacy of national policy documents impacts ambiguity of intent surrounding state actions, thus contributing to the perceived threat that fuels the escalatory cycle. This suggests that measures as simple as encouraging a greater number of countries to issue national policy documents or further clarify their existing policies can play an important role in mitigating the effects of the escalatory cycle.

Another example is that the lack or insufficiency of clear definitions of key terminology contributes to the lack of international agreements, which in turn fosters the ambiguity of intent and perceived threat that drive the escalatory cycle. One potential solution might be in ensuring better, agreed definitions. However, the presence of dual-use technology has revealed that unambiguous definitions are particularly difficult to achieve.

The flowchart therefore shows that another consequence of the paucity of key definitions is that it contributes to a lack of international cooperation, which also leads to the ambiguity of internet and perceived threat that reinforce the escalatory cycle. An alternative solution might be to take steps to promote international cooperation, which would act to decrease ambiguity of intent and the perceived threat fuelling the escalatory cycle, thereby counterbalancing the escalatory momentum generated by the lack of definitions of key terminology. The flowchart therefore also helps to convey how remedial actions in one area might be used to offset escalatory pressures in another area. There is growing concern within the cyber and space communities that both sectors are heading not only towards increasing militarization but a step beyond, towards increasing *weaponization*. It is therefore vital to take steps to break the escalatory cycle now, before it is too late.

CYBER SPACE - NATURE OF THREAT

Threat landscape

Existing and potential threats in the sphere of cyber security are among the most serious challenges of the 21st century. Threats emanate from a wide variety of sources, and manifest themselves in disruptive activities that target individuals, businesses, national infrastructures, and governments alike. Their effects carry significant risk for public safety, the security of nations and the stability of the globally linked international community as a whole. Malicious use of information technology can easily be concealed. The origin, identity of the perpetrator, or motivation for the disruption can be difficult to ascertain. Often, the perpetrators of these activities can only be inferred from the target, the effect or other circumstantial evidence. Threat actors can operate with substantial impunity from virtually anywhere. The motives for disruption vary widely, from simply demonstrating technical prowess, to the theft of money or information, or as an extension of state conflict. The source of these threats includes non-state actors such as criminals and, potentially, terrorists as well as States themselves. Many malicious tools and methodologies originate in the efforts of criminals and hackers. The growing sophistication and scale of criminal activity increases the potential for harmful actions.

International cooperation

Increasingly, nations are also concerned that the ICT supply chain could be influenced or subverted in ways that would affect normal, secure and reliable use of information technology. Inclusion of malicious hidden functions in information technology can undermine confidence in products and services, erode trust in commerce, and affect national security. As disruptive activities using information technology grow more complex and dangerous, it is obvious that no nation is able to address these threats alone. Confronting the challenges of the 21st century depends on successful cooperation among likeminded partners. Collaboration among nations, and between nations, the private sector and civil society, is important and the effectiveness of measures to improve cyber security requires broad international cooperation.

Securing cyber space - Scope of action

Cyber security and cyber defence

Cyber security is the activity of protecting information and information systems (networks, computers, data bases, data centers and applications) with appropriate procedural and technological security measures. In that sense, the notion of cyber security is quite generic and encompasses all protection activities.

Cyber defence relates to a much more specialized activity linked to particular aspects and organizations. The distinguishing factors between cyber security and cyber defence in a network environment are the nature of the threat, the assets that need to be protected and the mechanisms applied to ensure that protection. Cyber defence relates to defensive actions against activities primarily originating from hostile actors that have political, quasi-political or economic motivation that have an impact on national security, public safety or economic well being of the society. The cyber defence environment requires deployment of technologies and capabilities for real-time protection and incident response. Generally, cyber defence is driven by intelligence on the threat to achieve the kind of defence that directs, collects, analysis and disseminates the relevant actionable intelligence information to the stakeholders concerned for necessary proactive, preventive and protective measures. The effectiveness of cyber defence lies in the proactive nature of security counter measures as well as in ensuring resilience and continuity of operations, despite the possibilities of successful attacks.

Cyber intelligence and cyber defence

The value of collecting intelligence information about threat sources and possible cyber attacks cannot be underestimated.

A well-deployed cyber attack can yield vital information that compromises communication and encryption ciphers. It tends to project the power of the attacker and demoralize the victim. However, the changing phase of cyber attacks as well as ever-increasing sophistication of attack methods have complicated the efforts of collecting valuable intelligence information for effective proactive, preventive and protective measures. Generally, attacks directed against Govt. and critical information infrastructure can be categorized as either

massive attacks, aimed at disabling the infrastructure rendering it unusable or inaccessible to users; or targeted attacks, aimed at collecting sensitive/strategic information. Massive attacks generally take the form of denial of service attacks against the infrastructure. The targeted attacks involve a good deal of customization and personalization of attack methods and levels of technological and operational sophistication. Skillful execution of attack and the methodology used to conceal any traces of attack complicates the task of advance intelligence information collection and/or attack detection.

Priorities for action

Assuring security of cyber space requires careful and due attention to creation of well defined systems and processes, use of appropriate technology and more importantly, engaging right kind of people with suitable awareness, ethics and behavior. Considering the transnational character of information technology & the cyber space, the technical & legal challenges in ensuring security of information, information systems & networks as well as related impact on socio-economic life in the country, the priorities for action for creating a secure cyber eco-system include series of enabling processes, direct actions and cooperative & collaborative efforts within the country and beyond, covering:

- *Creation of necessary situational awareness regarding threats to ICT infrastructure for determination and implementation of suitable response*

- *Creation of a conducive legal environment in support of safe and secure cyber space, adequate trust & confidence in electronic transactions, enhancement of law enforcement capabilities that can enable responsible action by stakeholders and effective prosecution*
- *Protection of IT networks & gateways and critical communication & information infrastructure*
- *Putting in place 24 x 7 mechanism for cyber security emergency response & resolution and crisis management through effective predictive, preventive, protective, response and recovery actions*
- *Policy, promotion and enabling actions for compliance to international security best practices and conformity assessment (product, process, technology & people) and incentives for compliance.*
- *Indigenous development of suitable security techniques & technology through frontier technology research, solution oriented research, proof of concept, pilot development etc. and deployment of secure IT products/ processes*
- *Creation of a culture of cyber security for responsible user behavior & actions*
- *Effective cyber crime prevention & prosecution actions*
- *Proactive preventive & reactive mitigation actions to reach out & neutralize the sources of trouble and support for creation of global security eco system, including public-private partnership arrangements, information sharing, bilateral & multi-lateral agreements with overseas CERTs, security agencies and security vendors etc.*
- *Protection of data while in process, handling, storage & transit and protection of sensitive personal information to create a necessary environment of trust.*

Partnership and Collaborative Efforts

Government leadership catalyzes activities of strategic importance to the Nation. In cyber security, such leadership can energize a broad collaboration with private-sector partners and stakeholders to generate fundamental technological advances in the security of the Nation's IT infrastructure. First, in support of national and economic security, the Government should identify the most dangerous classes of cyber security threats to the Nation, the most critical IT infrastructure vulnerabilities, and the most difficult cyber security problems. Second, the Government can use these findings to develop and implement a coordinated R&D effort focused on the key research needs that can only be addressed with such leadership. While these needs will evolve over time, this cyber security policy provides a starting point for such an effort. Public- private partnership is a key component of this cyber security policy. These partnerships can usefully confront coordination problems. They can significantly enhance information exchange and cooperation. Public-private engagement will take a variety of forms and will address awareness, training, technological improvements, vulnerability remediation, and recovery operations. These actions will help in leveraging rapid technological developments and capabilities of private sector.

Security threat and vulnerability management

All infrastructure facilities face a certain level of risk associated with various threats. These threats may be result of natural events, accidents or intentional acts to cause harm. Regardless of the nature of the threat, facility owners have a responsibility to limit or manage risks from these threats to the extent possible. This is more so, if the facility is a part of nation's critical information infrastructure. As such focus of these efforts would be:

1) *To prevent cyber attacks on critical ICT infrastructure*
2) *Reduce vulnerability of critical ICT infrastructure to cyber attacks.*
3) *Enhancing the capability of critical ICT infrastructure to resist cyber attacks*
4) *Minimize damage and recovery in a reasonable time frame time*

The key actions to reduce security threats and related vulnerabilities are:

1) Identification and classification of critical information infrastructure facilities and assets.
2) Roadmaps for organization-wise security policy implementation in line with international security best practices standards and other related guidelines.
3) Process for national level security threat & vulnerability assessments to understand the potential consequences.
4) Use of secure products/services, protocols & communications, trusted networks and digital control systems. Internet Service Providers (ISPs) would be closely associated in providing for secure information flow through their networks and gateways. Appropriate legally binding agreements need to be in place to support law enforcement, information security incident handling and crisis management processes on a 24x7 basis.
5) Identification of national level security organization (CERT-In, DIT) to act as a nodal agency and co-ordinate all matters related to information security in the country, with clearly defined roles & responsibilities.
6) Emergency preparedness and crisis management (Mirror Centers, Hot/warm/cold sites, communication, redundancy, and disaster recovery plans, test & evaluation of plans etc.
7) Periodic as well as random verification of the level of emergency preparedness of critical information infrastructure facilities in resisting cyber attacks and minimize damage & recovery time in case cyber attacks do occur.
8) Development of comprehensive repair and maintenance policy so as to minimize false alarms and increase cyber resource availability to all users efficiently.

Security threat early warning and response a) National cyber alert system:

(i) Rapid identification, information exchange, and remediation can often mitigate the damage caused by malicious cyberspace activity. For these activities to take place effectively at a national level, it requires a central nodal agency (CERT-In, DIT) to perform analysis, issue warnings, and coordinate response efforts. Because no information security plan can be impervious to concerted and intelligent attacks, information systems must be able to operate while under attack and also have the resilience to restore full operations in reasonable time frame. The National Cyber Alert System will involve critical infrastructure organizations, public and private institutions to perform analysis, conduct watch and warning activities, enable information exchange, and facilitate restoration efforts.

(ii) The essential actions under National Cyber Alert System include:

- Identification of focal points in the critical infrastructure
- Establishment of a public-private architecture for responding to national-level cyber incidents
- Tactical and strategic analysis of cyber attacks and vulnerability assessments
- Expanding the Cyber Warning and Information Network to support the role of Government in coordinating crisis management for cyberspace security;
- Cyber security drills and exercises in IT dependent business continuity plans of critical sectors to assess the level of emergency preparedness of critical information infrastructure facilities in resisting cyber attacks and minimize damage & recovery time in case cyber attacks do occur.

Sectoral CERTS

In order to effectively deal with targeted cyber attacks on sensitive and strategic sectors, it is essential to operationalise sectoral CERTs in all identified critical sectors such as finance, defence, energy, transportation, telecommunication etc. These CERTs would be responsible for all coordination and communication actions within their respective sectors and should be in regular touch with CERT-In for any incidence resolution support as well as dealing with cyber crisis requiring broader action.

Local incident response teams

Each critical sector organisation should have an identified team of personnel who will be part of the respective local Incident Response Team. This team would:

- Identify the correctness of the severity level of any incident
- Contain, Eradicate and Recover
- Seek necessary resources and support from the corresponding Level II Incident Resolution Team
- Provide regular updates to higher management regarding progress of the incident handling process
- Escalate to an expert team/sectoral CERT or CERT-In, if unable to resolve within the prescribed time frame/ reasonable time frame.

Security best practices - compliance and assurance

Critical Information Infrastructure Protection

The primary focus of these efforts is to secure the information resources belonging to Government as well as those in the critical sectors. The critical sectors include Defence, Finance, Energy, Transportation and Telecommunications. Consequently, many in the industry and critical infrastructure organizations have come to recognize that their continued ability to gain consumer confidence will depend on improved software development, systems engineering practices and the adoption of strengthened security models and best practices. The designated agency of the Government would coordinate the efforts towards protection of critical information infrastructure in the country and enable development of expertise in communication, interception, monitoring and early warning, and surprise vulnerability checks with due authorization.

(a) Implementation of security best practices in Govt. and Critical sectors: In order to reduce the risk of cyber attacks and improve upon the security posture of critical information infrastructure, Government and critical sector organizations are required to do the following on priority:

1) Identify a member of senior management, as Chief Information Security Officer (CISO), knowledgeable in the nature of information security & related issues and designate him/her as a 'Point of contact', responsible for coordinating security policy compliance efforts and to regularly interact with the Indian Computer Emergency Response Team (CERT-In), Department of Information Technology (DIT), which is the nodal agency for coordinating all actions pertaining to cyber security
2) Prepare information security plan and implement the security control measures as per international security best practices standards and other guidelines, as appropriate
3) Carry out periodic IT security risk assessments and determine acceptable level of risks, consistent with criticality of business/functional requirements, likely impact on business/functions and achievement of organisational goals/objectives.
4) Periodically test and evaluate the adequacy and effectiveness of technical security control measures implemented for IT systems and networks. Especially, Test and evaluation may become necessary after each significant change to the IT applications/systems/networks and can include, as appropriate the following:
   - Penetration Testing (both announced as well as unannounced)

- Vulnerability Assessment
- Application Security Testing
- Web Security Testing

5) Carry out Audit of Information infrastructure on an annual basis and when there is major up gradation/ change in the Information Technology Infrastructure, by an independent IT Security Auditing organization
6) Report to CERT-In cyber security incidents, as and when they occur and the status of cyber security, periodically.

Government Networks

The government agencies need to set an example in the development and use of secure computer and communication networks. For this purpose, a part of departmental budget should be earmarked for IT and information security needs.

Besides this, all ministries/departments and other agencies of the government should ensure that they take necessary precautions and steps to promote the culture of information security amongst their employees and attached agencies. Necessary change in office procedure should be undertaken to bring in vogue, reliable and robust paperless offices where required.

Top-level management of government departments should pay attention to the development of suitable information security policy and guidelines and encourage the use of appropriate technology and applications in the organization.

Government secure intranet

There is a need for priority action to create a countrywide secure intranet for connecting strategic installations with CERT-In as the nodal centre for emergency response and coordination. This intranet will facilitate faster and efficient information sharing between strategic installations and CERT-In as well as supporting crisis management and disaster recovery during national IT security emergencies.

Information security Assurance Framework

In order to ensure implementation security best practices in critical sector organizations and periodic verification of compliance, there is a need to create, establish and operate a 'Information security Assurance Framework', including creation of national conformity assessment infrastructure. Information security Assurance Framework is aimed at assisting National level efforts in protecting critical information infrastructure. It supports Government, Critical Infrastructure Organizations and other key IT users of nation's economy through series of "Enabling and Endorsing" actions.

Enabling actions are essentially Promotional/Advisory/Regulatory in nature and involve publication of "National Security Policy Compliance requirements" and cyber security guidelines and supporting documents to facilitate cyber security implementation and compliance.

Endorsing actions are part of national conformity assessment infrastructure. These are essentially commercial in nature and may involve more than one service provider offering commercial services after having fulfilled requisite qualification criteria and demonstrated ability prior to empanelment. These include:

Assessment and certification of compliance to international IT security best practices, standards and guidelines (Ex. ISMS certification, Trusted company certification *for Data security and privacy protection*, IS system audits, Penetration testing/Vulnerability assessment etc.)

Government and critical infrastructure organizations can make use of CERT-In evaluated and empanelled third party agencies for their organisation/site specific IT security assessment services (including ISMS assessment, risk assessment, network security profiling, penetration testing, vulnerability assessment, application security testing etc.) under specific contract and pre-determined rules of engagement. Contact details of the agencies empanelled by CERT-In are available at 'http://www.cert-in.org.in')

IT Security product evaluation and certification as per accepted international standards.

These actions provide an assurance that the process of specification, implementation and evaluation of a IT security product has been conducted in a rigorous and acceptable manner.

IT security manpower training, qualification and other related services to assist user in IT security implementation and compliance.

Data security and privacy protection for 'Trust and Confidence': In order to stay competitive in the global market place, business entities have to continually generate adequate levels of trust & confidence in their services in terms of privacy and data protection through the use of internationally accepted best practices and ability to demonstrate where necessary.

Quality and protection of electronic records: Organizations need to ensure that important data/records are protected from loss, destruction and falsification, in accordance with statutory, regulatory, contractual, and business requirements.

Where a follow-up action against a person or organization involves legal action (either civil or criminal), electronic evidence needs to be properly collected, retained, and presented to conform to the rules for evidence laid down in the relevant jurisdiction(s).

It is a good practice to have audit logs recording user activities, exceptions, and information security events and retained for an agreed period to assist in future investigations.

E-governance

All e-governance initiatives in the country should be based on best information security practices. Government should encourage wider usage of Public Key Infrastructure (PKI) in its own departments.

There is a need to empanel Information Security professionals/ organizations to assist E-Governance initiatives and monitor quality of their performance/service through appropriate quality standards.

Secure software development and application

Software development process, whether in-house or outsourced, needs to be supervised and monitored using a system development life cycle methodology that includes information security considerations and selection of appropriate security controls and countermeasures.

Open standards: To minimize the risk of dependency on proprietary IT products, open standards need to be encouraged. A consortium of government and private sector needs to be created for enhancing the use of validated and certified IT products based on open standards.

2

Intelligence for Cyberspace Security Challenges

Although many of the intelligence methodologies and principles remain the same, new ways of thinking appropriate to the cyber-domain are essential. The lack of borders in cyber-space is a critical difference from the more familiar domains of intelligence. Indeed, geography and political borders often aided traditional military intelligence analysis-it is a simple thing to develop threat scenarios if the potential enemy can only use certain terrain or sea lines of communication and then, only at certain times of the year-while simple factors of physics such as time and distance also provided opportunities for warning. Within the Internet, however, these limiting factors are absent, (although other limiting factors, such as geometry of network connectivity, might exist in a form useful to be incorporated into intelligence analysis), contributing to what can appear to be "instantaneous threats".

Assessment of cyber-space threats requires not only a merger of old methodologies and new modes of thinking but also analysts willing and able to approach the art of threat assessment and warning from new perspectives. Only with a distinctive blend of the traditional and the new will it be possible to obtain real understanding of threats and vulnerabilities, to differentiate among types of intrusions and to forecast or anticipate specific incidents or clusters of incidents in ways that lengthen warning time. Enhancing the ability to identify perpetrators is also highly desirable: removing the cloak of anonymity would make perpetrators more concerned about the potential costs and risks of their actions and could have an important deterrent effect. In short, there are several fundamental questions at the heart of the intelligence process. They consist of variations on the who, what, when, where, why and how questions that are familiar parts of most research and analysis.

HISTORY OF CYBER SECURITY

The history of successful counterattacks in the world of cyber security is a short one. There are an increasing number of papers and publications which make proposals, but concerns over legal issues as well as technical challenges have kept the list of successes small. In Sept. 1998, the Pentagon is reported to have counterattacked some activists who were doing a Denial of Service attack of the Department of Defense's websites, responding to their requests with an applet which ran on the attackers' machines and forced them to reboot. In 1999, a California ISP Conxion wrote a script which caused DoS packets sent to the World Trade Organization's website to be sent back to the attackers. Of course, such an attack would not have worked if the attackers had used what's known as "IP address spoofing", which would have made the packets appear that they came from a different computer from where they did.

In 2001, several defences were created in response to the Code Red II worm. One, called CRclean, if it received a probe from the worm, would make use of a back door which the worm placed on the infected machine to load a neutralizing agent and halt the spread of the worm. But it would also install itself on that machine. Another, called CodeGreen, would actually scan the internet for computers with the IIS vulnerability that allowed CodeRed, then download the patch and place it on the machine, and clean up the back doors. It is clear that there are serious legal and ethical issues with both of these worms, even the former, which is still a worm even though it only reacts to attacks. In 2003, the Welchia worm was released onto the Internet. Welchia would remove the Blaster worm and patch the vulnerability that Blaster used to spread. However, Welchia also caused severe network congestion.

In late 2004, Lycos Europe got fed up with spammers and launched a popular campaign called "Make Love Not Spam" which attracted over 100,000 users. Users could install a screen saver on their desktop which would send requests to websites which were known to advertise via spam. This effort was sucessful in causing some of the sites to change locations. (http://www.makelovenotspam.com) Lycos reportedly got around the illegality of DDoS attacks by claiming to only take 95% of the target sites' bandwidth, though, David Dittrich finds this reasoning dubious at best. Lycos ended this campaign in December 2004.

Some companies such as Symbiot Security are currently developing counter attack tools and devices, but there is a lot of skepticism about deployment of devices because of liability concerns.

Cyber security Incident Response

Counter-attacks are part of the overall process of cyber security incident response. This consists of five stages:

1. Intrusion detection.
2. Identifying the attacker.
3. Defending against the attack.
4. Designing and deploying a counter attack.
5. Post-conflict investigation and support.

Intrusion Detection: Intrusion detection first identifies if there is an intrusion or intrusion attempt in the network or machine connected to network. Monitoring can be done on the network or on end-hosts. Firewalls and virus scanners also contribute. There are various techniques, such as anomaly detection, and policy-based approaches. Identifying the Attacker: This very important step towards counter-attack, basically knowing who your enemy is and where is he located. Identifying the attacker can be difficult, since an attacker may use one compromised host to attack another. Also, with today's network architecture it can be quite difficult to locate the real attacker. Packets can be sent with spoofed source addresses, and tracing them through multiple hops and different autonomous systems can be a complicated process. Finding out the specific server and location can be critical in determining what the counter attack would be.

Defending against the Attack: Before an attack, software patches are used to fix vulnerabillities. More interesting are defences once an attack against a real vulnerability has happened. Diversions can be set forth to surprise an attacker. Or once the attack has been detected, countermeasures can be put in place to stop further damage. Also, diversion tactics like Honey Pots can be used to keep the rest of the network safe. The information from these diversions (or information gained during the delays caused by these tactics) can be harnessed to engineer a specific counter attack. Designing and deploying a counter attack: Counterattacks take a surprising variety of forms. Designing a counter attack should take into account the following factors: the method of attack; the support of the network infrastructure (*i.e.* are ISPs performing egress filtering); collateral damage; and costs. Post Counter attack investigation and support: In order to aid the post counter attack investigation a counter attack should have inbuilt mechanism to log its trail and its operation history. Ideally, it will also provide a means of discovering the hacker's techniques and identity. The more risk hackers have of being discovered, the less likely they are to go hacking.

Anti-worms

A worm spreads itself by sending out packets which look for certain responses from computers. It will analyse those responses to deduce if it thinks the replying machine has the vulnerability that it exploits. These packets represent a worm's 'signature.' The machine the worm is targeting can detect the signature of the worm and thus know its mode of propagation. An anti-worm is generated, which exploits the same vulnerabilities as the original worm or uses the back doors opened by the original worm. The antiworm would either fix the attacking host, neutralize the worm, or bring it down gracefully, potentially informing the owner. It may also install itself for further propagation.

In addition to the stated goal, an antiworm adheres to following guidelines to minimize collateral damage:

- It is bug-free and does leave other vulnerabilities that could be exploited further.
- It can be uninstalled gracefully when owner asks for it.
- It makes minimal changes to host that it operates on.
- It should not be able to be used for propagating malicious content.

The countermeasure, or 'Neutralizing Agent' used, can take several forms. For example, it could patch the vulnerability and remove the botnet or worm. Less invasive changes include blocking the port over which the worm sends messages, or using a mutex and rebooting the machine to lock the botnet from being able to execute.

Also, one would have to remove any backdoors left by the worm.

In addition, deployment strategy of the antiworm will determine its effectiveness and collateral damage it may cause.

- *Active Deployment*: The antiworm is itself a worm; it propagates across the network by scanning and seeking exploited vulnerabilities. This is the fastest way to remove the original worm from the network, but this also causes the most collateral damage by affecting the network traffic a lot.
- *Passive Deployment*: The anti-worm waits on a host till another host attacks it, and then the antiworm cures only the attacking host. Collateral damage is bare minimum, but the anti-worm is left behind on the new host.
- *Controlled Deployment*: The anti-worm propagation is control via some statistic of number of infected/ vulnerable host to number host it cured. This can be very effective and efficient.

- *IDS base Deployment*: The anti-worm uses the intrusion detection sensors which monitor traffic and may deploy an anti-worm against an attacker. As with passive deployment, collateral damage is limited to computers actively launching attacks, but this is less invasive because it does not leave a worm, it just neutralizes the machine.

Spam

Spam is unsolicited e-mail. A virus is a programme which, when executed, installs malware such as root-kits, key-stroke loggers, etc. These programmes are then used to send sensitive information to the attacker without the user's consent. Both spam and viruses spread through e-mail and require human interaction to activate them. Email servers as well as the hosts can detect spam with the help of spam detectors like Symantec's TurnTide. Once the spam is identified one counter attack is achieved by automatic flooding of the Sender Server with bounced e-mails and mail notification to server's administrator. (Even if sender addresses are spoofed, one may be able to identify the last mail server that forwarded a message.)

Botnet

An attacker establishes a botnet by first spreading a virus or worm that takes over the vulnerable hosts. Each worm or virus then calls Home to tell that it has successfully captured the Host. It also establishes a command channel such that the Attacker through the home can control the host. Botnets can be used for DDOS attacks, phishing etc.

Counter Attack

- Counter attack involves identifying the attacker by monitoring the compromised Host and intercepting its communication to the Home machine. The Home machine is probably the attacker's base or intermediate node for communication between the host and the attacker base machines. Once that machine is identified, you hack back into that machine bring it down. For hacking back, you can use same techniques as used by the hackers to take control of the attacking machine.

- Taking down the Home machine only removes the attacker for a short duration, the network of compromised hosts still exists. A more effective counter attack would be to takeover or monitor the command channel for communication between the Home and other compromised hosts. If possible, identify other compromised hosts and fix them or take them down as preventive measure.

SECURITY CHALLENGING

Efforts to identify intruders are critical both to the assessment of the challenge and the nature of the response. Potential intruders run the gamut from young hobbyists engaged in the equivalent of joy riding to terrorist organizations and nations that are intent on maximizing damage to the target. The problem of identification is particularly difficult in a domain where maintaining anonymity is easy and there are sometimes time lapses between the intruder action, the intrusion itself, and the actual disruptive effects. Moreover, the consequences are not always commensurate with the objectives, in some cases falling short of what the intruders hoped to achieve, and in others going well beyond what they had envisaged.

There is a broad spectrum of potential intruders on the Internet and an almost equal number of motives for intrusions against organizations. Not surprisingly, this includes perpetrators conducting operations against other perpetrators. As enticing as this prospect is, it does not mitigate the effects of such internecine rivalry. New and more sophisticated tools are often the result of such interplay. This sort of jousting can also provide valuable insights to analysts once it is recognized, but does not simplify the analytic task and puts an incredible strain on limited analytic/warning resources. With the continuing proliferation of sophisticated computer technologies into the mainstream population, attribution for an intrusion becomes more difficult by the day.

The dynamism of the intruder population is itself a problem. On the one hand, success breeds imitation and the sophistication of readily available tools means that even those with limited skills can become intruders.

On the one hand, there is a certain degree of attrition in the intruder community. Indeed, there are many reasons why intruders might cease their activity, including increased maturity, a need to find gainful employment, and a perception of the rewards of working to increase network security rather than attack it. The implication, of course, is that the mix of agents threatening network security is changing as the nature of the Internet changes.

The vast majority of the intrusions are probably being conducted by nuisance hackers or "ankle-biters" who have limited objectives and are usually satisfied with the actual penetration of the system or conduct relatively harmless cyber-vandalism such as the defacement or alteration of web-sites. While aggravating to the target, no significant or lasting damage occurs. The more serious problem occurs when an intrusion is carried out by a more sophisticated intruder (either an individual or a group) whose objective is better defined and involves malicious intent. Motives for these sorts of intrusions are also as varied as the persons carrying them out. They range from greed to defined military strategy and doctrine, and all that falls in between.

Four of the more dangerous, and less well defined categories of intruder are governments conducting operations against other sovereign states, the organized terrorist group, insurgency or revolutionary groups, and organized crime. All these entities are beginning to appreciate the potential power, anonymity, and effectiveness of the Internet. There are myriad examples of governments instituting programmes for Computer Network Warfare. In the case of Russia, policy-makers consider the security of their information infrastructure so critical that–rhetorically at least-they equate an attack against it with a strategic nuclear strike (and have promised an appropriate response). As a result of the realization of the criticality of information infrastructures, computer warfare is now a part of the formal Russian Military Strategy and Doctrine. The same is true of organized terrorist groups. In fact, "most of the 30 top terrorist organizations identified by the U.S. government have web pages and use e-mail, and are ``fairly well developed" at using the Internet."[Casciano] In many cases, dependence on technology is viewed as an Achilles Heel to be exploited by terrorist organizations.

Within the U.S., many of the more militant indigenous groups have discovered the power of the Internet and have well designed and effective Web sites. Indeed, militia and supremacist groups have had significant increases in membership since developing their Web pages. It is a natural progression from using the Internet for propaganda and recruiting to exploiting its potential as a weapon. There is also growing evidence that some of the active insurgency groups around the world are discovering the potential of the computer. It is just a matter of time until they discover the effect of a computer-generated attack against the infrastructure of the government they are fighting. Once that realization is made, cyber-attacks will likely become a weapon of choice for organizations intent on overthrowing an existing government. Disturbingly, Aum Shinrikyo, the group responsible for the Sarin gas attack on the Japanese subway, has increasingly been involved in the Japanese software industry!

Organized crime probably was the first of the sophisticated intruder threats to realize the power and value of the computer. In 1995, it was discovered that the Cali cartel had sophisticated state-of-the-art equipment for electronic eavesdropping, while smaller drug trafficking organizations in Colombia are using the Internet to pressure the Colombian government to change the policy of extraditing traffickers to the United States. Furthermore, the use of computers by organized crime organizations to garner illicit profits is well documented. However, some criminal efforts have gone beyond simple siphoning of funds and money laundering. Extortion of money from financial institutions by threatening to destroy or modify their computer databases is also evident. It is probable that at least some of these extortion operations are conducted by transnational criminal groups. Some of the extortion efforts go wrong–as did the effort to extort Bloomberg. In other cases, however, large payoffs are almost certainly made to the extortionist. It seems likely, therefore, that larger and potentially more dangerous operations should be anticipated.

The obvious challenge is to develop a capacity to identify and track the activities of these potential intruders with the goal of being able to provide predictive analysis and warning of intrusions. Some of the traditional intelligence techniques should apply to these threats, but new methodologies and the ability to contemplate new and complex concepts have to be developed concurrently. This will become even more important (and difficult) as perpetrators of increasing sophistication operate on the Internet. As motivations vary, so will the efforts of the individuals behind malicious operations to either conceal or reveal their responsibility. All of this complicates efforts to track responsible parties determine attribution. Nations and transnational criminal organizations, by their nature, will be diligent in their efforts to maintain anonymity. In some of these cases, identifying the intended victim may give valuable insight into tracking the intruder. Sometimes the target of an intrusion allows the analyst to rule out certain possible perpetrators. A multi-million dollar extortion plot against a major financial institution is probably not the work of a 13-year-old hacker working out of his bedroom. At the same time, however, many victims, especially within government or sensitive industries such as banking or insurance, often complicate the effort to track intruders because of their reluctance to report the incident. In other cases, such as politically motivated attacks, the perpetrators may want their identity known, but not their location. As such operations become more sophisticated, tracking the attack back to its point of origin will be a major challenge to the intelligence analysts involved. What is clear from all of this is that tracking intruders and gaining attribution is much more than just a technical challenge.

One difficulty, of course, is that there are legal constraints on intelligence collection, especially by the military and the national security establishment. Traditionally the focus of intelligence has been on foreign threats, and there are restrictions on intelligence activities directed against individuals or groups that are domestic in nature. Insofar as these groups are the focus of government attention, it is from the law enforcement community. This points to yet another problem: that of coordination and information sharing between the traditional national security agencies and the law enforcement community. Generally law enforcement focuses on individual cases and wants evidence that stands up in court; intelligence agencies in contrast are concerned with protecting the sources of their information so that they can continue to use them. The problem with cyber-threats is that they fall in the gray area where crime and national security merge into one another.

Forms of Intrusion are Occurring

It is tempting to see intrusions in terms of a pyramid that goes from transient vulnerability probing and defacing websites at the base to large scale efforts to undermine the critical missions of an organization or the critical functions of a nation at the top-and to suggest that there is an inverse relationship between frequency and significance, with many trivial incidents and comparatively few of the more serious incidents. There are several difficulties with this however. The first is that probes that appear relatively insignificant could be a harbinger of more serious intrusions. The second is that there is sometimes a gap between intent and consequences–the effects and impact of an incident can either fall far short of what was intended, or far exceed what the perpetrator initially envisaged. This lack of congruence between limited intent and far-reaching consequences stems from the capacity of worms and viruses for infinite replication and multiplication combined with the seamless inter-connectivity of systems. Incidents such as the Love Bug cross the public-private divide and have an indiscriminate impact on corporations, governments, and private individuals irrespective of the initial target. In cases such as this, the consequences have less to do with targeting than with the ubiquity of a particular programme such as Microsoft Outlook that is used as the vector of transmission. In effect, the incident takes on its own momentum.

When the consequences are widespread, of course, the incident becomes very public and is the subject of much media and official commentary. In many other cases, however, there is far greater reticence about the scale, type and targets of attack. The analytic effort must successfully build a trust relationship for the collection of data across a broad variety of organizations. This trust relationship allows for observation of incidents from early probing and experimentation through widespread deployment of automated forms of intrusion. For example, in recent months (June and July 2000) CERTÒ/CC has received reports of intrusions involving a wide variety of automated tools, ranging from simple viruses and system corruption toolkits through complex viruses designed to attack relatively hardened sites with low probability of detection and distributed tools designed to crash network infrastructure. Roughly 10%-25% of the CERT/CC reports involve viruses. Roughly 20%-40% are intrusions where the victim site cannot discern the type of the intrusion from available data. The remaining intrusions are a large number of other forms of intrusion, including compromise of system administration accounts, web defacements, reconnaissance attempts and misuse of computing resources.

Being intruded Upon

Determining who are the victims of intrusions is, in some respects, an enormously significant part of the intelligence process. It is important-at least in those cases where attacks are not indiscriminate-to differentiate between public and private targets, to distinguish infrastructure targets from individual targets, to distinguish between intrusions that focus on targets of convenience and those that are much more precise and calculated. For example, existing analysis has shown a link between port scanning and certain types of later intrusions, but this needs to be more fully explored to provide for effective warnings. Profiling victims can sometimes play a critical role in determining the nature of the intrusion and the nature of the intruders. For this to be done, understanding is needed of the level of "background noise", probes and intrusion attempts occurring across the Internet. Once understood, it may be possible to isolate this activity from the more significant activity directed at a particular victim.

Victim profiles will be just as important, in terms of strategic intelligence analysis of the Internet, as profiling potential intruders. The more serious the intrusion, the more critical this sort of profiling will be. One of the potential hurdles to this effort, however, will be the natural tendency of the victim, whether private or public, to withhold sensitive or proprietary information. A few examples of this kind of reticence would be financial institutions withholding information about loses due to intrusions; companies failing to divulge the nature of an intrusion due to proprietary corporate data; or a government agency protecting information that is sensitive or even classified. Beyond simply protecting proprietary or sensitive data, there are also serious legal questions that have not yet been resolved in the courts or in the legislature. These include constitutional guarantees of privacy; contradictory national laws (or lack of laws) as perpetrators use the global network; laws limiting various governmental agency's efforts to track down the source of an intrusion, and the need to determine what is domestic and what is foreign.

If these barriers can be overcome, critical information will become available. Details of the victim's infrastructure, the nature of the intrusion, identity clues left by the intruder, network traffic flow as observed by the victim site, and intrusion tools left as artifacts on the victim hosts can all provide indispensable clues. Without such information, motivation becomes more difficult to define and profiling efforts will be seriously flawed. Some work has already been accomplished in this area by organizations involved in incident monitoring, including the members of the Forum of Incident Response and Security Teams (FIRST) community. Much more remains to be accomplished, however, as new cooperative agreements are forged and additional analytic efforts and methodologies are developed. Furthermore, while it is true that some of the legal restrictions are avoided by the voluntary nature of the cooperative relationships, they are by no means completely overcome. The keys to success seem to be twofold. First, the analytic organization has to prove itself to be a highly secure confidant, never disclosing victim identities while working to assist victims in recovering from intrusions. Second, it must return information that is of value to the victims, including information that might place the intrusion in a larger context as well as providing assistance in dealing with vendors or other sites. More simply put, the exchange of information must be in both directions. Experience with other organizations has shown that neither trustworthiness nor returned value alone is sufficient, but both appear to be required for effective information gathering with victims.

Beyond their reticence, victim organizations are often unaware of critical parts of their security stance. Available data suggests that victims are often not aware that their networks have been intruded upon. The effectiveness of installed security measures is often overestimated. Levels of trust given to users by computing practices are often unwarranted. All of this hampers both analysis and defence.

One of the reasons that profiling the victims is so critical is that it provides insights in to motivations that can greatly assist analysts in predicting future intrusions under similar circumstances. This insight will need to incorporate identification of circumstances that facilitate or hamper intrusion. For example, K-12 educational institutions might offer a significant opportunity for intruders to stage their attacks, since many such institutions lack knowledgeable system administrators. However, such hosts may be removed from the network during summer break and other times when school is not in session. During the Year 2000 rollover, conditions for system intrusion were relatively poor not only because of the active presence of a large number of system administrators, carefully monitoring their systems, but also the significant number of alternative activities available to potential intruders. These examples serve to identify that there exist time-varying circumstances; further analysis is required to delineate these factors more fully.

CAPABILITIES OF CYBER INTELLIGENCE

Individual cyber intelligence capabilities have been applied for decades, some since the earliest days of IT system design. Beyond the inflection point of a unified, comprehensive approach, there have been significant advancements in the overall discipline. Given the importance of cyber intelligence in today's environment, business executives should join their IT colleagues in understanding how this discipline is evolving. Here's a look at four critical topics:

Cyber Security

Many cyber security efforts were geared to detecting and protecting against intrusions of the perimeter. As threats shifted to inside the trust zone (*e.g.*, employees who inadvertently enable security breaches), new tools and techniques were needed. Identity and access management solutions were siloed systems—with isolated entitlements, activity logging, and controls. Pattern detection of higher-order threats was extremely difficult because these solutions had limited access to the context of external events. Technology solutions were manually operated, which the business perceived as a nuisance and often circumvented. The chief security officer (CSO) or chief information security officer (CISO), if they existed at all, were typically technologists with deep domain knowledge, but without a seat in the boardroom.

Today, cyber security is increasingly framed as a combination of architecture, practices, and processes—with equal focus on internal and external threats. Highly integrated tool sets and investments in cyber analytics have helped connect dots and identify previously undetectable exposures. Automated identity management tools are incorporated into day-to-day tasks, including smart cards, biometrics, fingerprint, and handprint scanners. The CSO role has become commonplace, requiring a mix of technology and leadership skills and gaining a seat at the boardroom table.

Cyber Forensics

In the past, incident investigations would conclude once a root-cause analysis was completed. These self-contained analyses were rarely used to augment existing controls or update policies. At best, a script was created to improve response in case a breach recurred.

Cyber forensics now looks beyond the host to the network layer, determining the source (inside or outside the organization) of the malware. This determination is correlated with other internal and known external threats using cyber analytics, in an attempt to identify future vulnerabilities. Forensics results are part of a closed-loop cycle in cyber intelligence, improving directly affected and associated controls.

Cyber Analytics

In the past, cyber analytics was a reactive approach based on situational awareness and descriptive analysis. It provided an understanding of the value of business analytics, but without the models to apply the patterns.

These days, this discipline is an established tradecraft of analytics, reinforced by the realization that threats and opportunities are often hidden in plain sight. Cyber analytics is predictive, prescriptive, and a part of a closed-loop cycle of continuous refinement based on other cyber intelligence activities.

Cyber Logistics

Supplier security reviews were typically limited to deal signings and cursory annual audits. Notably in manufacturing, companies relied on several ever-changing sub-contractors and small hardware providers, each with its own risk profile, which created potential weaknesses upstream in the supply chain.

Personnel checks occurred only during the hiring or contracting process, with clearance processing handled by largely unknown third parties.

Today, cyber logistics includes extensive analysis to identify, assess, and mitigate risks posed by vendors subject to foreign ownership, control or influence, or other significant concerns prior to a purchase or the awarding of a contract. It entails the continuous assessment of suppliers, including organization structures and corporate activity as well as ongoing confirmation of the integrity of goods. Cyber intelligence strategies include provisions for personnel security such as verifying the legitimacy of background investigation agencies, proactive foreign travel risk advisory, and automated reinvestigations of executives and privileged roles.

New Approach to IT Security

Intelligence expert Terry Roberts says cyber intelligence, a new approach to IT security, could make significant gains in the coming year. "The good thing is, this isn't really rocket science," says the chair of the Intelligence and National Security Alliance's Cyber Council.Pilot projects are underway to determine if methods employed by the 17 federal intelligence agencies could be adapted to safeguard non-classified but sensitive information in the private sector.

To succeed, Roberts says, the government and private sector must collaborate and share information. "In a year or two, we could actually have the private-public partnership established, with the beginnings of an unclassified cyber-intelligence approach," Roberts says in an interview with Information Security Media Group (select one of the Podcast Options at right to listen).

Roberts edited the alliance's just-issued paper, Cyber Intelligence: Setting the Landscape for an Emerging Discipline, which discusses how the current cyberthreat landscape requires a new way to share intelligence in unclassified cyberspace.

"It's important to understand that when we use the word *intelligence* that we're really talking about knowledge, not just information, and we're not necessarily talking about something that has to be classified," Robert says. "When we're talking about intelligence as an approach for the cyber arena, it's really about pulling together all the information that we know, processing it, analysing it and providing unclassified, situational awareness and situations of warning to both government and industry."

In the interview, Roberts discusses the:

- Difficulties of industry to adapt the highly sophisticated approach the federal intelligence agencies employ to share cyber intelligence. "What we are not doing really is applying those intelligence techniques and tradecraft to the unclassified arena," she says. "Think about it this way: 90 percent of infrastructure in the cyber arena is owned by industry, and 90 percent of the information or data of cyber activity is in the unclassified arena. But we're not focusing on that realm in a comprehensive, consistent manner that we can provide unclassified cyber intelligence to all of industry."
- Multidisciplinary skills that cyber intelligence requires. "In the beginning nuclear age, you brought in people with the technical body of knowledge, then your brought people with a body of knowledge on that particular adversary, the culture, the leadership, and you brought it all together so you would have a 360 view," she says. "We haven't been doing that in the (private-sector) cyber realm.

"Actually, in cyber intelligence, you need analytics types of folks, you need people who understand the network environment, that operational background; you need people with technical background who understand the particulars of an attack vector or a fraud approach or sabotage approach that's being used. And, those folks together, need to be looking at the data, analysing it and coming up with so what, the impact of what they're seeing today and what that means for the future."

CYBER-INTELLIGENCE AND TRADITIONAL APPROACHES

Cyber intelligence and their applicability to Internet security, it is tempting to suggest that cyber-space has so many unique characteristics that none of the traditional approaches is relevant. Such a temptation should be avoided. There are important parallels with, and critical lessons to be learned from, experience in other domains. One of the most notable parallels is between cyber-intelligence and business intelligence, particularly in product monitoring. In the case of intelligence for the Internet, it is the development and diffusion of tools for intrusion and disruption that need to be monitored. Yet, such efforts are not that different from monitoring the development and marketing of new products in the business world. Consequently, some of the methods and techniques developed in the world of competitive intelligence might be particularly helpful as one component of intelligence collection and analysis in relation to cyber-space threats.

The most serious and useful model for intelligence analysis of information threats, however, is probably intelligence methodologies in the area of national security intelligence, and specifically, counter-terrorism. The terrorism threat has several characteristics that are also apply to cyber-threats. The parallels include the diversity of the actors involved, the reliance of at least some of them on networks, the broad range of motivations, the anonymity of the perpetrators of terrorist incidents, (something that has become more pronounced in recent years as the traditional practice of claiming responsibility giving way to the cloak of silence) and the enormous array of potential targets and weapons. Terrorists can choose from a set of options that obviously include firearms and conventional explosives but could conceivably involve WMD capabilities. Not surprisingly, one of the major concerns of intelligence analysis in this domain is with predicting and either preventing or pre-empting terrorism incidents. The utility of early warning is hard to exaggerate as such warning facilitates preventive and defensive measures as well as damage mitigation efforts.

Whether the emphasis is on a single threat or multiple threats, however, crucial aspects of the intelligence task remain the same. Although the focus of the collection and analysis effort might shift, the intelligence process itself involves the same cycle of activities: focus on the mission, collection of sources and information, collation and management of the collected intelligence, analysis and assessment resulting in an intelligence product, and the dissemination of this product to the customer. The intelligence cycle remains constant whatever the target of the efforts. Similarly, good intelligence not only moves from data streams to data fusion but also from fused data to knowledge, and from knowledge to forecasting or prediction. And whatever the domain of activity, whether business intelligence, military intelligence, or cyber-intelligence, there is always a requirement to overcome pathologies and obstacles that can undermine the analytical process and dilute or distort finished intelligence products.

In terms of collection methods, however, a critical addition needs to be made. As well as traditional reliance on Comint, Humint, and Sigint, it might be necessary to develop a separate category of Cyberint. In effect, Cyberint would require a blending of Sigint, Humint, and Comint methodologies to be effective. Each of those traditional intelligence disciplines brings components that are critical for analysis of on-line threats. The Humint aspect would provide for the monitoring and profiling of potential threat groups. It could take the form of simple monitoring of intruder chat rooms and web sites or in-depth profiling of identified individuals or groups. It will require that analysts are able to identify which players, whether individuals or groups, have the technical expertise to carry out their intended operations. Consequently, much effort will need to be focused on existing use of the Net and identified intrusions to establish a baseline of data from which to proceed.

The Sigint perspective is useful from the point of analysing intruder tools and specific system vulnerabilities. This is not to say that an analytic organization would necessarily intercept and collect data being transmitted across targeted systems.

There are too many questions of legality and ethics to anticipate that sort of effort. However, studying identified tools and how they have been implemented does call for the utilization of existing Sigint methodologies to provide value added assessments. Similarly, one of the basic tenets of Comint analysis is to establish a communications activity baseline–this readily applies to various information and communication systems. Establishing baseline information on the normal data flow for a given system would make it easier and quicker to identify anomalies that could be indicative of probes or attempts at intrusion. As with the overall intelligence process, each of these recognized intelligence disciplines provide individual parts of a greater whole. They are the tools through which fusion intelligence of both current and future cyber-threats can be obtained. It goes without saying that collecting this sort of data will require a major cooperative effort between the analytic organization and past, as well as potential future, victims. In sum, cyberint would not supercede other collection methods but is likely to prove a crucial addition that would help to focus the intelligence effort and contribute significantly to the successful analysis of cyber-threats and intrusions.

Intelligence for Cyber-space

Although many of the intelligence methodologies and principles remain the same, new ways of thinking appropriate to the cyber-domain are essential. The lack of borders in cyber-space is a critical difference from the more familiar domains of intelligence. Indeed, geography and political borders often aided traditional military intelligence analysis-it is a simple thing to develop threat scenarios if the potential enemy can only use certain terrain or sea lines of communication and then, only at certain times of the year-while simple factors of physics such as time and distance also provided opportunities for warning. Within the Internet, however, these limiting factors are absent, (although other limiting factors, such as geometry of network connectivity, might exist in a form useful to be incorporated into intelligence analysis), contributing to what can appear to be "instantaneous threats".

Assessment of cyber-space threats requires not only a merger of old methodologies and new modes of thinking but also analysts willing and able to approach the art of threat assessment and warning from new perspectives. Only with a distinctive blend of the traditional and the new will it be possible to obtain real understanding of threats and vulnerabilities, to differentiate among types of intrusions and to forecast or anticipate specific incidents or clusters of incidents in ways that lengthen warning time. Enhancing the ability to identify perpetrators is also highly desirable: removing the cloak of anonymity would make perpetrators more concerned about the potential costs and risks of their actions and could have an important deterrent effect. In short, there are several fundamental questions at the heart of the intelligence process. They consist of variations on the who, what, when, where, why and how questions that are familiar parts of most research and analysis.

INTRUSIONS BEING IMPLEMENTED TAKING PLACE

This is both the most technical aspect of the problem and, for specialists in the area, the easiest question to answer. Methods of intrusion are the on-line equivalent of military tactics. And just as in the military world there has historically been a dialectic between defence and offence so on the Internet, there is a similar dialectic between protection and intrusion. One difference lies in the ability of intruders to obfuscate their methods of intrusion by manipulation of the sources of intrusion and of the on-line records of activity. The sources of intrusion are manipulated either by staging intrusions through a series of already-intruded and corrupted hosts, or by falsification of source information found in network traffic. Both of these methods are common in intrusions. The on-line records of activity are commonly falsified either by direct modification of the records themselves or by replacement of the monitoring software that produces these records. While there are analogies to these activities in the physical world, the ease, rate, and invisibility of these activities on the Internet especially complicates the analysis task.

The timing of intrusions might or might not be significant. It is possible, for example, that an intrusion on a particular company could have been precipitated by a particular action of the company, whether in the marketplace or in relation to one or more of its employees. Similarly, an intrusion on a country's infrastructure could come about in an international crisis, as part of an adversary's effort to prevent or disrupt military intervention in a specific region or country. A particular sequence of intrusions might also be important in determining whether probing activities are taking place as a preliminary to a more serious assault. Another important component is whether or not the intrusions are accompanied by any other actions–such as the demand for payment that would be an essential ingredient in any extortion contingency.

The timing of an intrusion, especially one that is more serious in nature will often have significance with regard to the motive for the intrusion, hence the importance of victim profiling. Given the global nature of business today and the amount of political upheaval throughout the world, myriad events must be examined on a daily basis for clues to possible impending intrusions. Awareness of upcoming political events, corporate announcements or openings of new industrial facilities will be essential to the analytic process. This sort of situational awareness, combined with the historical perspective provided by profiling, will have a major impact on the ability to provide predictive analysis and warning. There is a need for care here in distinguishing significant from background activity. Experience at the CERT/CC with informal measures of significance, as are used in generation of advisories, may be useful in facilitating this distinction.

Although the virtual world is borderless, the points at which it connects to the real world are geographic locations. Indeed, the simple question of "where?" has to be broken down into point(s) of origin, digital routing, and point(s) of attack. Indeed, it is physical actions at a particular location that start the attack process–even if there is sometimes a time lag prior to the implementation of the attack itself. This becomes particularly significant when the actions initiated at this location go beyond web defacement and involve more serious criminal, terrorist, and war-like actions. Tracing the attack back to source, therefore, becomes particularly important in determining both the responsibility for the action and the appropriate target for counter-measures or reprisals. Where the attacker is determined to be another nation then this has particularly important implications. Even in less extreme situations, however, location is critical–and because of law as well as geography. In some jurisdictions, for example, there are no laws against computer intrusions. This was why the Filipino perpetrator of the love bug was not placed on trial in the Philippines itself. In other jurisdictions, of course, the laws are quite severe.

For criminals and terrorists, these divergences offer opportunities to launch attacks at minimal risk–even if the source of the attack is somehow discovered. This suggests that there might be a form of jurisdictional arbitrage with potential attackers seeking out low risk jurisdictions from which to launch their attacks. Over the longer term, of course, the opportunities for arbitrage of this kind can be diminished through more inclusive laws criminalizing this kind of activity, through the harmonization of laws among states, and through the extension of extradition treaties and mutual legal assistance treaties.

As well as using jurisdictional arbitrage computer intruders also seek to cover their tracks by going through multiple jurisdictions. In some cases, this makes it impossible to track the activity back to source by complicating the digital trail. In others, it adds significant legal obstacles as some states are simply unwilling to cooperate in investigations There is also the potential for mischief with the possibility that skilful intruders might lay a false trail that lead to unwarranted but damaging accusations against innocent parties (whether individuals, groups or nations).

With respect to victim location, physical location can also provide key insights. Local threats might arise through local activism (such as the Sierra Club opposition to military exercises in California; this did not involve cyber threats, but analogous activities in the future might well do so). Beyond physical location, there is logical location. A site might come under attack because either its Internet service provider or a subsidiary site is vulnerable. This logical location could be entirely unrelated to physical location: a site in New York might be on a network logically associated with one in Florida. This could occur due to mergers and acquisitions, but more typically takes place due to the difficulties in securing Internet addresses. Whatever the cause, however, it adds yet another complication to the location issue.

Using either physical or logical locations, there are several sorts of victims that might be of interest. One is the intended target of the incident. Another is an intermediate site used as a means of access or interference to the intended target, which might be termed the vector for the incident. In some circumstances this can involve substantial collateral damage to the vector site (or sites) even though it is not the intended victim. Intruders on a vector might extract information, reconfigure computers and hamper desirable operation, all for the purpose of striking the intended target.

Actions Taking Place

From a predictive intelligence analysis perspective, threat is most simply defined as capability plus intent. Capabilities, in terms of more powerful computers and more malicious covert software, are expanding rapidly. Attacks that required deep technical expertise in the recent past are within the reach of casual users today. Malicious intent is less easy to pin down, but can be assumed to be widespread and varied. History alone teaches us that much. Determining those two factors is the foundation of strategic intelligence analysis. Categorization of the nature of attacks and of the victims is critical to the success of any analytic effort. Historically, the more serious attacks will often have a specific catalyst: a corporation builds a production facility in a third world country that is viewed as an exploitive action by one or more activist groups; a government sponsors a peace conference that is viewed as an attempt to subvert the political viability of a disaffected part of the population; a repressive regime massacres a band of rebels near the capital; an organized crime syndicate reacts to crack downs by law enforcement. These are just a handful of examples of motivations for more serious incidents. Just as importantly, a more serious incident, while probably more sophisticated, also has a greater potential for an unintended cascading effect.

Objectives can range from revenge (a disgruntled employee) to political statements (terrorism) to a full-scale attack on infrastructure as an act of warfare or at the very least part of "coercive diplomacy". Although the inference of intent is sometimes problematic (particularly where the damage or disruption is either less or more than the intruder intended), the effort is an essential component of the intelligence process. In many cases, intrusions that are politically motivated will be relatively easy to interpret. The effect of the intrusion will be muted if the underlying political intent is not publicized. Depending on the nature of the goal, this publication of intent may be quite localized and covert–*e.g.*, to gain power within the intruder organization. Nonetheless, such publication might be identifiable and could provide a historical perspective that will greatly assist in predicting possible future intrusions. On the other hand, activities by governments and criminal elements are, almost by definition, covert in nature. Intrusions of those types will provide a much greater challenge to the goal of providing predictive assessments and warnings. It also has to be recognized that in some incidents, there are no clear objectives. The lack of motive can be truly confounding.

In this connection, it is essential to acknowledge the limits of intelligence. No one has articulated these more effectively than Sherman Kent, formerly the Director of the Office of National Intelligence Estimates, who noted that intelligence consists of three kinds of information: "The first is easily disposed of; it is the statement of indisputable fact... The second and third kinds do not carry any such certainty; each rests upon a varying degree of uncertainty. They relate respectively (a) to things which are knowable but happen to be unknown to us, and (b) to things which are not known to anyone at all." In effect, much of the analysis process involves what Kent also called the "speculative-evaluative" component of intelligence–especially when it involves efforts to anticipate future behaviour and future threats, and when the targets of intelligence collection and analysis are engaging in systematic concealment or deception designed to thwart these efforts.

THE NATURE AND LEVELS OF INTELLIGENCE ANALYSIS

Intelligence analysis requires many of the same analytical methods and techniques, irrespective of domain. From this perspective, intelligence analysis for Internet security is no different from the intelligence task in any other area of national and international security.

The commonality is the concern with those who want to inflict harm and the vulnerabilities they can exploit to do this. Threats can come from many sources: the military activities of hostile nations; inimical economic strategies pursued by adversarial or even allied states; the activities of terrorist groups intent on inflicting harm on society in order to achieve political objectives; transnational criminal organizations pursuing the acquisition of large profits through illegal activities, violence, and corruption; and groups (including any of those just mentioned) and individuals with the ability and desire to distort, disrupt, degrade or destroy information and communications systems.

Whatever their source, threats are inextricably linked to vulnerabilities. Indeed, absolute security could only be achieved if there were no vulnerabilities to be exploited. It is crucial, therefore, not only to identify vulnerabilities but also to understand how hostile groups or individuals might exploit them. Strictly speaking, real security threats only come from those with a combination of hostile intent (*i.e.* a desire to do us harm) and the capacity to inflict harm (*i.e.* exploit vulnerabilities in ways that transform intent into reality).

In the realm of cyber-space, vulnerabilities are inescapable. There are many reasons for this, ranging from the inherent weaknesses in complex systems to specific problems in the creation of software code.

Even if protective security measures were an integral part of information systems rather than being subsequently grafted onto them, problems would remain. Some vulnerabilities stem from the underlying protocols used to communicate on the Internet, which were formulated when the Internet was a relatively small community of trusted systems, with connectivity determined by government contract.

Other vulnerabilities stem from development practices, which may ignore validation of input (or even length checking) and avoid controlling the environment in which programmes execute. Finally, vulnerabilities stem from the rapidly evolving use of software, in which programmes meant for a limited purpose are applied in ways not anticipated by their developers. The intruder community is constantly seeking to find interesting (and, from their point of view, profitable) ways to discover and exploit vulnerabilities.

This behaviour tends to be quite trend-driven. A newly discovered interesting vulnerability exploit in an application will spawn both intensive interest in other vulnerabilities in that application and an intensive search for similar vulnerabilities in other applications.

This results in waves of discovered vulnerabilities that impact both specific vendors and the community in general.

At the same time, the recognition that there are measurable trends in vulnerability exploitation are at least a temporary advantage to intelligence analysis efforts. From a tactical perspective, the recognition of a trend in intrusion tools and their applications may well allow for at least short-term predictive analysis and the potential for limited warning.

One of the greatest challenges to system owners and administrator is determining how much security is enough. Managing risks inherent in information systems is problem that changes as fast as new technologies are brought online. Intelligence analysis of the threats to information systems should, by definition, be a major component of the risk management process. Without application, intelligence analysis efforts are merely an intellectual exercise and have no value. It is only when the results of that analysis, the assessments derived from the analytic process, are provided to operators that they begin to have value.

Obtaining prior knowledge of both threats and vulnerabilities–as well as sensitivity to possible opportunities to exploit the vulnerabilities-is essential. Intelligence analysis, of course, operates at different levels, ranging from the specific to the general, and from short-term incidents and operations to long term patterns and challenges. Each form or level of analysis is crucial, and complements and supplements the others. Nevertheless, it is important to distinguish them from one another and to be clear at which level the activities are taking place.

It is also important to recognize that the most critical insights will be obtained from fusion efforts that combine these different levels. The several complementary levels of intelligence analysis are strategic analysis, tactical analysis and operational analysis. In practice, these categories shade into each other and are not always sharply differentiated, and differing definitions for these terms exist in the intelligence community. Nevertheless, they offer a useful framework within which intelligence tasks and requirements can initially be delineated.

Strategic Intelligence Analysis

Strategic analysis is perhaps the most important form of intelligence. It provides a framework within which other forms of intelligence collection and analysis take place, offers an overall assessment from the top down rather than from the bottom up, and helps to provide a basis for policy formulation, strategic planning, and resource allocation. Its weakness is its focus on macro-level issues rather than the more detailed levels of analysis.

On the Internet, such analysis is even more problematic, due to the rapidly evolving nature of Internet usage. Prior to 1994, for example, Internet commerce was illegal. Today it is a multi-billion dollar economic force. New methods of organizational and economic cooperation are constantly evolving, with greater or less security.

Maintaining continuity on this constantly shifting environment is one of the greatest challenges to conducting effective strategic analysis of cyber-threats. Furthermore, for many consumers, strategic intelligence is irrelevant to day-to-day tasks and needs. At the end of the day, however, the importance of strategic intelligence analysis is undeniable. Such an effort helps to discern and make sense of trends, to identify and extract patterns that would otherwise not be visible, and to provide an overall picture of the evolving threat environment and the level of damage that might be occurred in certain specified contingencies.

Analytical initiatives that would fall under the rubric of strategic intelligence analysis include:

- *Overall threat assessments.* These include in the analysis the vulnerabilities of critical missions (including levels of dependence), the kind of disruption and damage that could be caused to the implementation of these missions, the kinds of weapons/instruments that could be used to cause such disruptions, and the likelihood of such attacks and intrusions taking place
- *Sector threat assessments.* Such analyses focus on vulnerabilities and threats either in particular areas such as national infrastructure, or in particular sectors of the economy such as banking or e-commerce. In effect, a strategic analysis of this kind has to take account of changes in what can be a very dynamic environment.
- *Trend Analysis to highlight changing threats and vulnerabilities.* These might include base-line assessments so as to better recognize departures from the baseline. Alternatively, they might focus on future threats and vulnerabilities in an effort to determine in

what ways the problem is evolving–and what can be done to anticipate and contain future challenges. The way in which e-commerce has become a major issue suggests that the pace of change in the cyber-space environment is posing novel challenges that can best be understood through strategic intelligence analysis that is very forward looking. Indeed, trend analysis is likely to be most effective when it is linked with careful attention to drivers, *i.e.* fundamental trends in the political, economic, social and technological sectors that will shape the future threat and vulnerability environment of the future.

- *Potential Damage Assessments*. Because of the macro-level view taken by strategic analysis, it also offers the best approach for assessing potential cascade effects of intrusions. The specific target of a an intrusion might be a regional electric power grid, but the effects of a failure to that system can cascade to include telecommunications, public emergency services, water systems, etc. The potential for such wide-spread effects will be recognized most readily as a result of in-depth strategic analysis–which in turn would offer opportunities to develop both defensive and mitigation strategies. Crisis management, contingency planning, mitigation strategies, and disaster management would all be enhanced by strategic analysis of potential damage assessment. Indeed, the capacity for effective and rapid reconstitution might depend on such analysis.
- *Categorizing and differentiating attacks and attackers*. Intrusions in cyber-space can emanate from individuals, whether insiders or outsiders; from hacker groups intent on displaying their skills and capabilities; activist groups using direct action on the Internet to publicize their political cause; terrorist organizations using intrusions to create massive disruption or other forms of large-scale harm, and seeking to obtain widespread publicity and create a climate of fear; transnational criminal

organizations responding to law enforcement pressure with cyber-retaliation, and states using attacks on, or through, information systems as a form of asymmetric warfare. One of the most important tasks of intelligence analysis for the Internet is to discover ways of differentiating among intrusions from these various sources. This will be especially true as groups or individuals develop intrusion strategies that mimic other forms and thereby lessen their chances of identification or, in the case of nation states, provide plausible deniability of their actions. From the perspective of strategic intelligence analysis, this is critical in efforts to determine appropriate responses that might go beyond simply defensive or mitigation strategies. How specific attacks are categorized, of course, will also be an issue at the tactical and operational level. But the differentiating and categorization methodologies, initially at least, are a matter for strategic analysis.

- *Identification of Anomalies*. Searching for anomalies that provide indicators of emerging threats and problems is an important task of strategic intelligence analysis (albeit one that both feeds into and relies on tactical and operational efforts). Anomalies in this context can be understood as developments or events that do not fit typical or known patterns. The detection of anomalies or novel patterns can be a major element in anticipating new methods of intrusion, new targets, or even new classes of intruders. It is a macro-level task that requires careful and systematic "environmental scanning" as well as the coalescing of tactical and operational intelligence reports that identify and highlight specific aberrations from the norm.
- *Analysis of Future Net Environments*. The greatest constant about the Internet is change. Strategic intelligence analysis must take that into account and attempt to provide assessments of potential future environments on the Net and the potential impact of

malicious activity within those environments. Given the dramatic changes in technology within the recent past, and seeing the rapid pace with which innovation continues to grow, it seems a reasonable assumption that the Internet (in one form or another) will become more and more integrated into the fabric of society. As this occurs, intrusions or attacks will have far more wide-ranging consequences. Considerations of social as well as political and economic impacts will have to be factored into intelligence assessments.

It is clear from this discussion that not only does strategic intelligence analysis provide a framework for tactical and operational assessments, but that work done at these levels in turn helps to shape the strategic intelligence focus. As for the strategic assessments themselves they should be useful for consumers, providing forecasting estimates that help to reduce uncertainties in ways that feed into policy processes, providing a basis for more informed decision-making and more effective resource allocation.

As strategic analytic methodologies mature, they will also offer the basis for predictive or anticipatory assessments that can serve to provide warning of potential hostile operations. In effect, strategic intelligence assessments provide a basis for the development of high-level policy and strategy and for strategic responses to vulnerabilities, whether actual or potential.

Tactical Intelligence Analysis

Tactical analysis is a necessary and important complement to work done at the strategic level. It is the natural linking element between macro-level analysis and the micro-level focus on individual cases.

Among the kinds of studies that come under the level of tactical analysis would be:

- Cluster and pattern analysis designed to discern temporal patterns, the use of particular intrusion methods, commonalities of targets, and attempts to build profiles of perpetrators, whether hackers or insiders.

- Stimulus-response analysis designed to identify potential actions that could be taken by intruders in response to specific known or predicted events. This analysis could be used both proactively in development of warnings or reactively in lending significance to otherwise-unrecognized activity.
- Network environmental analysis methods will have to be developed. It is probable that in-depth analysis of the Internet will reveal patterns similar to those in the physical world. Net weather is already being discussed, and network terrain is a viable concept. Unlike physical environments, however, the Internet environment will probably be subject to much more rapid shifting. That places this sort of analytic effort squarely in the realm of Tactical Analysis.

In physical space, geography helps to differentiate tactical from strategic, but on the Internet this component is lacking, an absence that makes the distinction between strategic and tactical somewhat more tenuous than in other domains. At the same time, the strategic and tactical levels are mutually reinforcing: although strategic intelligence analysis provides the framework for tactical assessments, these assessments in turn help to feed strategic analysis. With a highly dynamic inter-relationship among the various levels of analysis, each level is strengthened by and strengthens the others.

THE CYBER INTELLIGENCE COMMUNITY

This unique, currently ad hoc, community is made up of government, telecommunication and internet providers, CERTs, and other formal information security entities, specialty companies, and vendors. The members of this community engage in a myriad of activities that could be the potential victim of a cyber threat. This "Cyber Intelligence Community" is currently an informal coalition of the willing that collects and analyses unclassified and classified cyber intelligence data and trends. There is no formal mechanism across industry and government cyber intelligence entities that successfully collects, processes, and analyses all identifiable key cyber threat behaviour and reports it at an unclassified or reasonable classification level to all appropriate customers. An effective connection between intelligence provider and the customer means that the customer has understood and internalized the intelligence resulting in action to work the intelligence and mitigate the threat. Good intelligence professionals relentlessly pursue interactions with customers to ensure that: the data is collected, analysed, and conveyed; the intelligence serves customers' purposes; and some action is being taken (or deliberately not taken). This cycle can be referred to as a constant process of story-finding, storytelling, story-updating, storylistening, and story-heeding. A concept to institutionalize this ad hoc community is currently missing.

Investing in Cyber Intelligence Tradecraft

A substantial and continuing investment in cyber intelligence should be a strategic imperative in the information age. It is also imperative to use that intelligence to safe guard our ability to maintain security. We must ensure that stable domestic and international economies are not jeopardized by possible conflict with rival powers, rogue states, failing or failed states, modern terrorists and thieves, and WMD proliferators.

All formal and informal intelligence disciplines contribute to these imperatives, including Signals Intelligence (SIGINT), Human Intelligence (HUMINT), open Source Intelligence (OSINT), geospatial and Measurement Intelligence (GEOINT), and the volumes of unclassified network data and behaviour being watched by global CERTs.

Continuous liaison among all related parties is critical so that sharing is seamless. This ensures an evolving, improved level of insight and reporting to an increasingly secure and highly performing cyber environment for all.

This evolving cyber intelligence tradecraft requires deep and powerful technical and analytic expertise at all levels. Such technical talent and related capabilities remain ill-defined and in short supply across government and industry.

An institution that has made some headway in this regard is the Information Assurance Directorate (IAD) at the national Security Agency.

IAD is the front line of the defensive cyber mission. It commands substantial resources, high performing talent, strong processes, and informed outreach.

It also works hand in hand with military, public, and private partners to ensure that our cyber capabilities and intellectual property are defended and that our defence is informing offence and vice versa. IAD is a good start, but we must emulate their good practices and innovativeness in defining professional attributes, associated education, and training goals for the unique career fields associated with the cyber realm.

TYPES OF CYBER SECURITY THREATS

Nation-sponsored hacking specifically-targeted cyber attacks will incorporate concepts and techniques from the commercial hacker industry. These campaigns will contain a different malware payload than the traditional attacks conducted for monetary gain. However, these attacks will use similar techniques.

These Advanced Persistent Threat (APT) attacks will borrow techniques, such as automation and viral distribution, making them all the more powerful and potentially more successful. An example of such an attack is Stuxnet, which was not searching for data to monetize, rather it was focused on gaining control of crucial infrastructure.

Both classes of attack (hacker industry and APT) are going to use some of the same techniques so some security controls are applicable to both. On the positive side, given you're covered against the cyber mafia you should have some of the controls to be protected from certain APT attacks. As APT is persistent, if a certain attack does not succeed, another one will come into play. The traditional security controls do not deter these relentless, state-sponsored hacker organizations. For the enterprise as well as government, this means increasing monitoring of traffic and setting security controls across all organization layers.

The insider Threat

In this upcoming year, we expect to see a growing awareness to security incidents of an "insider job" nature. Attention will grow as a consequence of an increased flow of incident reports where data theft and security breaches are tied to employees and other insiders. The cause of this trend will be the emphasis put on new regulations covering the act of notification and disclosure (rather on the actual protection of data).

To deter insider threats, organizations should therefore:

- Enforce access controls such that access is based only a business need-to-know level. This includes eliminating excessive privileges.
- Provide the proper access auditing tools to data centres. These auditing tools should monitor who accesses what data.

Man in the Browser Attacks will man Up

Man in the Browser (MitB) attack sophistication is going to increase, as well as moving forward to more types of online applications. As a consequence, more online service providers are going to include this in their list of priorities for 2011, shifting the responsibility for mitigating the risk from the consumers to the service providers.

While avoiding infection by proxy Trojans is presumably the responsibility of consumers, MitB attacks are quickly becoming a concern of online service providers. The actual rate of infection and the proliferation of the many types of MitB malware suggest that providers must be able to serve (and protect) customers who might be infected with one type of malware or another. Just as the evolution of vehicle safety drove manufacturers to include device such as ABS, Air Bags and ESP, rather than rely on us to drive carefully, so will online service providers need to invest in mechanisms that allow them to conduct business with allegedly infected consumers. Among the technologies that we foresee as helpful are strong device identification, client profiling, fast security code evolution, session flow tracking and site-to-client authentication.

Misanthropes and Anti-socials: Privacy vs. Security in Social Networks

In 2011, we will see prominent social networks, and tools, placing more efforts into security over privacy. This is not the result of resolved privacy issues, but rather an understanding of the real threats to the existence and proliferation of social networks.

There are two key factors at stake: security and trust. While privacy concerns the ability to keep personal information hidden from other application users, security controls the way in which people use the information of others. Trust impacts our ability to make decisions based on the information we receive through social networks.

In today's social networking platform, both security and trust are in danger. Cross-site scripting (XSS) and cross-site request forgery (CSRF) vulnerabilities are quickly translating into massive worm out brakes.

Next year, we expect social platforms to invest more resources in improving the security posture of the platform. These measures will provide improved protection against application layer attacks, stronger authentication and account control features, as well as better malware detection systems.

File Security takes Centre Stage

In 2011, we expect to see a growing number of data breaches where compromised data is in the form of files rather than database records. Consequently, organizations will rush to look for the proper tools to control access to repositories of unstructured data, mainly file servers. We estimate that the number of compromised files, and the number of organizations that suffer a massive file related security breach, will rise. Even PCI 2.0 has recognized the security aspect of storing data in different locations.

With today's available tools, controlling access and usage of these files can be an extremely daunting task. Since each file is an autonomous entity, with respect to content ownership and access control (contrary to a database record), maintaining control of who can access a file is almost impossible as is keeping track of access to those files that contain sensitive information.

The inability to maintain control may result in excessive access privileges and an inadequate audit trail of access to sensitive information.

Data Security goes to the Cloud

We expect to see more application security offerings in the cloud throughout 2011, and predict some early data security in the cloud offerings. Offerings will need to respond to private and public clouds that are either self-serviced or managed as a service.

This trend is a late response to the move of many applications and data stores to cloud technologies, and the industrialization of hacking, which dragged many smaller online businesses into the threat zone.

Taking together all the types of cloud forms (private and public, SaaS, PaaS and IaaS) we can see a set of challenges for both providers and consumers.

These can be summarized as following:

- Maintaining bulletproof partitions between datasets of different customers
- Providing different levels of data security to applications sharing the same logical or physical platforms
- Protecting customer data from the prying eyes of cloud administrators
- Providing solutions that operate over a specialized infrastructure (VM, Amazon AMI)
- Managing application and data security for a large number of applications inside the cloud.

We expect that in 2011 good technical solutions for application security in the cloud will be available and gain traction, while data security solutions (protecting data stores in the cloud) will lag behind.

Mobile Devices Compromise Data Security

The proliferation of sophisticated mobile devices is going to have a substantial effect on application and data security in the coming years. In particular, we will see organizations struggle to accommodate the increase in number and variety of these devices, while maintaining traditional data and application security practices.

The past couple of years have witnessed a dramatic surge in the number of sophisticated mobile devices being used as access points to online services and enterprise networks. Add to the mix a growing variety of applications that are a gateway to enterprise systems, including CRM, ERP, and document management.

While we are used to concerning ourselves with lost or stolen laptops, it turns out that missing mobile devices may be just as big of a pain point. As mobile devices become mainstream, online service providers will create a special version of the applications to match each device platform.

We anticipate this process, will cause older vulnerabilities to surface once again. In particular, mistakes around identification and authentication. Thus, the applications will become vulnerable to mistakenly trusting attributes of the data stream that can be forged by an attacker.

Furthermore, some assumptions regarding "strong" multifactor authentication schemes are becoming obsolete. Take, for example, applications that use a one-time password (OTP) for validation of sensitive transactions being defeated by a Trojan that is able to access the OTP delivered through SMS.

Mobile malware will proliferate as malicious code becomes available for these platforms (*e.g.* Zitmo) and the complex applications (not to mention the usual human flaws) make it easy, if not easier, to infect a mobile device with malware, as with any standard desktop platform.

We expect exponential growth in the number of incidents related to mobile devices in the next few years. Organizations need to start planning to secure the devices and their interaction with the enterprise networks.

Tools and procedures need to be put into place, such as anti-malware, encryption, and authentication. Special monitoring requirements should be set for access of these devices to enterprise resources (databases, files, intranets). On the other hand, application providers need to get their act together with respect to serving these devices, including vulnerability mitigation, reevaluation of trust, and incorporation of new authentication/authorization channels.

Hackers Feeling the Heat

In 2011, the cyber crime landscape will change in two ways. First, more and more smaller cyber gangs will go out of business. Why? Security researchers will continue to look into the hacker operations and will unearth the smaller or less diligent criminals.

In general, the hacker industry will react by investing more resources in their attack techniques and detection evasion. The hackers that cannot make this investment will go out of business. Other cyber-criminal organizations will "buy-out" other groups or merge their operations with other groups.

This will lead to the second change. The current powerful cyber crime organizations will consolidate their power and grow (after all, antitrust laws don't apply to them).

As the year 2010 draws to a close, it provides us with all the more examples of this accelerating trend:

- At the end of September, Zeus botnet ring leaders and operatives were arrested. This was the culmination of a year-long investigation that included the infiltration of the C&C servers by security researchers. Similarly, the master mind of the Bredolab botnet was arrested three weeks later.

- During mid October, the Avalanche phishing group completed their 2 year-long move from phishing techniques to distributing MitB Trojans.
- The end of October has seen the Iranian Cyber-Army (ICA), infamously known for engaging politically-motivated DDoS attacks, advertising their bots for rent.

Also, towards the end of October, the bot code developers of the ever-competing spyEye and Zeus bots were showing signs of an upcoming merger.

Cyber Security becomes a Business Process

The consolidation taking place with security vendors implies, as Intel CEO Paul Otellini put it, "We have concluded that security has become the third pillar of computing." Vendors are seeing a big shift in security, what about enterprises?

Today, cyber security can't be separated from business operations. For this reason, how security teams must view and approach their roles has changed dramatically. For example, in the past, a CIO's role was laptop distribution. Today, CIOs build supply chains.

In the past, CISOs distributed anti-virus and set up firewalls. Today, they must know where data resides, where it moves and how to protect it, which requires a serious, comprehensive data security practice. This means security teams need to become business process experts to keep the bad guys disarmed while keeping the good guys productive.

Convergence of Data Security and Privacy Regulation Worldwide

As newspapers features more companies that violate data privacy on its front page and security breaches appear daily, government regulators will continue to tighten the legal screws on enterprises.

Continuing data breaches force more and more governments—and even private industries—to consider more in-depth security regulations to protect citizens. But another interesting trend seems to be flying under the radar: as enterprises contend with additional data laws, a consolidation will take place across borders.

Recently, for instance, the FTC reached out to the EU to begin the process of investigating where both sides of the Atlantic can unify data security laws. Companies will comply, but will find the task of complying with multiple mandates across borders very difficult. Governments will respond—in fact already are—to define a common framework to make life easier for themselves and for enterprises housing data.

3

Basic Principles of the Cyber Security Strategy

The Federal Government aims at making a substantial contribution to a secure cyberspace, thus maintaining and promoting economic and social prosperity in Germany. Cyber security in Germany must be ensured at a level commensurate with the importance and protection required by interlinked information infrastructures, without hampering the opportunities and the utilization of the cyberspace. In this context the level of cyber security reached is the sum of all national and international measures taken to protect the availability of information and communications technology and the integrity, authenticity and confidentiality of data in cyberspace.

Cyber security must be based on a comprehensive approach. This requires even more intensive information sharing and coordination. The Cyber Security Strategy mainly focuses on civilian approaches and measures. They are complemented by measures taken by the Bundeswehr to protect its capabilities and measures based on mandates to make cyber security a part of Germany's preventive security strategy. Given the global nature of information and communications technology, international coordination and appropriate networks focusing on foreign and security policy aspects are indispensable. This includes cooperation not only in the United Nations, but also in the EU, the Council of Europe, NATO, the G8, the OSCE and other multinational organizations. The aim is to ensure the coherence and capabilities of the international community to protect cyberspace.

CYBER-SECURITY RISKS

New risk factors and challenges to data and communications networks seem to be evolving as rapidly as the spread of high-speed Internet infrastructure. Among these compelling risks are: Computer worms and viruses. Debilitating worms and computer viruses have demonstrated destructive capabilities for a number of years, as evidenced by the damage caused by such programmes as Sasser, Blaster, Netsky, Welchia and Code Red. Organized criminal activity. The booming growth of ICT-services has spawned new gray-and black-market opportunities that organized criminal elements are exploiting for huge financial advantage. Financial institutions, for example, have already experienced significant losses through "phishing" and "pharming" operations.

The more significant the volume of revenues that flow over ICT-based networks, the greater will be the incentive for organized criminal elements to corrupt or economically exploit high-value data resources.

A global "black economy" can, for example, generate financing for terrorism, as well as "off-budget" funding for military, police, or national security agencies of nation states.

A Network Model for Cyber Security

A well-balanced cyber security policy framework is highly complex. Such a policy framework has no bounds or limits—geographical or jurisdictional. It necessarily encompasses a full spectrum of business, societal, and governmental interests. Although cyber security policy will inevitably address grave concerns about national and global security, as well as well-organized criminal activity, it is fundamentally about creating the very underpinnings of stable economic growth and open, transparent, just, and vibrant societies. A "network model"—essentially, a communications network—illustrates how actors in the public and private sectors can work together to manage future cyber risks. Rather than focus on institutions and functions, the focus is on processes, procedures, and information flows within these sectors. In other words, the framework promotes thinking in terms of functions, rather than titles or national or international institutions.

The focus on information flows is intended to help policymakers and other stakeholders visualize the systemic, inter-related nature of cyber security and how the actions of individual entities are likely to impact the decisions and responses of other participants in the network. It should be noted that such a model may require significant changes in traditional roles of intelligence and (inter)national security agencies, requiring them to operate on a more collaborative, interinstitutional basis.

The network model is based on three types of nodes or groups of stakeholders (policymakers, policy implementers, and operational personnel), which exchange three types of information on cyber-security: assessments, responses, and policy. Information exchange occurs both among the nodes, as well as between individual nodes and their peers in outside organizations at all levels. The model operates in the same way at four different levels, as risk management generally has the same components, regardless of whether it is conducted at the level of a firm, industrial sector, nation, or international organization. First, it requires communications across "organizational" boundaries. Second, it requires information exchange between stakeholders at different levels in the same organization and with other organizations regarding threats that have been encountered and handled. Third, procedures for handling such incidents are required and, fourth, legal or law enforcement sanctions may need to be applied.

At the national level, the major network "nodes" are central coordinating bodies, telecommunications regulators and e-economy ministries, intelligence agencies, law enforcement bodies, and national and governmental Computer Emergency Response Teams (CERTs) and Information Sharing and Analysis

Centres (ISACs). The model works at the international level, where the top-level node is comprised of multinational firms, political and military alliances, which coordinate with such international bodies as the ITU, G8, and the United Nations and its specialized agencies.

The implementation node in the international model is comprised of individual national ministries (telecommunications, intelligence, e-economy, and defence ministries, together with law enforcement bodies) and the operational level of national firms (including software and hardware vendors), CERTs, and national defence organizations.

The drivers of various information exchanges—the factors that shape and influence critical flows of information—include regulatory requirements, liability obligations, and market signals (*e.g.*, risk-related information through which the performance of a network may be influenced). Each national networked relationship may operate with its own unique set of additional drivers. Policymakers may further shape certain drivers to influence node behaviour and performance. It may be possible, for example, to strengthen the influence of market-related drivers by using government procurement policies. Insurance and rating companies may use liability strategies to influence the cost of capital and the incentives for security-related investments.

DATABASE SECURITY

Database security concerns the use of a broad range of information security controls to protect databases (potentially including the data, the database applications or stored functions, the database systems, the database servers and the associated network links) against compromises of their confidentiality, integrity and availability.

It involves various types or categories of controls, such as technical, procedural/administrative and physical. *Database security* is a specialist topic within the broader realms of computer security, information security and risk management. Security risks to database systems include, for example:

- Unauthorized or unintended activity or misuse by authorized database users, database administrators, or network/systems managers, or by unauthorized users or hackers (e.g. inappropriate access to sensitive data, metadata or functions within databases, or inappropriate changes to the database programmes, structures or security configurations);
- Malware infections causing incidents such as unauthorized access, leakage or disclosure of personal or proprietary data, deletion of or damage to the data or programmes, interruption or denial of authorized access to the database, attacks on other systems and the unanticipated failure of database services;
- Overloads, performance constraints and capacity issues resulting in the inability of authorized users to use databases as intended;
- Physical damage to database servers caused by computer room fires or floods, overheating, lightning, accidental liquid spills, static discharge, electronic breakdowns/ equipment failures and obsolescence;
- Design flaws and programming bugs in databases and the associated programmes and systems, creating various security vulnerabilities (e.g. unauthorized privilege escalation), data loss/corruption, performance degradation etc.;
- Data corruption and/or loss caused by the entry of invalid data or commands, mistakes in database or system administration processes, sabotage/criminal damage etc.

Many layers and types of information security control are appropriate to databases, including:

- Access control
- Auditing
- Authentication
- Encryption
- Integrity controls
- Backups
- Application security

Traditionally databases have been largely secured against hackers through network security measures such as firewalls, and network-based intrusion detection systems. While network security controls remain valuable in this regard, securing the database systems themselves, and the programmes/functions and data within them, has arguably become more critical as networks are increasingly opened to wider access, in particular access from the Internet.

Furthermore, system, programme, function and data access controls, along with the associated user identification, authentication and rights management functions, have always been important to limit and in some cases log the activities of authorized users and administrators. In other words, these are complementary approaches to database security, working from both the outside-in and the inside-out as it were. Many organizations develop their own "baseline" security standards and designs detailing basic security control measures for their database systems.

These may reflect general information security requirements or obligations imposed by corporate information security policies and applicable laws and regulations (e.g. concerning privacy, financial management and reporting systems), along with generally-accepted good database security practices (such as appropriate hardening of the underlying systems) and perhaps security recommendations from the relevant database system and software vendors.

The security designs for specific database systems typically specify further security administration and management functions (such as administration and reporting of user access rights, log management and analysis, database replication/synchronization and backups) along with various business-driven information security controls within the database programmes and functions (e.g. data entry validation and audit trails). Furthermore, various security-related activities (manual controls) are normally incorporated into the procedures, guidelines etc. relating to the design, development, configuration, use, management and maintenance of databases.

Vulnerability Assessments and Compliance

One technique for evaluating database security involves performing vulnerability assessments or penetration tests against the database. Testers attempt to find security vulnerabilities that could be used to defeat or bypass security controls, break into the database, compromise the system etc. Database administrators or information security administrators may for example use automated vulnerability scans to search out misconfiguration of controls within the layers mentioned above along with known vulnerabilities within the database software.

The results of such scans are used to harden the database (improve the security controls) and close off the specific vulnerabilities identified, but unfortunately other vulnerabilities typically remain unrecognized and unaddressed. A programme of continual monitoring for compliance with database security standards is another important task for mission critical database environments. Two crucial aspects of database security compliance include patch management and the review and management of permissions (especially public) granted to objects within the database. Database objects may include table or other objects listed in the Table link.

The permissions granted for SQL language commands on objects are considered in this process. One should note that compliance monitoring is similar to vulnerability assessment with the key difference that the results of vulnerability assessments generally drive the security standards that lead to the continuous monitoring programme. Essentially, vulnerability assessment is a preliminary procedure to determine risk where a compliance programme is the process of on-going risk assessment. The compliance programme should take into consideration any dependencies at the application software level as changes at the database level may have effects on the application software or the application server. In direct relation to this topic is that of application security.

Abstraction

Application level authentication and authorization mechanisms should be considered as an effective means of providing abstraction from the database layer. The primary benefit of abstraction is that of a single sign-on capability across multiple databases and database platforms. A Single sign-on system should store the database user's credentials (login id and password), and authenticate to the database on behalf of the user.

Database Activity Monitoring (DAM)

Another security layer of a more sophisticated nature includes real-time database activity monitoring, either by analyzing protocol traffic (SQL) over the network, or by observing local database activity on each server using software agents, or both.

Use of agents or native logging is required to capture activities executed on the database server, which typically include the activities of the database administrator. Agents allow this information to be captured in a fashion that can not be disabled by the database administrator, who has the ability to disable or modify native audit logs. Analysis can be performed to identify known exploits or policy breaches, or baselines can be captured over time to build a normal pattern used for detection of anomalous activity that could be indicative of intrusion.

These systems can provide a comprehensive Database audit trail in addition to the intrusion detection mechanisms, and some systems can also provide protection by terminating user sessions and/or quarantining users demonstrating suspicious behaviour.

Some systems are designed to support separation of duties (SOD), which is a typical requirement of auditors. SOD requires that the database administrators who are typically monitored as part of the DAM, not be able to disable or alter the DAM functionality. This requires the DAM audit trail to be securely stored in a separate system not administered by the database administration group.

Native Audit

In addition to using external tools for monitoring or auditing, native database audit capabilities are also available for many database platforms. The native audit trails are extracted on a regular basis and transferred to a designated security system where the database administrators do not have access. This ensures a certain level of segregation of duties that may provide evidence the native audit trails were not modified by authenticated administrators.

Turning on native impacts the performance of the server. Generally, the native audit trails of databases do not provide sufficient controls to enforce separation of duties; therefore, the network and/or kernel module level host based monitoring capabilities provides a higher degree of confidence for forsenics and preservation of evidence.

Process and Procedures

A *database security* programme should include the regular review of permissions granted to individually owned accounts and accounts used by automated processes. The accounts used by automated processes should have appropriate controls around password storage such as sufficient encryption and access controls to reduce the risk of compromise.

For individual accounts, a two-factor authentication system should be considered in a database environment where the risk is commensurate with the expenditure for such an authentication system. In conjunction with a sound *database security* programme, an appropriate disaster recovery programme should exist to ensure that service is not interrupted during a security incident or any other incident that results in an outage of the primary database environment. An example is that of replication for the primary databases to sites located in different geographical regions. After an incident occurs, the usage of database forensics should be employed to determine the scope of the breach, and to identify appropriate changes to systems and/or processes to prevent similar incidents in the future.

CYBER-SECURITY AS SCIENCE

A science of cyber-security has to deal with a combination of peculiar features that are shared by no other area of study. First, the background on which events occur is almost completely created by humans and is digital. That is, people built all the pieces. One might have thought that computers, their software, and networks were therefore completely understandable. The truth is that the cyber-universe is complex well beyond anyone's understanding and exhibits behaviour that no one predicted, and sometimes can't even be explained well. On the positive side, the cyber-universe can be thought of as reduced to the 0s and 1s of binary data. Actions in this universe consist of sequences of changes to binary data, interleaved in time, and having some sort of locations in space. One can speculate as to why mathematics is so effective in explaining physics, but the cyber-world is inherently mathematical. Mathematics is a natural way for reasoning about it and this point of view is a theme that appears repeatedly in this report. Second, cyber-security has good guys and bad guys. It is a field that has developed because people have discovered how to do things that other people disapprove of, and that break what is thought to be an agreed-upon social contract in the material world. That is, in cyber-security there are adversaries, and the adversaries are purposeful and intelligent.

Thus, the reasoning in cyber-security has to be both about the constructed universe and the actions and reactions of the adversaries. Definitions and concepts will shift over time in cyber-security, as in all sciences. A successfully chosen name is a bridge between scientific knowledge and common sense, between new experience and old habits. The conceptual foundation of any science consists of a complicated network of names of things, names of ideas, and names of names. It evolves itself, and its projections on reality changes.

This quote echoes the observations of a presentation to JASON by Peter Gallison of Harvard in which he compared the type of science encountered in cyber security to a "Manichaean science" or science in the presence of adversaries. Particularly important for this type of science (and indeed any branch of science) was the development of a common language so that precise arguments could be formulated that addressed directly the problems of interest. We emphasize this point because the deninition of cyber-security itself is imprecise. The subject includes correctness properties like condentiality and integrity, and liveness properties such as are associated with denial-of-service attacks, together with a growing set of unpleasant surprises.

Security Degrades Over Time

We observed earlier that success in cyber-security requires constant attention. Not only do the threats and attacks change, but the old techniques tend to become less effective. Technology advances, and the properties of the security system become better understood.

Unix Passwords

The original UNIX passwords were up to 8 ASCII non-control characters. The passwords aren't stored directly. Rather hashes (some one-way function) are stored. In modern systems these hashes aren't easily read, but if a machine is compromised, then the hashes can be taken away, and one can attempt to break passwords by making up likely candidates, applying the one-way function, and seeing if the result matches any of the hashes. There are about 2 original UNIX passwords, which seemed like quite a lot at the time. Nowadays, one could imagine trying about 32 million guesses (2) per second on a single CPU core, so testing the entire space would only take about 3 days on 1,000 cores. That's not a particularly large computer, but the calculation is also embarrassingly parallel, so the 1,000 cores could be 1,000 machines in a (small) botnet. Or one could use 9,000 machines, still not a large botnet, and do the whole calculation in one night. For completeness we note that there has been a lot of work on making it harder to guess passwords; for instance, by using much slower one-way functions and much larger spaces. Another approach is to force people to use more complex passwords, but that has other sociological ramications which are unfortunately very difcult to deal with in terms of any science. An extreme version turned up in the recent Russian spy case, where "Ricci said the steganographic programme was activated by pressing controlalt-E and then typing in a 27-character password, which the FBI found written down on a piece of paper during one of its searches."

Lock Bumping

A second example of security decreasing over time comes from the common locks people use on doors. A simple technique called "lock bumping" makes all these locks quite easy to open with just a little practice. The locks were, of course, vulnerable, but it didn't much matter until the technique was popularized starting about 2005. There are plenty of explanatory videos online. The implication for cyber-security is that the nature of the attack can change over time. It will not in general be possible to anticipate all attacks. For this reason it becomes necessary to constantly survey the extant modes of attack to understand the nature of current technology as well as continually attack one's own systems in the hopes of finding heretofore undiscovered attacks.

The Role of Secrecy

All security regimes include some secrets. The TSA doesn't explain everything it is looking for; the credit card processors don't fully explain their criteria, and so on. In the computer science community, security by obscurity is generally considered bad, probably based on examples of awed cryptography. There seems to be little theoretical work on this subject. We mention a few examples of keeping (and not keeping) secrets.

Commercial anti-virus programmes, of the sort that run on your home computer, reveal some of the weaknesses of totally public defences. In principal, a malware author could just buy these, and adjust the malware until none of them detect it. The market has made this easier; there are online services that for a fee will run uploaded malware through a large number of commercial programmes, and report the result.

Game theory and economics teach us that keeping our private valuations secret sometimes adds value. Much effort has gone into auction mechanisms that get bidders to reveal their private valuations.

On the other hand, under various circum stances, this "asymmetric information" can lead to lemon markets, where either no market exists, or only people who are forced to will trade in the market.

Secrecy might also be required by the rules. For instance, the DoD might use logs of network trafc to tune its network defences. These logs might easily contain material that should not be made public. For these reasons, there may be some benefit in exploring the role an enhanced role for secrecy and obfuscation, particularly for DOD systems.

Finally, one might ask if keeping the source code secret adds much to security. First, there may be other reasons for keeping source code secret, such as the trade secrets incorporated in it. Certainly attackers with source code are likely to proceed differently, as they have a better chance of finding attacks based on logical errors, and this would be especially valuable for targeted attacks.

On the other hand, there seems to be no particular shortage of effective attacks when source code is unavailable. But the code owner may have no realistic alternatives to making the source available. As an example consider the following announcement: "The agreement that we signed with the FSB is an extension of Microsoft's Government Security Programme (GSP)," Microsoft said in a statement on Friday. "The purpose of the GSP is to increase trust with national governments.

In the case of the Russian agreement, GSP participation will facilitate the development of the next generation of secured solutions for Russian government agencies based on the latest Microsoft technologies and Russian cryptography."

THE FUTURE OF CYBER SECURITY

The product of human ingenuity and innovation, cyberspace now delivers a range of critical services to more citizens around the world than ever before. Yet, the online world as we know it stands at the threshold of unprecedented change.

Being invited to speak at the EastWest Institute's Worldwide Security Conference in Brussels this week provided an opportunity to examine the needs faced by the global security community as we prepare to meet the needs of the Internet's next billion users.

The International Telecommunication Union (ITU) reported that the number of Internet users reached the two billion threshold in March of this year and according to a Boston Consulting Group report, another billion are expected to come online in the next four years, bringing the total number of Internet users worldwide to about three billion by 2015.

Planning to ensure that our online world—cyberspace—is trustworthy, resilient and secure as we move into this uncertain future, policy leaders need to consider the fundamental changes that are occurring in cyberspace, and the policy issues that these changes will likely present and that will need to be addressed. Looking towards the future of three billion users, four factors will fundamentally change the future of cyberspace security: people, devices, data, and cloud services.

The Global Online Population Expands

The emergence of the next billion Internet users will impact security in two ways. Most important will be the impact of the demographic characteristics of these users. Consider that the next billion users will (1) be younger, (2) spend more time online, (3) be more mobile, (4) see the world through social media and apps, and (5) make greater use of natural interfaces. These five factors could hasten the onset of totally digital lifestyles making connectivity seemingly as essential as oxygen. The next billion could also help foster new innovation in the development and application of technology.

Separately, however, this emerging user population also represents a greatly expanded "target rich" environment for cybercriminals that want to exploit their data, social networks, and devices via botnets or other means.

Internet of Things to Immersive Computing

These new users will require new devices. According to The Boston Consulting Group, the number of Internet-connected devices is predicted to exceed 15 billion—twice the world's population–by 2015, and to soar to 50 billion devices by 2020. "Devices" of course refers to more than smart phones, netbooks and tablets. It also systems such as smart grids, intelligent transportation, healthcare monitoring, smart manufacturing, and environmental sensors.

The advent of powerful wireless devices that both run infrastructure and deliver infrastructure services, including providing access to cloud services, means that cybercriminals and other threat actors need not merely target traditional, and increasingly protected, commercial software and consumer applications to execute attacks with significant consequences. Attackers may well target the embedded software, firmware and hardware in these devices to attack the infrastructure or seize control of the devices and turn them into sensors that can report status, collect personally identifiable information, or conduct other espionage.

Data: Rapid increases in Understanding

The striking growth in the number of users and devices will also produce an exponential growth in the amount of data that is being generated, stored, analysed and transformed into innovation and knowledge. Analysing large data sets—so-called big data—will become a key basis of competition, underpinning new waves of productivity growth, innovation, and consumer surplus, according to research by MGI and McKinsey's Business Technology Office. However, such data sets also represent attractive targets for organized cyber criminals and other threat actors. From a security standpoint, safeguarding these huge data sets, protecting privacy and integrity, will require concerted global effort requiring collaboration among governments, the private sector, and users.

Cloud Computing: The Information Society Enabler

With an exponentially growing community of increasingly mobile users, cloud computing will commensurately grow in importance. It will fundamentally change how businesses operate, how every manner of services are delivered, and even how lives are lived. On the positive side, the security best practices implemented by an effective cloud provider may rival or surpass the measures that cloud customers might themselves be able to provide, resulting in enhanced security. Yet there are global issues that will need to be addressed in terms of transparency and jurisdiction to enable cloud services that are both secure and scalable to service the needsof this expanded user community across multiple countries.

Reducing the Cyber-attack Surface

Reducing the cyber-attack surface can be achieved by industry and government working inpartnership to make the ICT infrastructure less susceptible to attack and compromise. One important way to achieve this is through concerted action to address risks in the supply chain for information and communications technology products and services. Vendors and service providers need to build and maintain world-class approaches to secure software and hardware development methodologies. Microsoft began this journey over 10 years ago and has openly shared its Security Development Lifecycle. The nonprofit alliance SAFECode provides a platform for companies toshare, both within the software development community and more broadly, information on secure software development techniques that have proven to be effective as well as those that have not. Industry needs to do more.

For their part, governments need to understand the nature of ICT supply chain risk more clearly and work collaboratively with one another and with vendors to develop a common risk management framework rooted in core principles that both address supply chain integrity concerns and preserve the fruits of global free trade. Such a system should be risk-based,transparent, flexible, and should recognize the realities of reciprocal treatment in the global economic environment.

Improving Internet Health

Improving Internet health requires a global, collaborative approach to protecting people from the potential dangers of the Internet. Despite the best efforts at education and protection, many consumer computers host malware and may be part of a "botnet," unbeknownst to their legitimate owners. There is currently no concerted mechanism to shield users from or help them mitigate these risks. Such infected computers do not simply expose their owners'valuable information and data; they place others at risk too. This threat to greater society makes it is essential that the technology ecosystem take collective action to combat it.

Work has been underway in industry circles to build cooperation among various stakeholder groups including ISPs, software vendors, and others; to leverage investments made in key regions of the world; and to create a future roadmap for an Internet health system. The active discussions of cyber security policy and legislation now underway in many nations afford a ripe opportunity to promote this Internet health model. As part of this discussion, it is important to focus on building a socially acceptable model. While the security benefits may be clear, it is important to achieve those benefits in a way that does not erode privacy or otherwise raise concern.

CYBER SECURITY SYSTEM

Cyber security standards are security standards which enable organizations to practice safe security techniques to minimize the number of successful cyber security attacks. These guides provide general outlines as well as specific techniques for implementing cyber security. For certain specific standards, cyber security certification by an accredited body can be obtained. There are many advantages to obtaining certification including the ability to get cyber security insurance.

History

Cyber security standards have been created recently because sensitive information is now frequently stored on computers that are attached to the Internet. Also many tasks that were once done by hand are carried out by computer; therefore there is a need for Information Assurance (IA) and security. Cyber security is important in order to guard against identity theft. Businesses also have a need for cyber security because they need to protect their trade secrets, proprietary information, and personally identifiable information (PII) of their customers or employees. The government also has the need to secure its information. One of the most widely used security standards today is ISO/IEC 27002 which started in 1995. This standard consists of two basic parts. BS 7799 part 1 and BS 7799 part 2 both of which were created by (British Standards Institute) BSI. Recently this standard has become ISO 27001. The National Institute of Standards and Technology (NIST) has released several special publications addressing cyber security.

Three of these special papers are very relevant to cyber security: the 800-12 titled "Computer Security Handbook;" 800-14 titled "Generally Accepted Principles and Practices for Securing Information Technology;" and the 800-26 titled "Security Self-Assessment Guide for Information Technology Systems". The International Society of Automation (ISA) developed cyber security standards for industrial automation control systems (IACS) that are broadly applicable across manufacturing industries. The series of ISA industrial cyber security standards are known as ISA-99 and are being expanded to address new areas of concern.

ISO 27002

ISO 27002 incorporates both parts of the BS 7799 standard. Sometimes ISO/IEC 27002 is referred to as BS 7799 part 1 and sometimes it refers to part 1 and part 2. BS 7799 part 1 provides an outline for cyber security policy; whereas BS 7799 part 2 provides a certification.

The outline is a high level guide to cyber security. It is most beneficial for an organization to obtain a certification to be recognized as compliant with the standard. The certification once obtained lasts three years and is periodically checked by the BSI to ensure an organization continues to be compliant throughout that three year period. ISO 27001 (ISMS) replaces BS 7799 part 2, but since it is backward compatible any organization working toward BS 7799 part 2 can easily transition to the ISO 27001 certification process. There is also a transitional audit available to make it easier once an organization is BS 7799 part 2-certified for the organization to become ISO 27001-certified. ISO/IEC 27002 states that information security is characterized by integrity, confidentiality, and availability. The ISO/IEC 27002 standard is arranged into eleven control areas; security policy, organizing information security, asset management, human resources security, physical and environmental security, communication and operations, access controls, information systems acquisition/development/ maintenance, incident handling, business continuity management, compliance.

Standard of Good Practice

In the 1990s, the Information Security Forum (ISF) published a comprehensive list of best practices for information security, published as the *Standard of Good Practice* (SoGP). The ISF continues to update the SoGP every two years; the latest version was published in February 2007. Originally the *Standard of Good Practice* was a private document available only to ISF members, but the ISF has since made the full document available to the general public at no cost. Among other programmes, the ISF offers its member organizations a comprehensive benchmarking programme based on the SoGP.

NERC

The North American Electric Reliability Corporation (NERC) has created many standards. The most widely recognized is NERC 1300 which is a modification/update of NERC 1200. The newest version of NERC 1300 is called

CIP-002-1 through CIP-009-2 (CIP=Critical Infrastructure Protection). These standards are used to secure bulk electric systems although NERC has created standards within other areas. The bulk electric system standards also provide network security administration while still supporting best practice industry processes.

NIST

1. Special publication 800-12 provides a broad overview of computer security and control areas. It also emphasizes the importance of the security controls and ways to implement them. Initially this document was aimed at the federal government although most practices in this document can be applied to the private sector as well. Specifically it was written for those people in the federal government responsible for handling sensitive systems.
2. Special publication 800-14 describes common security principles that are used. It provides a high level description of what should be incorporated within a computer security policy. It describes what can be done to improve existing security as well as how to develop a new security practice. Eight principles and fourteen practices are described within this document.
3. Special publication 800-26 provides advice on how to manage IT security. This document emphasizes the importance of self assessments as well as risk assessments.
4. Special publication 800-37, updated in 2010 provides a new risk approach: "Guide for Applying the Risk Management Framework to Federal Information Systems"
5. Special publication 800-53 rev3, "Guide for Assessing the Security Controls in Federal Information Systems", updated in August 2009, specifically addresses the 194 security controls that are applied to a system to make it "more secure."

ISO 15408

This standard develops what is called the "Common Criteria". It allows many different software applications to be integrated and tested in a secure way.

RFC 2196

RFC 2196 is memorandum published by Internet Engineering Task Force for developing security policies and procedures for information systems connected on the Internet. The RFC 2196 provides a general and broad overview of information security including network security, incident response or security policies. The document is very practical and focusing on day-to-day operations.

ISA-99

ISA99 is the Industrial Automation and Control System Security Committee of the International Society for Automation (ISA). The committee is developing a multi-part series of standards and technical reports on the subject, several of which have been publicly released. Work products from the ISA99 committee are also submitted to IEC as standards and specifications in the IEC 63443 series.

- ISA-99.01.01 (formerly referred to as "Part 1") (ANSI/ ISA 99.00.01) is approved and published.
- ISA-TR99.01.02 is a master glossary of terms used by the committee.
- ISA-99.01.03 identifies a set of compliance metrics for IACS security. This document is currently under development.
- ISA-99.02.01 (formerly referred to as "Part 2") (ANSI/ ISA 99.02.01-2009) addresses how to establish an IACS security programme. This standard is approved and published. It has also been approved and published by the IEC as IEC 62443-2-1
- ISA-99.02.02 addresses how to operate an IACS security programme. This standard is currently under development.

- ISA-TR99.02.03 is a technical report on the subject of patch management. This report is currently under development.
- ISA-TR99.03.01 ()is a technical report on the subject of suitable technologies for IACS security. This report is approved and published.
- ISA-99.03.02 addresses how to define security assurance levels using the zones and conduits concept. This standard is currently under development.
- ISA-99.03.03 defines detailed technical requirements for IACS security. This standard is currently under development.
- ISA-99.03.04 addresses the requirements for the development of secure IACS products and solutions. This standard is currently under development.
- Standards in the ISA-99.04.xx series address detailed technical requirements at the component level. These standards are currently under development.

Risks to Internet Privacy

In today's technological world, millions of individuals are subject to privacy threats. Companies are hired not only to watch what you visit online, but to infiltrate the information and send advertising based on your browsing history. People set up accounts for Facebook; enter bank and credit card information to various websites. Those concerned about Internet privacy often cite a number of *privacy risks* — events that can compromise privacy — which may be encountered through Internet use. These methods of compromise can range from the gathering of statistics on users, to more malicious acts such as the spreading of spyware and various forms of bugs (software errors) exploitation. Privacy measures are provided on several social networking sites to try to provide their users with protection for their personal information. On Facebook for example privacy settings are available for all registered users. The settings available on Facebook include the ability to block certain individuals from seeing your profile, the ability to choose your "friends," and the ability to limit who has access to your pictures and videos. Privacy settings are also available on other social networking sites such as E-harmony and MySpace. It is the user's prerogative to apply such settings when providing personal information on the internet. In late 2007 Facebook launched the Beacon programme where user rental records were released on the public for friends to see. Many people were enraged by this breach in privacy, and the*Lane v. Facebook, Inc.* case ensued.

HTTP Cookies

An HTTP cookie is data stored on a user's computer that assists in automated access to websites or web features, or other state information required in complex web sites. It may also be used for user-tracking by storing special usage history data in a cookie. Cookies are a common concern in the field of privacy. As a result, some types of cookies are classified as a *tracking cookie*. Although website developers most commonly use cookies for legitimate technical purposes, cases of abuse occur. In 2009, two researchers noted that social networking profiles could be connected to cookies, allowing the social networking profile to be connected to browsing habits. Systems do not generally make the user explicitly aware of the storing of a cookie. (Although some users object to that, it does not properly relate to Internet privacy. It does however have implications for computer privacy, and specifically for computer forensics. The original developers of cookies intended that only the website that originally distributed cookies to users so they could retrieve them, therefore returning only data already possessed by the website. However, in practice programmers can circumvent this restriction. Possible consequences include:

- the placing of a personally-identifiable tag in a browser to facilitate web profiling, or,
- use of cross-site scripting or other techniques to steal information from a user's cookies.

Some users choose to disable cookies in their web browsers – as of 2000 a Pew survey estimated the proportion of users at 4%. Such an action eliminates the potential privacy risks, but may severely limit or prevent the functionality of many websites. All significant web browsers have this disabling ability built-in, with no external programme required. As an alternative, users may frequently delete any stored cookies. Some browsers (such as Mozilla Firefox and Opera) offer the option to clear cookies automatically whenever the user closes the browser. A third option involves allowing cookies in general, but preventing their abuse. There are also a host of wrapper applications that will redirect cookies and cache data to some other location. The process of *profiling* (also known as "tracking") assembles and analyses several events, each attributable to a single originating entity, in order to gain information (especially patterns of activity) relating to the originating entity. Some organizations engage in the profiling of people's web browsing, collecting the URLs of sites visited. The resulting profiles can potentially link with information that personally identifies the individual who did the browsing.

Some web-oriented marketing-research organizations may use this practice legitimately, for example: in order to construct profiles of 'typical Internet users'. Such profiles, which describe average trends of large groups of Internet users rather than of actual individuals, can then prove useful for market analysis.

Although the aggregate data does not constitute a privacy violation, some people believe that the initial profiling does. Profiling becomes a more contentious privacy issue when data-matching associates the profile of an individual with personally-identifiable information of the individual. Governments and organizations may set up honeypot websites – featuring controversial topics – with the purpose of attracting and træking unwary people. This constitutes a potential danger for individuals.

4

Issues and Laws of Cyberspace

The rapid development of Information technology poses new challenges before the law. These challenges are not confined to any single traditional legal category but arise in, for example, Criminal Law, Intellectual Property Law, Contract and Tort. One such challenge is the growing menace of "Data Theft". It is the term used when any information in the form of data is illegally copied or taken from a business or other individual without his knowledge or consent.

Data as a Valuable Asset

Data is a valuable asset in this modern era of Information Technology (IT). Data is an important raw-material for Call Centers and I.T. Companies. Data has also become an important tool and weapon for Corporates to capture larger market shares. Due to the importance of Data in this new era, its security has become a major issue with the I.T. industry. The piracy of data is a threat, faced by the I.T. players, who spend millions to compile or buy data from the market. Their profits depend upon the security of the Data.

Issues

The major issue regarding Data Theft is its International character, for example Systems may be accessed in USA, the data manipulated in China and the consequences felt in India.

The result of this ability is that different sovereignties, jurisdictions, laws and rules will come into play which again is an issue in itself.

Further, collection of evidence in such circumstances become another issue as investigation in three different countries, all of whom may not be in talking terms, is almost impossible and poor technical know-how of our cops adds to the woes. Also, the lack of coordination between different investigating agencies and a not-so-sure extradition process is another head ache. However the biggest of all these issues is the lack of specific laws in the country dealing with this crime, so even if the culprit is caught he can easily get away by picking and choosing any of the of various loopholes in our law.

DOES INDIA HAVE SUFFICIENT LAWS?

The problem of data theft which has emerged as one of the major cyber crimes worldwide has attracted little attention of law makers in India. Unlike U.K which has The Data Protection Act, 1984 there is no specific legislation in India to tackle this problem, though India boasts of its Information Technology Act, 2000 to address the ever growing menace of cyber crimes, including data theft. The truth is that our IT Act, 2000 is not well equipped to tackle such crimes. The various provisions of the IT Act, 2000 which deal with the problem to some extent are briefly discussed below.

Section 43:- This section provides protection against destruction and unauthorized access of the computer system by imposing heavy penalty up to one crore. The unauthorized downloading, extraction and copying of data are also covered under this section. Clause 'C' of this section imposes penalty for unauthorized introduction of computer viruses of contaminants. Clause 'G' provides penalties for assisting the unauthorized access.

Section 65:- This section provides for computer source code. If anyone knowingly or intentionally conceals, destroys, alters or causes another to do as such shall have to suffer imprisonment of up to 3 years or fine up to 2 lakh rupees. Thus protection has been provided against tampering of computer source documents.

Section 66:- Protection against hacking has been provided under this section.

As per this section, hacking is defined as any act with an intention to cause wrongful loss or damage to any person or with the knowledge that wrongful loss or damage will be caused to any person and information residing in a computer resource must be either destroyed, deleted, altered or its value and utility get diminished. This section imposes the penalty of imprisonment of up to three years or fine up to two lakh rupees or both on the hacker.

Section 70:- This section provides protection to the data stored in the protected system. Protected systems are those computers, computer system or computer network to which the appropriate government, by issuing gazette information in the official gazette, declared it as a protected system. Any access or attempt to secure access of that system in contravention of the provision of this section will make the person accessed liable for punishment of imprisonment which may extend to ten years and shall also be liable to fine.

Section 72:- This section provides protection against breach of confidentiality and privacy of the data. As per this, any person upon whom powers have been conferred under IT Act and allied rules to secure access to any electronic record, book, register, correspondence, information document of other material discloses it to any other person, shall be punished with imprisonment which may extend to two years or with fine which may extend to one lakh rupees or both.

Can Data Theft be Covered under IPC?

Section 378 of the Indian Penal Code, 1860 defines 'Theft' as follows:-

Theft – Whoever, intending to take dishonestly any movable property out of the possession of any person without that person's consent, moves that property in order to such taking, is said to commit theft.

Section 22 of I.P.C., 1860 defines "movable property" as follows:-

"The words "movable property" are intended to include corporeal property of every description, except land and things attached to the earth or permanently fastened to anything which is attached to the earth."

Since Section 378 I.P.C., only refers to "Movable Property" i.e. Corporeal Property, and Data by itself is intangible, it is not covered under the definition of "Theft". However, if Data is stored in a medium (CD, Floppy etc.) and such medium is stolen, it would be covered under the definition of 'Theft', since the medium is a movable property. But, if Data is transmitted electronically, i.e., in intangible form, it would not specifically constitute theft under the IPC.

"Data", in its intangible form, can at best be put at par with electricity. The question whether electricity could be stolen, arose before the Hon'ble Supreme Court in the case "Avtar Singh vs. State of Punjab" (AIR 1965 SC 666). Answering the question, the Supreme Court held that electricity is not a movable property, hence, is not covered under the definition of 'Theft' under Section 378 IPC.

However, since Section 39 of the Electricity Act extended Section 378 IPC to apply to electricity, so it so became specifically covered within the meaning of "Theft". It is therefore imperative that a provision like in the Electricity Act be inserted in the IT Act, 2000 to extend the application of section 378 IPC to data theft specifically.

What do we need and why do we need?

It is imperative in today's world that an emerging IT super power like India has a comprehensive legislation to protect its booming IT and BPO Industries (worst affected industries) against such crimes. Though the IT Act may appear sufficient in this regard but it is not comprehensive enough to tackle the minute technological intricacies involved in such a crime which leaves loopholes in the law and the culprits get away easily. Since this problem is not confined to one nation and has international dimensions, India must look forward to be a signatory to any international convention or treaty in this regard. Also it high time that our national police organizations are trained to deal with such crimes.

IPR And Enforcement Mechanism: Problem And Prospects

"Determine that things can and shall be done and then we shall find the way" - *Abraham Lincoln*

The objective of IPR is to give the greatest good to greatest number. In other words this approach states that these rights induce people to behave in the ways that increase socially valuable goods and services and distribute these goods and services in the fashion that maximizes the net profit that people reap from them. The distinctive characteristics of most intellectual products are that they are easily replicated eg.Copyright and this can be easily done when a person is working in digital environment. Digital environment is intrinsically different from print and mass media. The digital environment can be characterized as ephemeral and ethereal. In the words of Benkler," There are three attributes of information society:

1. Plasticity
2. Transmissibility
3. Processibility

The plasticity, transmissibility and processibility are unique to digital environment. These characteristics are the product of electric impulses of binary language of 0's and 1's.At best, they are symbols and therefore intangibles. These symbols are converted in human readable forms and also know no borders. Written and printed texts, sounds, speech and pictures can be reduced to 0's and 1's and once reduced they become signals and hence vulnerable to mutations by the use for multimedia, become capable of being combined, separated or manipulated in any or all forms of expressions in ways which were never thought of. However it is not the intangibility alone which is problematic because Common Law incorporates incorporeal rights. The problem is intangibility plus plasticibility, transmissibility and processibility which require law and legal institutions for remapping of the contours of digital environment.

The digital environment offers a wide range of possibilities to all stake holders. In particular, the technical development has moved the internet increasingly from a centralized structure where the users utilizes those contents offered by website to one where more powerful devices with cheaper connectivity and faster transmission speeds, offer consumers access to richer online contents. The advent of broadband promised ubiquitous access to all types of intellectual property in a manner previously not possible. This permits not only a greater dissemination of such Intellectual Property, but also stimulates consumer demands for the services that enabled access. The problem arises just after the contents take the digital form and are put on internet. There are some inherent weaknesses associated with the management of digital rights as the same being prone to violation by use of technology itself. There have been several efforts to overcome the problem and find a way for the efficient management and the protection of digital rights. It has rightly been recognized that digital rights neither be protected nor be enforced unless solution for the problem is sought in the technology itself.

As with the ever developing technological advancement the number of people using internet services is increasing so is the malpractices to negate the interests of IPR and to reproduce the contents available thereon. The most common act of violation is observed as piracy, which has not earlier been specifically defined in the Copyright Act 1957 or in any other legislation dealing in Intellectual Property Rights. Even IT Act, 2000 does not provide specific provision dealing with piracy.

This paper is an attempt to analyze the Intellectual Property violation with special reference to digital rights management. Copyright and its related rights are essential to human creativity, by giving creators incentives in the form of recognition and fair economic rewards. Under this system of rights, creators are assured that their works can be disseminated without fear of unauthorized copying or piracy. This in turn helps increased access to the work and further enhances enjoyment of culture, knowledge and entertainment all over the world. It is recognized worldwide that copyright piracy is a serious crime which not only adversely affects the creative potential of society by denying the creators their legitimate dues, but also causes economic losses to all those who had invested their money in bringing out copyrighted material in various forms for use by the end users.

With advancement in technology new techniques have been developed to control the internet piracy on copyrighted contents. Digital Rights Management is an impressive attempt amongst such techniques. DRM is primarily a process of insertion of particulars of the intellectual property into it. And, therefore it is an aid to curb the piracy practices.

Digital Rights and Information Management is usually construed as protection of copyright and controlling internet piracy but our submission identifies DRM as a technology used to identify, describe, distribute and trading of contents and regulation and enforcement policies on digital media. Information stored on electronic form is cheaper, easy to store, retrieve and speedier to communicate. These advantages of Web have attracted many people and easy access to information on the website may result in conflict with their copyright interests.

COUNTERING THREATS THROUGH CYBER SPACE

In the United States, surveillance has been at the heart of changes in traditional defence, as well as attempts to counter so-called "asymmetric" security threats. Guided by the principle that "what can be seen can be hit," battlefield surveillance was at the heart of the U.S., "revolution in military affairs" during the 1970s, 1980s, and 1990s. Two asymmetric threats in particular have caught the imaginations of those within the United States who have worked consistently to increase government surveillance capabilities: the threats of terrorism and cyber attack.

The idea that information-age conflict in general, and the fight against terrorism in particular, constitute a global "battle for hearts and minds" has been popular among U.S., defence and security professionals for at least a decade. Various observers have worried about terrorist use of the Internet as a tool for fundraising, organising, recruiting, and propaganda. It is in this spirit that Arquilla has urged the U.S., government to remove terrorist web sites from the Internet. Likewise, it is in this spirit that groups of self-organised, online volunteers engage in various types of online activities in support of the U.S., "war on terrorism," including intelligence gathering and counter-propaganda activities.

The work of Shannen Rossmiller and her group Phoenix Global Information Systems is the most notable example of intelligence-focused, volunteer cyber-counterterrorism. In response to the terrorist attacks of September 11, 2001, Rossmiller, a municipal judge from a small town in Montana, began trolling jihadist web sites to learn more about those who had attacked the United States and what they might be planning next. In January 2003, Rossmiller joined forces with at least six other individuals whom she met in the online discussion forum. They created a web site and began calling themselves 7-Seas Global Intelligence.

Members of 7-Seas live in the United States, Canada, Australia, and Singapore and include an economist, a physicist, a computer systems engineer, a corporate security consultant, and a private investigator. Rossmiller and members of 7-Seas have used a number of techniques to gather intelligence about terrorists online. These have included creating multiple false personas complete with pictures and detailed life histories. To appear as convincing as possible to her targets, Rossmiller has learned Arabic, studied the Quran, and read Arabic literature. They also employ translation software, tools to map the IP addresses of the online jihadists with whom they interact, software to mask their own IP addresses and make it appear that they are located in the Middle East or South Asia, and even spyware that is remotely installed on the computers of some of those that they investigate.

While their initial goal was to predict future terrorist attacks, they soon shifted to gathering and analysing information from terrorist web sites, forums, and chat rooms, and then turning that information over to authorities. Rossmiller's efforts in particular have contributed to two high-profile arrests of would-be terrorists, including the 2004 case of Specialist Ryan Anderson, a Washington state National Guardsman who attempted to sell classified information about vulnerabilities of U.S., weapons systems to an al-Qa'ida member that he met online.

That al-Qa'ida member was actually Rossmiller. Anderson is now in prison serving five consecutive life sentences, the harshest penalty yet dealt to an American in the war on terrorism. In another case, and again posing online as a member of al- Qa'ida, Rossmiller uncovered a plot by Pennsylvania resident and al-Qa'ida sympathiser, Michael Reynolds, to blow up several gas pipelines and oil refineries in the United States. Reynolds was convicted and is now serving fifty seven years in prison. Rossmiller is reported to have provided information to U.S., law enforcement or intelligence in as many as 240 other cases, leading to the detention of dozens of suspects worldwide and even some arrests and deportations of terrorism suspects from the United States.

For all the success that Rossmiller and 7-Seas has had, there remains a great deal of ambivalence, ambiguity, and tension in their relationship with authorities. On the one hand, the volunteers are motivated in part by calls by authorities to be vigilant. They believe authorities' claims about the seriousness of the threat of terrorism and want to help. One the other hand, they are also motivated by feelings that the government is either unable or unwilling to counter extremists' use of the Internet. Similarly, while Rossmiller has received a great deal of praise and assistance from authorities—the FBI has compensated her for her expenses, provided her with Arabic translation services, and provided her with security, a former Secretary of Commerce has said that she deserves a medal, she has been consulted by the Defence Intelligence Agency, and she has been an invited speaker at an FBI cyber security conference—these agencies have also sometimes expressed concern or doubt about her work and the work of others like her.

For her part, Rossmiller has at times complained that her work is being undervalued by authorities and has been clear to assert her independence from the state. But for all the tensions between authorities and volunteers, and for all that Rossmiller and 7-Seas have tried to distance themselves from the authorities, they nonetheless seek both approval and profit from the authorities.

Both 7-Seas and later Phoenix Global Intelligence Systems have sought government contracts and intelligence and security consulting work for government clients.

In 2009, Rossmiller announced at an FBI-sponsored cyber security conference that she had formed a company and was seeking a partnership with a defence contractor to offer cyber-intelligence training and services to the government. She has been encouraged to do so by former CIA Director, James Woolsey. In the end, there are real reasons for tension and for concern. Both sides are right. The authorities likely cannot monitor and analyse that much Web content, making the work of the volunteers indispensable.

However, the volunteers do not have the ability to physically arrest suspects or materially disrupt terrorist planning or operations in any significant way, making the capabilities of the state indispensable in achieving their goals. Additionally, there are clear difficulties in making the relationship work. Sometimes authorities and volunteers can work at cross purposes. If authorities rely too much on volunteers, or if the role of volunteers becomes formally institutionalised, then their main value can be compromised. Finally, Michael Reynolds' defence strategy—i.e., claiming that he too was just trying to catch terrorists online like Rossmiller—also points to some of the potential difficulties in this new relationship between producers and consumers of security online.

THE INDIAN CYBERSPACE

The National Informatics Centre (NIC) was set up as early as 1975 with the goal of providing IT solutions to the government. Between 1986 and 1988, three NWs were set up: INDONET, connecting the IBM mainframe installations that made up India's computer infrastructure; NICNET (the NIC Network), being a nationwide very small aperture terminal (VSAT) NW for public sector organisations as well as to connect the central government with the state governments and district administrations; and the Education and Research Network (ERNET), to serve the academic and research communities.

Policies such as the New Internet Policy of 1998 paved the way for multiple Internet service providers (ISPs) and saw the Internet user base grow from 1.4 million in 1999 to over 15 million by 2003. Though the rate of growth has slowed subsequently, with Internet users now approximately numbering 100 million, exponential growth is again expected as Internet access increasingly shifts to mobile phones and tablets, with the government making a determined push to increase broadband penetration from its present level of about 6%.

The target for broadband is 160 million households by 2016 under the National Broadband Plan. Despite the low numbers in relation to the population, Indians have been active users of the Internet across various segments. The two top e-mail providers, Gmail and Yahoo, had over 34 million users registered from India.

Similar figures have also been seen in the social networking arena, which is the most recent entrant to the cyber platform. India currently has the fastest growing user base for Facebook and Twitter, the two top social networking sites. An indication of the rapid pace of adaptation to the Internet in India is that Indian Railways, India's top e-commerce retailer, saw its online sales go up from 19 million tickets in 2008 to 44 million in 2009, with a value of Rs. 3800 crore ($875 million).

Even though the Indian government was a late convert to computerisation, there has been an increasing thrust on e-governance, seen as a cost-effective way of taking public services to the masses across the country. Critical sectors such as Defence, Energy, Finance, Space, Telecommunications, Transport, Land Records, Public Essential Services and Utilities, Law Enforcement and Security all increasingly depend on NWs to relay data, for communication purposes and for commercial transactions. The National e-governance Programme (NeGP) is one of the most ambitious in the world and seeks to provide more than 1200 governmental services online.

Looking to the future, the Cisco Visual Networking Index estimates that India's Internet traffic will grow nine-fold between now and 2015, topping out at 13.2 Exabytes in 2015, from 1.6 Exabytes in 2010. That will be the equivalent of the data contained in 374,372 DVDs being carried every hour through these NWs. In terms of contribution to the economy, the ICT sector has grown at an annual compounded rate of 33% over the last decade.

The contribution of the IT-ITeS industry to GDP increased from 5.2% in 2006-7 to 6.4% in 2010-11. Much of the activities of the IT/BPO sector, which was responsible for putting India on the services export map, would not have been possible but for the cost-efficiencies provided through the expansion of global data NWs.

The government has ambitious plans to raise cyber connectivity. There has been a boom in e-commerce, and many activities related to e-governance are now being carried out over the Internet. As we grow more dependent on the Internet for our daily activities, we also become more vulnerable to any disruptions caused in and through cyberspace. The rapidity with which this sector has grown has meant that governments and private companies are still trying to figure out both the scope and meaning of security in cyberspace and apportioning responsibility. As in other countries, much of the infrastructure related to cyberspace is with the private sector, which also provides many of the critical services, ranging from banking, to electricity to running airports and other key transportation infrastructure.

Taking telecommunications as a case in point, CII in India comprises around 150 Internet and telecom service providers, offering Internet, mobile and wireless connectivity to a user base of nearly 800 million. A major portion of data communication is facilitated by submarine cables. India has landing points for major submarine cable systems which are minimally protected. A preview of what could happen by way of these cables being disabled took place in 2008 when a series of outages and cable cuts in undersea cables running through the Suez Canal, in the Persian Gulf and Malaysia caused massive communications disruptions to India and West Asia.

Other sectors that could be subject to serious threats include the financial sector, which has largely transferred operations online. Stock exchanges in the United States and Hong Kong have reportedly been subject to cyber attacks. The electricity grid is also vulnerable with the inevitable move towards a smart grid, given the economic and efficiency factors. The protection of critical infrastructure is a complex task requiring forethought, planning, strong laws, technologies, PPP and resources. For all these reasons it needs to be given top priority by the government. The country cannot afford to wait indefinitely for a robust policy to protect this critical infrastructure.

Need for a Comprehensive Cyber Security Policy

As in most countries around the world, the cyber security scenario in India is one of relative chaos and a sense of insecurity arising out of the periodic reports of cyber espionage, cyberterrorism, cyber warfare and cyber crime. The complexity of the issue has resulted in a virtual paralysis. Legal and law enforcement mechanisms have not shifted gears fast enough to grapple with growing cyber crime. Periodic newspaper reports indicate that a wide variety of offensive measures are being contemplated by various agencies, but that is all. The lack of a coherent cyber security policy will seriously interfere with India's national security and economic development.

It is essential that more attention at the highest levels is paid to ensuring that cyber-related vulnerabilities that can impact on critical sectors are identified and removed. A coherent and comprehensive cyber security policy will have several major elements, including accurate conceptualisation of cyberspace threats; building of robust cyberspace through a variety of measures, including technical, legal, diplomatic, international cooperation; creation of adequate organisational structures; strengthening of PPPs; HR development; and implementation of best practices and guidelines. The list is only illustrative. India's approach to cyber security has so far been ad hoc and piecemeal. A number of organisations have been created but their precise roles have not been defined nor synergy has been created among them. As it transcends a vast domain, this falls within the charter of the NSCS.

However, there appears to be no institutional structure for implementation of policies. Neither the private sector nor government has been able to build information systems that can be described as reasonably robust. There has not been enough thinking on the implications of cyber warfare.

Meanwhile, many countries are seriously engaged in attending to their cyber security doctrines and strategies. The US, Russia, UK, France, Australia, Germany, New Zealand, South Korea, China, Brazil, South Africa, Denmark, Sweden, EU, Singapore, Malaysia–the list is long and growing–are actively engaged in ensuring a safe and secure cyber environment for their citizens. The international community is also engaged in a variety of discussions. NATO has taken the task of creating cyber security institutions in member countries. A group of governmental experts (GGE), set up by the UN Secretary General, gave a report in 2010 on "developments in the field of ICT in the context of international security". The report noted that there was increasing evidence that states were developing ICTs as "instruments of warfare and intelligence, and for political purposes". To confront challenges in cyberspace, the GGE recommended cooperation among likeminded partners, among states, between states, and between states and civil society and the private sectors. The draft cyber security policy document put out by the DIT for public discussion is an important step but it is essentially a departmental effort, not taking a whole of-government approach. DIT does not have jurisdiction over departments. The document lists a number of major stakeholders, including: (1) National Information Board (NIB); (2) National Crisis Management Committee (NCMC); (3) NSCS; (4) Ministry of Home Affairs (MHA); (5) Ministry of Defence; (6) DIT; (7) DoT; (8) National Cyber Response Centre (NCRC); (9) CERT-In; (10) National Information Infrastructure Protection Centre (NIIPC); (11) National Disaster Management Authority (NDMA); (12) Standardisation, Testing and Quality Certification (STQC) Directorate; and (13) sectoral CERTs. However, only CERT-In is mandated under the IT Amendment Act, 2008 to serve as the national agency in charge of cyber security. The Act also provided for a national nodal agency for protection of CII but it is not clear whether such an organisation exists other than on paper; NDMA and some others play only a peripheral role; and many of the sectoral CERTs are yet to come up. In the meantime, real oversight over cyber security may be said to be distributed amongst the Ministries of Communication and Technology, Home Affairs and Defence, and the office of the NSA.

CYBER LAWS AND LEGAL ISSUES

Cyberlaw is a term that encapsulates the legal issues related to use of communicative, transactional, and distributive aspects of networked information devices and technologies. It is less a distinct field of law in the way that property or contract are, as it is a domain covering many areas of law and regulation. Some leading topics include intellectual property, privacy, freedom of expression, and jurisdiction.

Jurisdiction and Sovereignty

Issues of jurisdiction and sovereignty have quickly come to the fore in the era of the Internet. The Internet does not tend to make geographical and jurisdictional boundaries clear, but

Internet users remain in physical jurisdictions and are subject to laws independent of their presence on the Internet. As such, a single transaction may involve the laws of at least three jurisdictions: 1) the laws of the state/nation in which the user resides, 2) the laws of the state/nation that apply where the server hosting the transaction is located, and 3) the laws of the state/nation which apply to the person or business with whom the transaction takes place. So a user in one of the United States conducting a transaction with another user in Britain through a server in Canada could theoretically be subject to the laws of all three countries as they relate to the transaction at hand.

Jurisdiction is an aspect of state sovereignty and it refers to judicial, legislative and administrative competence. Although jurisdiction is an aspect of sovereignty, it is not coextensive with it. The laws of a nation may have extraterritorial impact extending the jurisdiction beyond the sovereign and territorial limits of that nation.

This is particularly problematic as the medium of the Internet does not explicitly recognize sovereignty and territorial limitations. There is no uniform, international jurisdictional law of universal application, and such questions are generally a matter of conflict of laws, particularly private international law. An example would be where the contents of a web site are legal in one country and illegal in another. In the absence of a uniform jurisdictional code, legal practitioners are generally left with a conflict of law issue.

Another major problem of cyberlaw lies in whether to treat the Internet as if it were physical space (and thus subject to a given jurisdiction's laws) or to act as if the Internet is a world unto itself (and therefore free of such restraints). Those who favour the latter view often feel that government should leave the Internet community to self-regulate. John Perry Barlow, for example, has addressed the governments of the world and stated, "Where there are real conflicts, where there are wrongs, we will identify them and address them by our means. We are forming our own Social Contract. This governance will arise according to the conditions of our world, not yours. Our world is different".· A more balanced alternative is the Declaration of Cyber secession: "Human beings possess a mind, which they are absolutely free to inhabit with no legal constraints. Human civilization is developing its own (collective) mind. All we want is to be free to inhabit it with no legal constraints. Since you make sure we cannot harm you, you have no ethical right to intrude our lives. So stop intruding!" Other scholars argue for more of a compromise between the two notions, such as Lawrence Lessig's argument that "The problem for law is to work out how the norms of the two communities are to apply given that the subject to whom they apply may be in both places at once" (Lessig, Code 190).

Though rhetorically attractive, cyber secession initiatives have had little real impact on the Internet or the laws governing it. In practical terms, a user of the Internet is subject to the laws of the state or nation within which he or she goes online. Thus, in the U.S., Jake Baker faced criminal charges for his e-conduct, and numerous users of peer-to-peer file-sharing software were subject to civil lawsuits for copyright infringement. This system runs into conflicts, however, when these suits are international in nature. Simply put, legal conduct in one nation may be decidedly illegal in another. In fact, even different standards concerning the burden of proof in a civil case can cause jurisdictional problems. For example, an American celebrity, claiming to be insulted by an online American magazine, faces a difficult task of winning a lawsuit against that magazine for libel. But if the celebrity has ties, economic or otherwise, to England, he or she can sue for libel in the British court system, where the standard of "libelous speech" is far lower.

Net Neutrality

Another major area of interest is net neutrality, which affects the regulation of the infrastructure of the Internet. Though not obvious to most Internet users, every packet of data sent and received by every user on the Internet passes through routers and transmission infrastructure owned by a collection of private and public entities, including telecommunications companies, universities, and governments, suggesting that the Internet is not as independent as Barlow and others would like to believe. This is turning into one of the most critical aspects of cyberlaw and has immediate jurisdictional implications, as laws in force in one jurisdiction have the potential to have dramatic effects in other jurisdictions when host servers or telecommunications companies are affected.

Free Speech in Cyberspace

In comparison to traditional print-based media, the accessibility and relative anonymity of cyber space has torn down traditional barriers between an individual and his or her ability to publish.

Any person with an internet connection has the potential to reach an audience of millions with little-to-no distribution costs. Yet this new form of highly-accessible authorship in cyber space raises questions and perhaps magnifies legal complexities relating to the freedom and regulation of speech in cyberspace.

Recently, these complexities have taken many forms, three notable examples being the Jake Baker incident, in which the limits of obscene Internet postings were at issue, the controversial distribution of the DeCSS code, and Gutnick v Dow Jones, in which libel laws were considered in the context of online publishing. The last example was particularly significant because it epitomized the complexities inherent to applying one country's laws (nation-specific by definition) to the internet (international by nature). In 2003, Jonathan Zittrain considered this issue in his paper, "Be Careful What You Ask For: Reconciling a Global Internet and Local Law".

In many countries, speech through cyberspace has proven to be another means of communication which has been regulated by the government.

The Open Net Initiative, whose mission statement is "to investigate and challenge state filtration and surveillance practices" in order to "...generate a credible picture of these practices," has released numerous reports documenting the filtration of internet-speech in various countries. While China has thus far proven to be the most rigorous in its attempts to filter unwanted parts of the internet from its citizens, many other countries-including Australia, Singapore, Iran, Saudi Arabia, and Tunisia-have engaged in similar practices of internet censorship. In one of the most vivid examples of information-control, the Chinese government for a short time transparently forwarded requests to the Google search engine to its own, state-controlled search engines.

These examples of filtration bring to light many underlying questions concerning the freedom of speech, namely, does the government have a legitimate role in limiting access to information? And if so, what forms of regulation are acceptable? The recent blocking of "blogspot" and other websites in India failed to reconcile the conflicting interests of speech and expression on the one hand and legitimate government concerns on the other hand. In the UK the case of Keith-Smith v Williams confirmed that existing libel laws applied to internet discussions.

Governance

The unique structure of the Internet has raised several judicial concerns. While grounded in physical computers and other electronic devices, the Internet is independent of any geographic location. While real individuals connect to the Internet and interact with others, it is possible for them to withhold personal information and make their real identities anonymous. If there are laws that could govern the Internet, then it appears that such laws would be fundamentally different from laws that geographic nations use today. In their essay "Law and Borders — The Rise of Law in Cyberspace", David Johnson and David Post offer a solution to the problem of Internet governance. Given the Internet's unique situation, with respect to geography and identity, Johnson and Post believe that it becomes necessary for the Internet to govern itself.

Instead of obeying the laws of a particular country, Internet citizens will obey the laws of electronic entities like service providers. Instead of identifying as a physical person, Internet citizens will be known by their usernames or email addresses. Since the Internet defies geographical boundaries, national laws will no longer apply. Instead, an entirely new set of laws will be created to address concerns like intellectual property and individual rights. In effect, the Internet will exist as its own sovereign nation.

Even if the Internet represents a legal paradigm shift, Johnson and Post do not make clear exactly how or by whom the law of the Internet will be enforced. Instead, the authors see market mechanisms, like those that Medieval merchants used, guiding Internet citizens' actions like Adam Smith's invisible hand. Yet, as more physical locations go online, the greater the potential for physical manifestation of electronic misdeeds. What do we do when someone electronically turns off the hospital lights?

However, there is also substantial literature and commentary that the internet is not only "regulable," but is already subject to substantial regulation, both public and private, by many parties and at many different levels. Leaving aside the most obvious examples of internet filtering in nations like China or Saudi Arabia or Iran (that monitor content), there are four primary modes of regulation of the internet described by Lawrence Lessig in his book, Code and Other Laws of Cyberspace:

1. Law: Standard East Coast Code, and the most self-evident of the four modes of regulation. As the numerous statutes, evolving case law and precedents make clear, many actions on the internet are already subject to conventional legislation (both with regard to transactions conducted on the internet and images posted). Areas like gambling, child pornography, and fraud are regulated in very similar ways online as off-line. While one of the most controversial and unclear areas of evolving laws is the determination of what forum has subject matter jurisdiction over activity (economic and other) conducted on the internet, particularly as cross

border transactions affect local jurisdictions, it is certainly clear that substantial portions of internet activity are subject to traditional regulation, and that conduct that is unlawful off-line is presumptively unlawful online, and subject to similar laws and regulations. Scandals with major corporations led to US legislation rethinking corporate governance regulations such as the Sarbanes-Oxley Act.

2. Architecture: West Coast Code: these mechanisms concern the parameters of how information can and cannot be transmitted across the internet. Everything from internet filtering software (which searches for keywords or specific URLs and blocks them before they can even appear on the computer requesting them), to encryption programs, to the very basic architecture of TCP/IP protocol, falls within this category of regulation. It is arguable that all other modes of regulation either rely on, or are significantly supported by, regulation via West Coast Code.
3. Norms: As in all other modes of social interaction, conduct is regulated by social norms and conventions in significant ways. While certain activities or kinds of conduct online may not be specifically prohibited by the code architecture of the internet, or expressly prohibited by applicable law, nevertheless these activities or conduct will be invisibly regulated by the inherent standards of the community, in this case the internet "users." And just as certain patterns of conduct will cause an individual to be ostracised from our real world society, so too certain actions will be censored or self-regulated by the norms of whatever community one chooses to associate with on the internet.
4. Markets: Closely allied with regulation by virtue of social norms, markets also regulate certain patterns of conduct on the internet. While economic markets will have limited influence over non-commercial portions of the internet, the internet also creates a virtual

marketplace for information, and such information affects everything from the comparative valuation of services to the traditional valuation of stocks. In addition, the increase in popularity of the internet as a means for transacting all forms of commercial activity, and as a forum for advertisement, has brought the laws of supply and demand in cyberspace.

INDIAN CYBER LAW OR IT ACT OF INDIA

Cyber laws are meant to set the definite pattern, some rules and guidelines that defined certain business activities going on through internet legal and certain illegal and hence punishable . The IT Act 2000, the cyber law of India , gives the legal framework so that information is not denied legal effect, validity or enforceability, solely on the ground that it is in the form of electronic records. One cannot regard government as complete failure in shielding numerous e-commerce activities on the firm basis of which this industry has got to its skies, but then the law cannot be regarded as free from ambiguities.

MMS porn case in which the CEO of bazee.com(an Ebay Company) was arrested for allegedly selling the MMS clips involving school children on its website is the most apt example in this reference.

Other cases where the law becomes hazy in its stand includes the case where the newspaper Mid-Daily published the pictures of the Indian actor kissing her boyfriend at the Bombay nightspot and the arrest of Krishan Kumar for illegally using the internet account of Col. (Retd.) J.S. Bajwa.

The IT Act 2000 attempts to change outdated laws and provides ways to deal with cyber crimes. Let's have an overview of the law where it takes a firm stand and has got successful in the reason for which it was framed.

1. The E-commerce industry carries out its business via transactions and communications done through electronic records . It thus becomes essential that such transactions be made legal . Keeping this point in the

consideration, the IT Act 2000 empowers the government departments to accept filing, creating and retention of official documents in the digital format. The Act also puts forward the proposal for setting up the legal framework essential for the authentication and origin of electronic records / communications through digital signature.

2. The Act legalizes the e-mail and gives it the status of being valid form of carrying out communication in India . This implies that e-mails can be duly produced and approved in a court of law , thus can be a regarded as substantial document to carry out legal proceedings.
3. The act also talks about digital signatures and digital records . These have been also awarded the status of being legal and valid means that can form strong basis for launching litigation in a court of law. It invites the corporate companies in the business of being Certifying Authorities for issuing secure Digital Signatures Certificates.
4. The Act now allows Government to issue notification on the web thus heralding e-governance.
5. It eases the task of companies of the filing any form, application or document by laying down the guidelines to be submitted at any appropriate office, authority, body or agency owned or controlled by the government. This will help in saving costs, time and manpower for the corporates.
6. The act also provides statutory remedy to the coporates in case the crime against the accused for breaking into their computer systems or network and damaging and copying the data is proven. The remedy provided by the Act is in the form of monetary damages, not exceeding Rs. 1 crore($200,000).
7. Also the law sets up the Territorial Jurisdiction of the Adjudicating Officers for cyber crimes and the Cyber Regulations Appellate Tribunal.

8. The law has also laid guidelines for providing Internet Services on a license on a non-exclusive basis.

The IT Law 2000, though appears to be self sufficient, it takes mixed stand when it comes to many practical situations. It looses its certainty at many places like:

1. The law misses out completely the issue of Intellectual Property Rights, and makes no provisions whatsoever for copyrighting, trade marking or patenting of electronic information and data. The law even doesn't talk of the rights and liabilities of domain name holders , the first step of entering into the e-commerce.
2. The law even stays silent over the regulation of electronic payments gateway and segregates the negotiable instruments from the applicability of the IT Act , which may have major effect on the growth of e-commerce in India . It leads to make the banking and financial sectors irresolute in their stands .
3. The act empowers the Deputy Superintendent of Police to look up into the investigations and filling of charge sheet when any case related to cyber law is called. This approach is likely to result in misuse in the context of Corporate India as companies have public offices which would come within the ambit of "public place" under the Act. As a result, companies will not be able to escape potential harassment at the hands of the DSP.
4. Internet is a borderless medium ; it spreads to every corner of the world where life is possible and hence is the cyber criminal. Then how come is it possible to feel relaxed and secured once this law is enforced in the nation??

The Act initially was supposed to apply to crimes committed all over the world, but nobody knows how can this be achieved in practice , how to enforce it all over the world at the same time.

* The IT Act is silent on filming anyone's personal actions in public and then distributing it electronically. It holds

ISPs (Internet Service Providers) responsible for third party data and information, unless contravention is committed without their knowledge or unless the ISP has undertaken due diligence to prevent the contravention .

* For example, many Delhi based newspapers advertise the massage parlors; and in few cases even show the 'therapeutic masseurs' hidden behind the mask, who actually are prostitutes. Delhi Police has been successful in busting out a few such rackets but then it is not sure of the action it can take...should it arrest the owners and editors of newspapers or wait for some new clauses in the Act to be added up?? Even the much hyped case of the arrest of Bajaj, the CEO of Bazee.com, was a consequence of this particular ambiguity of the law. One cannot expect an ISP to monitor what information their subscribers are sending out, all 24 hours a day.

Cyber law is a generic term, which denotes all aspects, issues and the legal consequences on the Internet, the World Wide Web and cyber space. India is the 12th nation in the world that has cyber legislation apart from countries like the US, Singapore, France, Malaysia and Japan .

But can the cyber laws of the country be regarded as sufficient and secure enough to provide a strong platform to the country's e-commerce industry for which they were meant?? India has failed to keep in pace with the world in this respect, and the consequence is not far enough from our sight; most of the big customers of India 's outsourcing company have started to re-think of carrying out their business in India .Bajaj's case has given the strongest blow in this respect and have broken India 's share in outsourcing market as a leader.

If India doesn't want to loose its position and wishes to stay as the world's leader forever in outsourcing market, it needs to take fast but intelligent steps to cover the glaring loopholes of the Act, or else the day is not far when the scenario of India ruling the world's outsourcing market will stay alive in the dreams only as it will be overtaken by its competitors.

INTERNATIONAL LAWS AND STANDARDS

International Laws

In the UK, the Data Protection Act is used to ensure that personal data is accessible to those whom it concerns, and provides redress to individuals if there are inaccuracies. This is particularly important to ensure individuals are treated fairly, for example for credit checking purposes. The Data Protection Act states that only individuals and companies with legitimate and lawful reasons can process personal information and cannot be shared.

International Standards

The International Standard ISO/IEC 17799 covers data security under the topic of information security, and one of its cardinal principles is that all stored information, i.e. data, should be owned so that it is clear whose responsibility it is to protect and control access to that data. The Trusted Computing Group is an organization that helps standardize computing security technologies.

Database Model

A '*database model*'is the theoretical foundation of a database and fundamentally determines in which manner data can be stored, organized and manipulated in a database system. It thereby defines the infrastructure offered by a particular database system. The most popular example of a database model is the relational model.

A database model is a theory or specification describing how a database is structured and used. Several such models have been suggested. Common models include:

- Hierarchical model
- Network model
- Relational model
- Entity-relationship
- Object-relational model

- Object model

A data model is not just a way of structuring data: it also defines a set of operations that can be performed on the data. The relational model, for example, defines operations such as select, project, and join. Although these operations may not be explicit in a particular query language, they provide the foundation on which a query language is built.

MODELS

Various techniques are used to model data structure. Most database systems are built around one particular data model, although it is increasingly common for products to offer support for more than one model. For any one logical model various physical implementations may be possible, and most products will offer the user some level of control in tuning the physical implementation, since the choices that are made have a significant effect on performance. An example of this is the relational model: all serious implementations of the relational model allow the creation of indexes which provide fast access to rows in a table if the values of certain columns are known.

Flat Model

The flat (or table) model consists of a single, two-dimensional array of data elements, where all members of a given column are assumed to be similar values, and all members of a row are assumed to be related to one another. For instance, columns for name and password that might be used as a part of a system security database. Each row would have the specific password associated with an individual user. Columns of the table often have a type associated with them, defining them as character data, date or time information, integers, or floating point numbers. This may not strictly qualify as a data model, as defined above.

Hierarchical Model

In a hierarchical model, data is organized into a tree-like structure, implying a single upward link in each record to describe the nesting, and a sort field to keep the records in a particular order in each same-level list. Hierarchical structures were widely used in the early mainframe database management systems, such as the Information Management System (IMS) by IBM, and now describe the structure of XML documents. This structure allows one 1:N relationship between two types of data. This structure is very efficient to describe many relationships in the real world; recipes, table of contents, ordering of paragraphs/verses, any nested and sorted information. However, the hierarchical structure is inefficient for certain database operations when a full path (as opposed to upward link and sort field) is not also included for each record. Parent–child relationship: Child may only have one parent but a parent can have multiple children. Parents and children are tied together by links called "pointers". A parent will have a list of pointers to each of their children.

Network Model

The network model (defined by the CODASYL specification) organizes data using two fundamental constructs, called *records* and *sets*. Records contain fields (which may be organized hierarchically, as in the programming language COBOL). Sets (not to be confused with mathematical sets) define one-to-many relationships between records: one owner, many members. A record may be an owner in any number of sets, and a member in any number of sets.

The network model is a variation on the hierarchical model, to the extent that it is built on the concept of multiple branches (lower-level structures) emanating from one or more nodes (higher-level structures), while the model differs from the hierarchical model in that branches can be connected to multiple nodes. The network model is able to represent redundancy in data more efficiently than in the hierarchical model.

The operations of the network model are navigational in style: a programme maintains a current position, and navigates from one record to another by following the relationships in which the record participates. Records can also be located by supplying key values. Although it is not an essential feature of the model, network databases generally implement the set relationships by means of pointers that directly address the location of a record on disk. This gives excellent retrieval performance, at the expense of operations such as database loading and reorganization.

Most object databases use the navigational concept to provide fast navigation across networks of objects, generally using object identifiers as "smart" pointers to related objects. Objectivity/DB, for instance, implements named 1:1, 1:many, many:1 and many:many named relationships that can cross databases. Many object databases also support SQL, combining the strengths of both models.

Relational Model

The relational model was introduced by E.F. Codd in 1970 as a way to make database management systems more independent of any particular application. It is a mathematical model defined in terms of predicate logic and set theory. The products that are generally referred to as relational databases in fact implement a model that is only an approximation to the mathematical model defined by Codd. Three key terms are used extensively in relational database models: *relations*, *attributes*, and *domains*. A relation is a table with columns and rows. The named columns of the relation are called attributes, and the domain is the set of values the attributes are allowed to take.

The basic data structure of the relational model is the table, where information about a particular entity (say, an employee) is represented in rows (also called tuples) and columns. Thus, the "relation" in "relational database" refers to the various tables in the database; a relation is a set of tuples. The columns enumerate the various attributes of the entity (the employee's name, address or phone number, for example), and a row is an actual instance of the entity (a specific employee) that is represented by the relation. As a result, each tuple of the employee table represents various attributes of a single employee. All relations (and, thus, tables) in a relational database have to adhere to some basic rules to qualify as relations. First, the ordering of columns is immaterial in a table. Second, there can't be identical tuples or rows in a table. And third, each tuple will contain a single value for each of its attributes. A relational database contains multiple tables, each similar to the one in the "flat" database model. One of the strengths of the relational model is that, in principle, any value occurring in two different records (belonging to the same table or to different tables), implies a relationship among those two records. Yet, in order to enforce explicit integrity constraints, relationships between records in tables can also be defined explicitly, by identifying or non-identifying parent-child relationships characterized by assigning cardinality (1:1, (0)1:M, M:M). Tables can also have a designated single attribute or a set of attributes that can act as a "key", which can be used to uniquely identify each tuple in the table. A key that can be used to uniquely identify a row in a table is called a primary key. Keys are commonly used to join or combine data from two or more tables. For example, an *Employee* table may contain a column named *Location* which contains a value that matches the key of a *Location* table. Keys are also critical in the creation of indexes, which facilitate fast retrieval of data from large tables.

Any column can be a key, or multiple columns can be grouped together into a compound key. It is not necessary to define all the keys in advance; a column can be used as a key even if it was not originally intended to be one. A key that has an external, real-world meaning (such as a person's name, a book's ISBN, or a car's serial number) is sometimes called a "natural" key. If no natural key is suitable (think of the many people named *Brown*), an arbitrary or surrogate key can be assigned (such as by giving employees ID numbers). In practice, most databases have both generated and natural keys, because generated keys can be used internally to create links between rows that cannot break, while natural keys can be used, less reliably, for searches and for integration with other databases.

(For example, records in two independently developed databases could be matched up by social security number, except when the social security numbers are incorrect, missing, or have changed.)

Dimensional Model

The dimensional model is a specialized adaptation of the relational model used to represent data in data warehouses in a way that data can be easily summarized using OLAP queries. In the dimensional model, a database consists of a single large table of facts that are described using dimensions and measures. A dimension provides the context of a fact (such as who participated, when and where it happened, and its type) and is used in queries to group related facts together. Dimensions tend to be discrete and are often hierarchical; for example, the location might include the building, state, and country. A measure is a quantity describing the fact, such as revenue. It's important that measures can be meaningfully aggregated - for example, the revenue from different locations can be added together. In an OLAP query, dimensions are chosen and the facts are grouped and added together to create a summary. The dimensional model is often implemented on top of the relational model using a star schema, consisting of one table containing the facts and surrounding tables containing the dimensions. Particularly complicated dimensions might be represented using multiple tables, resulting in a snowflake schema. A data warehouse can contain multiple star schemas that share dimension tables, allowing them to be used together. Coming up with a standard set of dimensions is an important part of dimensional modeling.

Objectional Database Models

In recent years, the object-oriented paradigm has been applied to database technology, creating a new programming model known as object databases. These databases attempt to bring the database world and the application programming world closer together, in particular by ensuring that the database uses the same type system as the application programme. This aims to avoid the overhead (sometimes referred to as the *impedance mismatch*) of converting information between its representation in the database (for example as rows in tables) and its representation in the application programme (typically as objects). At the same time, object databases attempt to introduce the key ideas of object programming, such as encapsulation and polymorphism, into the world of databases. A variety of these ways have been tried for storing objects in a database. Some products have approached the problem from the application programming end, by making the objects manipulated by the programme persistent.

This also typically requires the addition of some kind of query language, since conventional programming languages do not have the ability to find objects based on their information content. Others have attacked the problem from the database end, by defining an object-oriented data model for the database, and defining a database programming language that allows full programming capabilities as well as traditional query facilities. Object databases suffered because of a lack of standardization: although standards were defined by ODMG, they were never implemented well enough to ensure interoperability between products. Nevertheless, object databases have been used successfully in many applications: usually specialized applications such as engineering databases or molecular biology databases rather than mainstream commercial data processing. However, object database ideas were picked up by the relational vendors and influenced extensions made to these products and indeed to the SQL language.

5

Cyber Protection and Cyber Security

The dawn of the internet provided many new avenues for doing business, and the protection of computer data has become a main concern in today's working environment.

"Cyber Liability," as it is called, encompasses a gamut of new risks for businesses that not only conduct business over the internet, but that also may store private confidential information subject to several federal laws.

To provide some insurance protection for these new risks, most insurance companies have developed cyber security liability policies which cover both first party "the insured" and third party liabilities which can arise because of attacks by outside parties or because of losing of sensitive data due to mistakes on the part of the insured.

Up until a few years ago, these policies were available under most property and general liability policies. However, since 2005 the loss of intangible property has been excluded under standard property policies; likewise, bodily injury or property damage, previously covered under the general liability policy, is also excluded if it emanates from a cyber breach or error.

Some examples of the claims that have occurred are as follows:

Theft of Digital Assets

A regional retailer contracted with a third party service provider. A burglar stole two laptops from the service provider containing the data of over 800,000 clients of the retailer. Under applicable notification laws, the retailer-not the service provider-was required to notify affected individuals. The total expenses incurred for crisis management notification of customers cost nearly $5 million.

In a second example a home health care organization had backup data, laptops and disks containing social security numbers, clinical and demographic information. In a small number of cases, patient financial data was stolen. In total, over 365,000 patient records were exposed. The organization settled with the State Attorney General and provided patients with free credit monitoring, credit restoration to patients that were victims of identity fraud, and reimbursement to patients for direct losses that resulted from the data breach.

Human Error

An employee of a private high school mistakenly distributed via e-mail the names, social security numbers, birth dates and medical information of students and faculty creating a privacy breach. Overall, 1,250 individuals' information was compromised.

Malicious Code

A juvenile released a computer worm that caused a launch of denial of service attack against a regional computing consulting and application outsourcing firm. The infection caused an 18 hour shut down of the entity's computer systems. The computer firm incurred extensive cost and expenses to repair and restore their systems, as well as business income expenses which totaled approximately $875,000.

The cyber liability policy is sufficiently flexible so that a business can buy either third party or first party coverages, or both. Here is an example of how the language in a carrier's insurance policy protects first party assets:

Loss of Digital Assets

"We will indemnify you for loss you incur, in excess of the deductible, as a result of damage, alteration, corruption, distortion, theft, misuse, or destruction of your digital assets directly caused by a covered cause of loss". In this case, digital assets mean electronic data and computer programmes that exist in a computer system. Please note that digital assets do not include computer hardware. In addition to this, protection can be provided for the business income loss that may result from any direct first party claims.

Here is an example of the coverage grants available for third party protection under a typical insurance carrier's policy:

Network Security and Privacy Liability Coverage

The insurance company "will pay on your behalf those amounts, in excess of the applicable deductible, which you are legally obligated as damages on claim expenses arising from your acts, errors or omissions or from acts, errors or omissions for others for whom you are legally responsible, including outsourcers, or vendors provided such acts, errors or omissions follow a security breach or privacy breach". An example of this claim is the loss of a laptop containing sensitive information, which results in the public disclosure of a person's private information. Also, this insuring agreement would cover unauthorized access into your computer system, a denial of service attack against your computer system, or an infection of your computer system by malicious code.

There are a number of other coverage protection grants available on most policies, which The Fedeli Group, after an assessment of your risks, can review with you. Please contact The Fedeli Group team to arrange for this type of risk assessment and possible valuable insurance protection.

MODEL OF CYBER-PROTECTION

The cyber-threat to British business and government is growing. Statistics from Symantec, the internet protection software company, show that during 2010 over 286 million unique malicious internet threats were observed globally, with a 93 per cent increase in the volume of web-based attacks from the previous year.

This translates to a growing economic threat, with the UK's Office of Cyber Security and Information Assurance estimating the cost of cyber-crime to British business at over £20 billion a year. This rising burden on the British economy cannot be ignored or dismissed as an acceptable cost of conducting business online.

There is also widespread acknowledgement that better public-private cooperation is an important element in improving security in cyberspace. At a meeting in February hosted by the Prime Minister, representatives from a cross section of British industry and government ministers agreed on the need for increased information sharing as part of a new approach to protecting the UK's economic and national security interests against cyber threats.

Research conducted by RUSI's Cyber-Security Programme has confirmed the need for sharing information on threats and responses, not just between government and industry, but between companies and other organisations, especially across sector boundaries. This research has also shown that it is vital to extend protection beyond what is traditionally perceived to be national infrastructure (*e.g.*, defence, telecommunications, food and water supply) to include often neglected sectors. These overlooked areas of vulnerability encompass those sectors which act as service providers (*e.g.*, lawyers and accountants) and collaborators (in particular academia), and potentially represent weak links in the cyber-security chain.

Moreover, these sectors also represent vital components of the economy, and should be protected accordingly. Any critical breach of security from these companies, such as the theft of sensitive client data from a law firm or a doctor's practice, could have a damaging impact upon public confidence in the industry as a whole.

Furthermore, sectors such as academia are entirely based upon the knowledge they generate through research, and hence it is vital to safeguard this from theft. There is therefore a clear need to extend protection across and within sectors to provide collective security.

RUSI's research has, however, also revealed equally widespread agreement among stakeholders and others that effective information sharing is hard to achieve, and that the costs often outweigh the benefits, as highlighted in Thomas and Walport's Data Sharing Review for the Ministry of Justice. This problem afflicts many areas where collective action is crucial for security (not just cyberspace), but is rarely acknowledged publicly. The idea is attractive, but there are many examples in various fields of systems that fail to deliver. However, RUSI's research into models for information sharing shows that, whilst it is undoubtedly challenging to do it well, outstandingly effective and efficient systems do exist, and a study of these can help identify the criteria that are key to success.

Understanding the Requirement

The overarching problem for security in cyberspace is that whilst a networked world brings many benefits, those benefits are accompanied by risks. How do we manage those risks intelligently and efficiently? The immediate problem is that our knowledge of those risks is dispersed, and our understanding fragmentary.

Without adequate knowledge, countermeasures will be ineffectual, if not counter-productive, and policy will be based merely on plausible ideas and guesswork. Success will be the result of luck, not judgement. But from greater shared knowledge will follow better countermeasures (both in their design and implementation) and better policy. Thus the absolutely necessary precursor to any sensible intervention in cyber-security is: Get knowledge.

Genuine knowledge is rooted in accurate, timely information, but how are we to understand 'information sharing'? It covers a wide range of actions, from the exchange of high-level generalised conclusions (*e.g.* at conferences or liaison meetings) to the automated transfer of large volumes of data.

We would suggest that the latter is not appropriate in this instance, two major objections being the horrendous privacy implications and the technical infrastructure needed. High-level exchanges have their place but experience (*e.g.* from financial crime) suggests that by themselves they are inadequate.

The answer lies somewhere between these two extremes: in essence, the reporting of incidents by individuals at the operational level. This does not rule out deeper analysis and higher level exchanges, but is a necessary precursor: a firm foundation of hard information on which they can be based.There is, indeed, much good co-operation and information sharing already in the field of cyber-security, often of an informal sort. But this activity tends to be confined to a particular sector (*e.g.*, banking or academia) and even then it is rarely comprehensive.

The sharing of knowledge is fairly high level or anecdotal: what is lacking is a foundation of hard information upon which a solid body of knowledge can be built. It will be important, however, to ensure that any new initiative(s) do not harm or disrupt the good work that is already being done: they should enhance and improve, not replace. Especially important will be avoiding a form of moral hazard where reporting, analysing and solving problems become 'someone else's business'. This will easily happen if the wrong model is adopted. Systemic flaws produce perverse outcomes, no matter how commendable the aims or how strong the commitment to them.

Principles

There are several guiding principles upon which we believe any solution to the problem of wider cyber-security should be based. The first is that the process should be fundamentally based upon active collaboration between the public and private sectors, whereby the government and its relevant agencies are equal stakeholders rather than controlling entities. This is designed to ensure a more level playing field to engender trust between public and private agencies, and to help facilitate greater information sharing, to the mutual benefit of all.

The second principle concerns the shifting of responsibility for cyber-security from central government agencies to companies themselves. This is designed to empower companies so that they may look after their own interests and not have to rely on the resources and direction of some central entity. This will help overcome the crucial time delay which occurs whenever companies at the periphery have to defer to the centre, thus reducing the vital time between detection and response to cyber incidents, where action will need to be taken within minutes rather than hours. Therefore companies should be provided with the tools and education to protect themselves from the most prevalent threats, and also trained to recognise serious incursions so that the rest of the community can be alerted and the relevant government agencies quickly involved.

In relation to this, the third principle argues for the creation of an environment which encourages collective security that can be collectively enforced, rather than security controlled and enforced from a central entity. An ideal model of cyber-security would facilitate, rather than direct, information-sharing between companies across non-traditional sector boundaries, and would encourage a culture of 'cyber-hygiene' amongst its members. Member organisations would thus be nudged into practicing better cyber-security as part of a collective community of security, with any central agency only intervening when necessary.

The fourth and perhaps the most important principle concerns the operator 'at the coalface'. This is the person who will spot and report incidents. If the system is designed so that their interest and intelligence is engaged, it will succeed. If not, a 'box-ticking' mentality will prevail and the information entering the system will be of poor quality, which will be devastating. Positive and negative factors come into play. The most important positive factor is that the system helps the operator to do their job better: they have access to the reports it contains and can use them to locally implement better countermeasures. This is a powerful incentive to contribute to the body of information themselves. On the negative side there must be no undue obstacles or disincentives to report. Reporting must be easy, quick, not (primarily) a compliance issue, and not governed by arbitrary targets.

Comparable Models

When considering the feasibility of putting these principles into practice, it is instructive to look towards existing collective security and information sharing arrangements. Public sector models such as the Serious Organised Crime Agency's Suspicious Activities Reports (SAR) system whilst playing a vital role in combating financial crime in the UK, are incompatible with our stated principles because they employ a top-down centralised approach, with private companies relegated to merely passing on information to assist law enforcement. Furthermore the SARs regime is part of a large and costly public-sector body, which is at odds with our vision of a small and nimble public-private sector collaborative entity.

A workable model can be found in Information Sharing and Analysis Centres (ISACs), which are organisations usually set up by the owners and operators of an infrastructure within a sector to provide information analysis and data dissemination. An example of this model that can be seen in practice in the UK is CIFAS-the UK's Credit Industry Fraud Advisory Service, which is a privately run organisation consisting of over 260 UK organisations, predominantly drawn from the private sector, and is the world's first non-profit fraud prevention data-sharing scheme. This model closely adheres to our stated principles as a relatively small organisation, entirely funded through membership fees, which facilitates information sharing between public and private agencies and across different sectors such a retail and finance. It also helps to empower and educate its members about fraud prevention by providing them with reports concerning the latest fraud trends and threats, and offers a multitude of staff training and even (jointly with a university) a foundation degree in Fraud Management. CIFAS provides an attractive model of collective security whereby the system empowers and educates its members whilst also facilitating information sharing, with the centre intervening and disciplining members only in cases of serious misconduct.

CRITICAL INFRASTRUCTURE PROTECTION

The Internet infrastructure relies on primarily on the Border Gateway Protocol (BGP) and the Domain Name System (DNS). The secure remote administration of routers relies mostly on the Secure Shell (SSH) protocol. Attacks against any of these technologies may impact on the availability of Internet-based services. As we do not know how to guarantee software correctness, it is a reasonable to assume that exploitable programming errors exist in applications.

To reduce the ability of an adversary to cause damage, we need to limit the impact of such programming errors. We offer *Privilege Separation* as one solution. Services that authenticate remote users to system resources are difficult to contain via external application confinement mechanisms. Privilege Separation is a protection mechanism at the application level that separates the privileged code path from the unprivileged code path. An adversary interacts with the unprivileged part only; an exploitable programming error in the unprivileged code path does not lead to immediate privilege escalation.

Privilege separation may also be employed to increase the resilience of domain name service implementations like bind. Privilege Separation is very portable as most modern Unix operating system provide address space protection between processes and inter-process communication, privilege separation.

Intrusion Prevention

While Privilege Separation increases an application's resilience against programming errors, it does not prevent all possible intrusions. Many system services and applications perform specific tasks. By confining applications to only those operations that required for its correct execution, we prevent adversaries who gain control over these system services from causing damage to the system.

In Unix operating systems, persistent changes are possibly only via *System Calls*. By carefully monitoring and restricting an application's system calls, we can limit or even prevent an adversary from causing damage. We offer *Systrace* as solution. Systrace provides fine-grained application confinement based on configurable security policies. Additionally, it can detect and prevent intrusions. It also records audit trails that can used in forensic analysis.

Threat Assessment

The impact of new security problems can be reduced by early threat detection. Threat detection and assessment allows us to quickly identify so far unknown attacks, prioritize their threat and protect vulnerable systems. Honeypot technology serves this purpose by providing computer systems that we expect to be compromised. The honeypot systems are network sensors that allows us to detect new attacks.

As computer security problems are inherently repeatable, we obtain threat detection by populating our network with honeypots. New attacks can easily be identified by monitoring the state of deployed honeypots including new worms or widespread scans for vulnerabilities.

CYBER SECURITY AND CRITICAL INFRASTRUCTURE PROTECTION IN INDIA

Cyber Security of India is an essential part of National ICT Policy and Strategy of India. Despite some very good suggestions and critical evaluations, the Government of India (GOI) has not considered it necessary to take some action in this regard. There has been repetitive wake up calls given to the GOI but it seems the GOI is in indefinite sleep.

On the other hand, the International Community is stressing really hard to make cyber security an essential part of their day to day lives. Dartmouth's Institute for Information Infrastructure Protection (I3P) has recently provided its cyber security research recommendations.

They are in the form of a set of recommendations for advancing research in cyber security that can be implemented in the next five to 10 years. The report recognises four areas of need that emerged during the forum:

(1) A coordinated and collaborative approach is needed.

(2) Metrics and assessment tools must be developed.

(3) An effective legal and policy framework for security must be created.

(4) The human dimension of security must be addressed.

It may be a coincidence that similar suggestions were provided by Mr. Praveen Dalal, Managing Partner of Perry4Law to the Government of India. He has also provided the Indian Policies and Strategies for Critical ICT Infrastructure Protection and Management in India. The stress upon Legal Enablement of ICT Systems in India is very important to make Cyber Law of India strong and effective.

There are lot of Problems through which the present Cyber Law of India is passing through. A good account of the same can be found at this nice piece of work.

The problem still remains the same. In India we don't have a dedicated resource that is taking care of Techno-Legal Laws of India in a holistic manner. Of course, we have a Cyber Law Database of India.

We also have a Techno-Legal ICT Regulations Database in India. These two resources are tracing back the history of cyber law in India. However, we need a resource that can trace both history of cyber law in India as well as its current position and the prospective future of the same. The task is very difficult but it has been successfully achieved by Mr. Praveen Dalal, Managing Partner of Perry4Law. He has successfully come out with a "Dedicated Resource" on cyber law in India.

The same is titled "Legal Enablement Of ICT Systems in India" and is the exclusive, most comprehensive and holistic web resource in India dealing with Techno-Legal ICT Laws and Regulations in India. All the cyber law observers can now access information about cyber law in India and the changes that are proposed or actually made from time to time. The resource is very futuristic and promising in nature and it would be good idea if the Government of India (GOI) consults the same while making, amending or reformulating techno-legal laws in India.

One of the important aspects of this resource is that it is the exclusive resource that is providing a "Constitutional Analysis" of the present as well as proposed techno-legal laws in India. Therefore all of the "Civil Liberty Crusaders" keep a close eye upon this resource for issues like Privacy Rights, Life and Liberty, Right to Speech and Expressions, etc.

For instance, surveillance has become a controversial issue since the Information Technology (Amendment) Bill, 2008 (Bill, 2008) has been proposed. Surprisingly some people are justifying these wide and unregulated powers as justified under the garb of security that does not exists at all in India. There is only one answer to the pro surveillance argument and it is a Benjamin Franklin quote: Those who would give up essential liberty to purchase a little temporary safety deserve neither liberty nor safety.

E-Surveillance should not be a substitute for cyber security and cyber forensics capabilities. Privacy Rights must be respected and followed in both letter and spirit in India. He Bill, 2008 has seriously compromised these Fundamental Rights. So friends, wake up and be a vigilant and legally aware citizens. We will keep on spreading the "Cyber Law Awareness" in India so that we may have an informed citizenry.

COMPUTER INSECURITY

Security and Systems Design

Most current real-world computer security efforts focus on external threats, and generally treat the computer system itself as a trusted system. Some knowledgeable observers consider this to be a disastrous mistake, and point out that this distinction is the cause of much of the insecurity of current computer systems - once an attacker has subverted one part of a system without fine-grained security, he or she usually has access to most or all of the features of that system. [citation needed] Because computer systems can be very complex, and cannot be guaranteed to be free of defects, this security stance tends to produce insecure systems.

The 'trusted systems' approach has been predominant in the design of many Microsoft software products, due to the long-standing Microsoft policy of emphasizing functionality and 'ease of use' over security. Since Microsoft products currently dominate the desktop and home computing markets, this has led to unfortunate effects. However, the problems described here derive from the security stance taken by software and hardware vendors generally, rather than the failing of a single vendor. Microsoft is not out of line in this respect, just far more prominent with respect to its consumer marketshare.

It should be noted that the Windows NT line of operating systems from Microsoft contained mechanisms to limit this, such as services that ran under dedicated user accounts, and Role-Based Access Control (RBAC) with user/group rights, but the Windows 95 line of products lacked most of these functions. Before the release of Windows 2003 Microsoft has changed their official stance, taking a more locked down approach.

On 15 January 2002, Bill Gates sent out a memo on Trustworthy Computing, marking the official change in company stance. Regardless, Microsoft's operating system Windows XP is still plagued by complaints about lack of local security and inability to use the fine-grained user access controls together with certain software (esp. certain popular computer games).

Financial Cost

Serious financial damage has been caused by computer security breaches, but reliably estimating costs is quite difficult. Figures in the billions of dollars have been quoted in relation to the damage caused by malware such as computer worms like the Code Red worm, but such estimates may be exaggerated. However, other losses, such as those caused by the compromise of credit card information, can be more easily determined, and they have been substantial, as measured by millions of individual victims of identity theft each year in each of several nations, and the severe hardship imposed on each victim, that can wipe out all of their finances, prevent them from getting a job, plus be treated as if they were the criminal. Volumes of victims of phishing and other scams may not be known.

Individuals who have been infected with spyware or malware likely go through a costly and time-consuming process of having their computer cleaned. Spyware and malware is considered to be a problem specific to the various Microsoft Windows operating systems, however this can be explained somewhat by the fact that Microsoft controls a major share of the PC market and thus represent the most prominent target.

Reasons

There are many similarities (yet many fundamental differences) between computer and physical security. Just like real-world security, the motivations for breaches of computer security vary between attackers, sometimes called hackers or crackers. Some are teenage thrill-seekers or vandals (the kind often responsible for defacing web sites); similarly, some web site defacements are done to make political statements. However, some attackers are highly skilled and motivated with the goal of compromising computers for financial gain or espionage. An example of the latter is Markus Hess who spied for the KGB and was ultimately caught because of the efforts of Clifford Stoll, who wrote an amusing and accurate book, The Cuckoo's Egg, about his experiences. For those seeking to prevent security breaches, the first step is usually to attempt to identify what might motivate an attack on the system, how much the continued operation and information security of the system are worth, and who might be motivated to breach it. The precautions required for a home PC are very different for those of banks' Internet banking system, and different again for a classified military network. Other computer security writers suggest that, since an attacker using a network need know nothing about you or what you have on your computer, attacker motivation is inherently impossible to determine beyond guessing. If true, blocking all possible attacks is the only plausible action to take.

Vulnerabilities

To understand the techniques for securing a computer system, it is important to first understand the various types of "attacks" that can be made against it. These threats can typically be classified into one of these seven categories:

Exploits

Software flaws, especially buffer overflows, are often exploited to gain control of a computer, or to cause it to operate in an unexpected manner. Many development methodologies rely on testing to ensure the quality of any code released; this process often fails to discover extremely unusual potential exploits. The term "exploit" generally refers to small programs designed to take advantage of a software flaw that has been discovered, either remote or local. The code from the exploit program is frequently reused in trojan horses and computer viruses. In some cases, a vulnerability can lie in certain programs' processing of a specific file type, such as a non-executable media file.

Eavesdropping

Any data that is transmitted over a network is at some risk of being eavesdropped, or even modified by a malicious person. Even machines that operate as a closed system (ie, with no contact to the outside world) can be eavesdropped upon via monitoring the faint electro-magnetic transmissions generated by the hardware such as TEMPEST. The FBI's proposed Carnivore program was intended to act as a system of eavesdropping protocols built into the systems of internet service providers.

DATA SAFETY AND PRIVACY PROTECTION

As the situation now warranty legislation of data protection in India, visitors to any website want reassurances that privacy rights will be respected when they engage in eCommerce. It is part of the confidence-creating role that successful eCommerce businesses have to convey to the consumer. If industry doesn't make sure it's guarding the privacy of the data it collects, it will be the responsibility of the government and it's their obligation to enact legislation. The problem that arises in eCommerce is that the Internet is in itself global. Generally the actions in regulating by the Indian Govt will have very little impact unless they are part of a larger international setting.

The protection of personal data has never been a purely national problem; it was always a global issue. Here we are trying no to not deal with privacy issues relating to internal use by employees, sending personal data or using the employers Internet for personal purposes. It is to focus on issues relating to the collection, storage, accuracy and use of data provided by Net users in the use of the World Wide Web

Information that could be collected by Operating Websites and what way it can be Used?

The type of information that could be collected and can be classified as either individually identifiable information or Mass undisclosed information.

Individually Identifiable Information

Individually identifiable information can be defined as information that can be used to identify an individual, that consist of information like name, address, telephone number, credit card number, or email address And other consumer specific information. This information is linked with identifiable information from other sources, or from which other personally identifiable information can easily be found, including, but not limited to, name, address, phone number, fax number, email address, financial profiles, credit card information. And also IP address is associated with Personally Identifiable Information, unless you have affirmatively disclosed this information. The Internet generates an elaborate trail of data every stop a person makes. Pentium III processor identifier chip called Processor Serial Number or PSN, It is a number tied to the individual and used to validate one's identity through a range of interactions with any organization or demographic.

Mass Undisclosed Information

Mass undisclosed information" can be defined as information that: a website or third party on its behalf aggregates and categorizes by established geographical areas, such as postal codes and contains non-consumer specific information created from anonymous transactions for use by merchants in better managing their businesses and conducting mass media advertising.

There is a abundant of technologies that are utilized to collect both Classes of information on consumers. One of these tools are called "Cookies" Which is simply a piece of information [computer code] that is saved on your own Computer or your browser. It contains information as to the personal preferences exhibited when visiting a website. As it is impossible to differentiate between Visitors to a Web site, the server will somehow mark the visitor by storing information on them.

While Cookies themselves are not gathering the data, they are used as tracking devices to help people who are collecting information.

Any information gathered is associated with the value they keep in any Cookie. A Cookie cannot read hard drive to find out who they are, or there incomes or place of residence, However, that information could end up in a Cookie if you provided it to a site and that site saved it in a Cookie.

Policies to Protect Privacy

Accountability by organizations for information within their possession Limit the collection of the information.Revelation of personal data to the declared purpose except with the consent of the individual.

Organization should retain information only as long as necessary. Information in possession of an organization should be accurate and up-to-date Security should be the Priority Organizations collecting should be transparent in their policy and practice Organizations should allow individuals access and the ability to rectify errors.

Fair information practices: Web sites would be required to provide consumers notice of what information they collect and how they use it. Web sites would be required to offer consumers choices as to how that information is to be used beyond the use for which the information was provided. Web sites would be required to offer consumers reasonable access to that information and an opportunity to correct inaccuracies. Web sites would be required to take reasonable steps to protect the security and integrity of that information. Websites that collect personal identifying information from children 12 and under need to provide actual notice to the parent and obtain parental consent as follows.

The agency should issue interpretive rules defining fair information practices with greater specificity, taking into account industry-specific differences.

The purpose is to prevent violations of fundamental human rights such as unlawful storage of personal data, or the abuse or unauthorized disclosure of such data.

THE LEGAL LANDSCAPE FOR THE PROTECTION OF PRIVACY

Although not specifically referenced in the Constitution, the Right to Privacy is considered a 'penumbral right' under the Constitution, *i.e.*, a right that has been declared by the Supreme Court as integral to the Fundamental Right to Life and Liberty. In addition, although no single statute confers a cross-cutting 'horizontal' right to privacy various statutes contain provisions which either implicitly or explicitly preserve this right.

Constitutional Protections for Privacy

Although the Indian Constitution does not contain an explicit reference to a Right to Privacy, this right has been read in to the constitution by the Supreme Court as a component of two

Fundamental Rights: the right to freedom under Article 19 and the right to life and personal liberty under Article 21. It would be instructive to provide a brief background to each of these Articles before delving deeper into the privacy jurisprudence expounded by the courts under them. Part III of the Constitution of India is titled 'Fundamental Rights' and lists out several rights which are regarded as fundamental to all citizens of India.

Article 13 forbids the State from making "any law which takes away or abridges" the fundamental rights. Article 19(1)(a) stipulates that "All citizens shall have the right to freedom of speech and expression". However this is qualified by Article 19(2) which states that this will not "affect the operation of any existing law, or prevent the State from making any law, in so far as such law imposes *reasonable restrictions* on the exercise of the right ... in the interests of the sovereignty and integrity of India, the security of the State, friendly relations with foreign States, public order, decency or morality, or in relation to contempt of court, defamation or incitement to an offence". Thus the Freedom of Expression guaranteed by Article 19(1)(a) is not absolute, but a qualified right that is susceptible, under the Constitutional scheme, to being curtailed under specified conditions.

The other important Fundamental Right from the perspective of privacy jurisprudence is Article 21 which reads "21. No person shall be deprived of his life or personal liberty except according to procedure established by law." Where Article 19 contains a detailed list of conditions under which Freedom of Expression may be curtailed, by contrast Article 21 is thinly-worded and only requires a "procedure established by law" as a pre-condition for the deprivation of life and liberty. However, the Supreme Court has held in a celebrated case *Maneka Gandhi vs. Union of India* that any procedure "which deals with the modalities of regulating, restricting or even rejection of a fundamental right falling within Article 21 has to be fair, not foolish, carefully designed to effectuate, not to subvert, the substantive right itself.

Thus, understood, "procedure" must rule out anything arbitrary, freakish or bizarre." Shortly after independence, in a case challenging the constitutionality of search and seizure provisions, the Supreme Court dealt a blow to the right to privacy in India, holding that "When the Constitution makers have thought fit not to subject to Constitutional limitations by recognition of a fundamental right to privacy, analogous to the American Fourth Amendment, we have no justification to import it, into a totally different fundamental right."

Notwithstanding this early setback, five decisions by the Supreme Court in the succeeding 5 decades have established the Right to Privacy in India as flowing from Article 19 and 21. The first was a seven-Judge bench decision in *Kharak Singh V. The State of U.P* decided in 1964. The question for consideration in this case was whether "surveillance" under Chapter XX of the U.P.Police Regulations constituted an infringement of any of the fundamental rights guaranteed by Part III of the Constitution. Regulation 236(b) which permitted surveillance by "domiciliary visits at night" was held to be violative of Article 21. The meanings of the word "life" and the expression "personal liberty" in Article 21 were elaborately considered by this court in Kharak Singh`s case. Although the majority found that the Constitution contained no explicit guarantee of a "right to privacy", it read the right to personal liberty expansively to include a right to dignity. It held that "an unauthorised intrusion into a person's home and the disturbance caused to him thereby, is as it were the violation of a common law right of a man -an ultimate essential of ordered liberty, if not of the very concept of civilization".

In a minority judgement in this case, Justice Subba Rao held that "the right to personal liberty takes in not only a right to be free from restrictions placed on his movements, but also free from encroachments on his private life. It is true our Constitution does not expressly declare a right to privacy as a fundamental right but the said right is an essential ingredient of personal liberty Every democratic country sanctifies domestic life; it is expected to give him rest, physical happiness, peace of mind and security. In the last resort, a person's house, where he lives with his family, is his "castle" " it is his rampart against encroachment on his personal liberty."

This case, especially Justice Subba Rao's observations, paved the way for later elaborations on the right to privacy using Article 21. In 1972, the Supreme Court decided one of its first cases on the constitutionality of wiretapping. In *R. M. Malkani vs State Of Maharashtra* the petitioner's voice had been recorded in the course of a telephonic conversation where he was attempting blackmail.

He asserted in his defence that his right to privacy under Article 21 had been violated. The Supreme Court declined his plea holding that "The telephonic conversation of an innocent citizen will be protected by Courts against wrongful or high handed' interference by tapping the conversation. *The protection is not for the guilty citizen against the efforts of the police to vindicate the law and prevent corruption of public servants.*" The third case in the series, *Govind vs. State of Madhya Pradesh*, decided by a three- Judge Bench of the Supreme Court, is regarded as being a setback to the right to privacy jurisprudence.

Here, the court was evaluating the constitutional validity of Regulations 855 and 856 of the Madhya Pradesh Police Regulations which provided for police surveillance of habitual offenders which including domiciliary visits and picketing of the suspects. The Supreme Court desisted from striking down these invasive provisions holding that "It cannot be said that surveillance by domiciliary visit-, would always be an unreasonable restriction upon the right of privacy. It is only persons who are suspected to be habitual criminals and those who are determined to lead a criminal life that are subjected to surveillance."

The court went on to make some observations on the right to privacy under the constitution:

- "Too broad a definition of privacy will raise serious questions about the propriety of judicial reliance on a right that is not explicit in the Constitution. The right to privacy will, therefore, necessarily, have to go through a process of case by case development. Hence, assuming that the right to personal liberty. the right to move freely throughout India and the freedom of speech create an independent fundamental right of privacy as an emanation from them it could not he absolute. It must be subject to restriction on the basis of compelling public interest. But the law infringing it must satisfy the compelling state interest test. *It could not be that under these freedoms the Constitution-makers intended to protect or protected mere personal sensitiveness."*

This case is important since, it marks the beginning of a trend in the higher judiciary to regard the right to privacy as "not being absolute". From *Govind* onwards, 'non-absoluteness' becomes the defining feature and the destiny of this right. This line of reasoning was continued in *Malak Singh v State Of Punjab and Haryana* where the Supreme Court held that surveillance was lawful and did not violate the right to personal liberty of a citizen as long as there was no 'illegal interference' and it was "unobstrusive and within bounds". Nearly fifteen years separate this case from the Supreme Court's next major elaboration of the right to privacy in *R. Rajagopal vs. State of Tamil Nadu*. Here the court was involved a balancing of the right of privacy of citizens against the right of the press to criticise and comment on acts and conduct of public officials. The case related to the publication by a newspaper of the autobiography of Auto Shankar who had been convicted and sentenced to death for committing six murders.

In the autobiography, he had commented on his contact and relations with various high-ranking police officials – disclosures which would have been extremely sensational. Sometime before the publication, he appears to have been induced to write a letter disclaiming his authorship of the autobiography. On this basis, the Inspector General of Prisons issued a letter forbidding the newspaper from publishing the autobiography claiming, inter alia, that the publication of the autobiography would violate the prisoner's privacy. Curiously, neither Shankar himself, nor his family were made parties to this petition. The Court decided to presume, somewhat oddly, that he had "neither written his autobiography" nor had he authorised its publication. The court then proceeded on this assumption to enquire whether he had any privacy interests that would be breached by unauthorised publication of his life story.

The right of privacy of citizens was dealt with by the Supreme Court in the following terms:

- The right to privacy is implicit in the right to life and liberty guaranteed to the citizens of this country by Article 21. It is a "right to be let alone". A citizen has a right to safeguard the privacy of his own, his family, marriage, procreation, motherhood, childbearing and education among other matters. None can publish anything concerning the above matters without his consent - whether truthful or otherwise and whether laudatory or critical. If he does so, he would be violating the right to privacy of the person concerned and would be liable in an action for damages. Position may, however, be different, if a person voluntarily thrusts himself into controversy or voluntarily invites or raises a controversy.
- The rule aforesaid is subject to the exception, that any publication concerning the aforesaid aspects becomes unobjectionable if such publication is based upon public records including court records. This is for the reason that once a matter becomes a matter of public record, the right to privacy no longer subsists and it becomes a legitimate subject for comment by press and media among others. We are, however, of the opinion that in the interests of decency an exception must be carved out to this rule, viz., a female who is the victim of a sexual assault, kidnap, abduction or a like offence should not further be subjected to the indignity of her name and the incident being publicised in press/media.

On this reasoning, the court upheld that the newspaper's right to publish Shankar's autobiography, even without his consent or authorisation, to the extent that this story was able to be pieced together from public records. However, if they went beyond that, the court held, "they may be invading his right to privacy and will be liable for the consequences in accordance with law." Importantly, the court held that "the remedy of the affected public officials/public figures, if any, is *after the publication*". The final case that makes up the 'privacy quintet' in India was the case of *PUCL v. Union of India*, a public interest litigation, in which the court was called upon to consider whether wiretapping was an unconstitutional infringement of a citizen's right to privacy. The case was filed in light of a report brought out by the Central Bureau of Investigation on the 'Tapping of politicians' phones' which disclosed several irregularities in the tapping of telephones.

On the concept of the 'right to privacy' in India, the Court made the following observations:

- The right privacy - by itself - has not been identified under the Constitution. As a concept it may be too broad and moralistic to define it judicially. Whether right to privacy can be claimed or has been infringed in a given case would depend on the facts of the said case.

However, the Court went on to hold that "the right to hold a telephone conversation in the privacy of ones home or office without interference can certainly be claimed as right to privacy". This was because "conversations on the telephone are often of an intimate and confidentialcharacter...Telephone conversation is an important facet of a man's private life. Right to privacy would certainly include telephone-conversation in the privacy of one's home or office. Telephone-tapping would, thus, infract Article 21 of the Constitution of India unless it is permitted under the procedure established by law." The court also read this right to privacy as deriving from Article 19. "When a person is talking on telephone, he is exercising his right to freedom of speech and expression", the court observed, and therefore "telephone-tapping unless it comes within the grounds of restrictions under Article 19(2) would infract Article 19(1)(a) of the Constitution."

This case made two important contributions to communications privacy jurisprudence in India – the first was its rejection of the contention that 'prior judicial scrutiny' should be mandated before any wiretapping could take place. Instead, the court accepted the contention that administrative safeguards would be sufficient. Secondly, the Court prescribed a list of procedural guidelines, the observance of which would save the wiretapping power from unconstitutionality. In 2007, these safeguards were formally incorporated into the Rules framed under the Telegraph Act.

Thus, it may be observed that the right to privacy in India is, at its foundations a *limited* right rather than an absolute one. This limited nature of the right provides a somewhat unstable assurance of privacy since, it is frequently made to yield to a range of conflicting interests – rights of paternity, national security etc. which happen to have a more pronounced standing in law. In March 2002, the National Commission to Review the Working of the Constitution submitted its report and recommended amending the Constitution to include a slew of new rights including the Right to Privacy.

The new Right to Privacy would be numbered Article 21-B and would read:

1. "Every person has a right to respect for his private and family life, his home and his correspondence.
2. Nothing in clause (1) shall prevent the State from making any law imposing reasonable restrictions on the exercise of the right conferred by clause (1), in the interests of security of the State, public safety or for the prevention of disorder or crime, or for the protection of health or morals, or for the protection of the rights and freedoms of others."

There has, so far been no move to amend the constitution to give effect to this recommendation.

Statutory Protections for Privacy

Although such a move is under consideration, India does not currently have a sui-generis statute that safeguards privacy horizontally across different contexts. However various statutes dealing with issues as diverse as banking and finance, professional ethics of lawyers, doctors and chartered accountants, information technology and telephony etc. contain provisions which either explicitly or impliedly protect privacy and offer victims remedies for their breach. We propose to deal mainly with privacy protections under the Information Technology Act, with special focus on Data Protection provisions and certain other miscellaneous laws which protect privacy.

The Information Technology Act

The Information Technology Act 2000 contains a number of provisions which can be used to safeguard against online/ computer related privacy. The Act provides for civil and criminal liability with respect to hacking and imprisonment of up to three years with fine for electronic voyeurism, Phishing and identity theft, Offensive e-mail. Disclosure by the government of information obtained in the course of exercising its interception powers under the IT Act is punishable with imprisonment of up to two years and fine Section 72A of the IT Act penalises the unauthorised disclosure of "personal information" by any person who has obtained such information while providing services under a lawful contract. Such disclosure must be made with the intent of causing wrongful loss or obtaining a wrongful gain and is punishable with imprisonment which may extend to 3 years or a fine of Rs. 500,000 or both.

6

Terrorism Moved into Cyberspace

Terrorists have moved into cyberspace to facilitate traditional forms of terrorism such as bombings. They use the Internet to communicate, coordinate events, and advance their agenda. While such activity does not constitute cyberterrorism in the strict sense, it does show that terrorists have some competency using the new information technologies.

By 1996, the headquarters of terrorist financier Osama bin Laden in Afghanistan was equipped with computers and communications equipment. Egyptian "Afghan" computer experts were said to have helped devise a communication network that used the Web, e-mail, and electronic bulletin boards. Hamas activists have been said to use chat rooms and e-mail to plan operations and coordinate activities, making it difficult for Israeli security officials to trace their messages and decode their contents. The Revolutionary Armed Forces of Columbia (FARC) uses e-mail to field inquiries from the press.

The Web is especially popular as a medium for reaching a global audience. For example, after the Peruvian terrorist group Tupac Amaru stormed the Japanese Ambassador's residence in Lima on December 17, 1996 and took 400 diplomatic, political, and military officials as hostage, sympathizers in the United States and Canada put up solidarity Web sites. One site included detailed drawings of the residence and planned assault.

In February 1998, Hizbullah was operating three Web sites: one for the central press office (www.hizbollah.org), another to describe its attacks on Israeli targets (www.moqawama.org), and the third for news and information (www.almanar.com.lb). That month, Clark Staten, executive director of the Emergency Response & Research Institute (ERRI) in Chicago, testified before a U.S. Senate subcommittee that "even small terrorist groups are now using the Internet to broadcast their message and misdirect/misinform the general population in multiple nations simultaneously." He gave the subcommittee copies of both domestic and international messages containing anti-American and anti-Israeli propaganda and threats, including a widely distributed extremist call for "jihad" (holy war) against America and Great Britain.

In June 1998, *U.S. News & World Report* noted that 12 of the 30 groups on the U.S. State Department=s list of terrorist organizations are on the Web. Now, it appears that virtually every terrorist group is on the Web. Forcing them off the Web is impossible, because they can set up their sites in countries with free-speech laws. The government of Sri Lanka, for example, banned the separatist Liberation Tigers of Tamil Eelam, but they have not even attempted to take down their London-based Web site.

Even in democracies, however, there are limits to what terrorists can post on the Net. After a group of anti-abortionists put up a Web site terrorizing doctors who performed abortions, a federal jury ordered the pages be taken down and damages of more than $100 million paid. The Nuremberg Files site had listed the names of about 200 abortion providers under the heading of "baby butchers." Readers were invited to send in such personal details as the doctors' home addresses, license plate numbers, and the names of their children. Three doctors whose names appeared on the list were killed, and after each, the doctor's name was promptly crossed out. Doctors named on the site testified that they lived in constant fear and used disguises, bodyguards, and bulletproof vests. In ordering the site down, the federal jury said the site and "wanted" posters amounted to death threats against the doctors.

Many terrorists are using encryption to conceal their communications and stored files, compounding the difficulties of providing effective counter-terrorism. Hamas, for example, reportedly has used encrypted Internet communications to transmit maps, pictures, and other details pertaining to terrorist attacks. Ramsey Yousef, a member of the international terrorist group responsible for bombing the World Trade Centre in 1994 and a Manila Air airliner in late 1995, encrypted files on his laptop computer. The files, which U.S. government officials decrypted, contained information pertaining to further plans to blow up eleven U.S.-owned commercial airliners in the Far East. The Aum Shinrikyo cult, which gassed the Tokyo subway in March 1995, killing 12 people and injuring 6,000 more, also used encryption to protect their computerized records, which included plans and intentions to deploy weapons of mass destruction in Japan and the United States.

Cyberspace Attacks

Cyberspace is constantly under assault. Cyber spies, thieves, saboteurs, and thrill seekers break into computer systems, steal personal data and trade secrets, vandalize Web sites, disrupt service, sabotage data and systems, launch computer viruses and worms, conduct fraudulent transactions, and harass individuals and companies. These attacks are facilitated with increasingly powerful and easy-to-use software tools, which are readily available for free from thousands of Web sites on the Internet.

Many of the attacks are serious and costly. The ILOVEYOU virus and variants, for example, was estimated to have hit tens of millions of users worldwide and cost billions of dollars in damage. Denial-of-service attacks against Yahoo, CNN, eBay, and other e-commerce Web sites were estimated to have caused over a billion in losses. They also shook the confidence of business and individuals in e-commerce. Governments are particularly concerned with terrorist and state-sponsored attacks against the critical infrastructures that constitute their national life support systems. The Clinton Administration defined eight: telecommunications, banking and finance, electrical power, oil and gas distribution and storage, water supply, transportation, emergency services, and government services.

There have been numerous attacks against these infrastructures. Hackers have invaded the public phone networks, compromising nearly every category of activity, including switching and operations, administration, maintenance, and provisioning (OAM&P). They have crashed or disrupted signal transfer points, traffic switches, OAM&P systems, and other network elements. They have planted "time bomb" programs designed to shut down major switching hubs, disrupted emergency 911 services throughout the eastern seaboard, and boasted that they have the capability to bring down all switches in Manhattan. They have installed wiretaps, rerouted phone calls, changed the greetings on voice mail systems, taken over voice mailboxes, and made free long-distance calls at their victims= expense — sticking some victims with phone bills in the hundreds of thousands of dollars. When they can=t crack the technology, they use "social engineering" to con employees into giving them access.

In March 1997, one teenage hacker penetrated and disabled a telephone company computer that serviced the Worcester Airport in Massachusetts. As a result, telephone service to the Federal Aviation Administration control tower, the airport fire department, airport security, the weather service, and various private airfreight companies was cut off for six hours. Later in the day, the juvenile disabled another telephone company computer, this time causing an outage in the Rutland area. The lost service caused financial damages and threatened public health and public safety. On a separate occasion, the hacker allegedly broke into a pharmacist=s computer and accessed files containing prescriptions.

Banks and financial systems are a popular target of cyber criminals. The usual motive is money, and perpetrators have stolen or attempted to steal tens of millions of dollars. In one case of sabotage, a computer operator at Reuters in Hong Kong tampered with the dealing room systems of five of the company=s bank clients. In November 1996, he programmed the systems to delete key operating system files after a delay long enough to allow him to leave the building. When the "time bombs" exploded, the systems crashed. They were partially restored by the next morning, but it took another day before they were fully operational. However, the banks said the tampering did not significantly affect trading and that neither they nor their clients experienced losses. In another act of sabotage against a critical infrastructure, a fired employee of Chevron's emergency alert network disabled the firm=s alert system by hacking into computers in New York and San Jose, California, and reconfiguring them so they=d crash. The vandalism was not discovered until an emergency arose at the Chevron refinery in Richmond, California, and the system could not be used to notify the adjacent community of a noxious release. During the 10-hour period in 1992 when the system was down, thousands of people in 22 states and 6 unspecified areas of Canada were put at risk.

An overflow of raw sewage on the Sunshine Coast of Australia in June was linked to a 49-year-old Brisbane man, who allegedly penetrated the Maroochy Shire Council's computer system and used radio transmissions to create the overflows. The man faced 370 charges that included stealing, computer hacking, and use radio communications equipment without authority.

Government computers, particularly Department of Defence computers, are a regular target of attack. Detected attacks against unclassified DoD computers rose from 780 in 1997 to 5,844 in 1998 and 22,144 in 1999.

The most damaging and costly attacks have been conducted for reasons other than the pursuit of terrorism. As the above cases illustrate, they have been motivated by greed, thrills, ego, revenge, and a variety of other non-ideological factors. They are properly classified as cybercrimes, but not cyberterrorism

Politically and Socially Motivated Cyberattacks

Terrorism is normally associated with attacks conducted in furtherance of political and social objectives. Numerous cyberattacks have been so motivated. For example, in 1998, ethnic Tamil guerrillas swamped Sri Lankan embassies with 800 e-mails a day over a two-week period. The messages read "We are the Internet Black Tigers and we=re doing this to disrupt your communications." Intelligence authorities characterized it as the first known attack by terrorists against a country=s computer systems.

Also in 1998, Spanish protestors bombarded the Institute for Global Communications (IGC) with thousands of bogus e-mail messages. E-mail was tied up and undeliverable to the San Francisco based ISP=s users, and support lines were tied up with people who couldn=t get their mail. The protestors also spammed IGC staff and member accounts, clogged their Web page with bogus credit card orders, and threatened to employ the same tactics against organizations using IGC services. They demanded that IGC stop hosting the Webs site for the *Euskal Herria Journal*, a New York-based publication supporting Basque independence. Protestors said IGC supported terrorism because a section on the Web pages contained materials on the terrorist group Fatherland and Liberty, or ETA, which claimed responsibility for assassinations of Spanish political and security officials, and attacks on military installations. IGC finally relented and pulled the site because of the "mail bombings."

During the Kosovo conflict in 1999, NATO computers were blasted with e-mail bombs and hit with denial-of-service attacks by hacktivists protesting the NATO bombings. In addition, businesses, public organizations, and academic institutes received highly politicized virus-laden e-mails from a range of Eastern European countries, according to reports. Web defacements were also common. After the Chinese Embassy was accidentally bombed in Belgrade, Chinese hacktivists posted messages such as "We won=t stop attacking until the war stops!" on U.S. government Web sites.

Since December 1997, the Electronic Disturbance Theater (EDT), a New York City based activist group, has been conducting Web sit-ins against various sites in support of the Mexican Zapatistas. At a designated time, thousands of protestors point their browsers to a target site using software that floods the target with rapid and repeated download requests. EDT=s software has also been used by animal rights groups against organizations said to abuse animals. Electrohippies, another group of hacktivists, conducted Web sit-ins against the WTO when they met in Seattle in late 1999. These sit-ins all require mass participation to have much effect, and thus are more suited to use by activists than by relatively small groups of terrorists operating in secrecy.

While the above incidents were motivated by political and social reasons, whether they were sufficiently harmful or frightening to be classified as cyberterrorism is a judgement call. To the best of my knowledge, no attack so far has led to violence or injury to persons, although some may have intimidated their victims. Both EDT and the Electrohippies view their operations as acts of civil disobedience, analogous to street protests and physical sit-ins, not as acts of violence or terrorism. This is an important distinction. Most activists, whether participating in a street march or Web sit-in, are not terrorists.

However, there are a few indications that some terrorist groups are pursuing cyberterrorism, either alone or in conjunction with acts of physical violence. In February 1998, Clark Staten told the Senate Judiciary Committee Subcommittee on Technology, Terrorism, and Government Information that it was believed that "members of some Islamic extremist organizations have been attempting to develop a 'hacker network' to support their computer activities and even engage in offensive information warfare attacks in the future."

In November 1998, the *Detroit News* reported that Khalid Ibrahim, who claimed to be a member of the militant Indian separatist group Harkat-ul-Ansar, had tried to buy military software from hackers who had stolen it from Department of Defence computers they had penetrated. The attempted purchase was discovered when an 18-year-old hacker calling himself Chameleon attempted to cash a $1,000 check from Ibrahim. Chameleon said he did not have the software and did not give it to Ibrahim, but Ibrahim may have obtained it or other sensitive information from one of the many other hackers he approached. Harkat-ul-Ansar declared war on the United States following the August cruise-missile attack on a suspected terrorist training camp in Afghanistan run by bin Laden, which allegedly killed nine of their members.

The Provisional Irish Republican Army employed the services of contract hackers to penetrate computers in order to acquire home addresses of law enforcement and intelligence officers, but the data was used to draw up plans to kill the officers in a single "night of the long knives" if the British government did not meet terms for a new cease-fire. As this case illustrates, terrorists may use hacking as a way of acquiring intelligence in support of physical violence, even if they do not use it to wreak havoc in cyberspace.

Terrorists might also engage in computer network attacks as a way of financing physical operations. For example, they could penetrate an e-commerce Web site and steal credit card numbers, conduct fraudulent transactions against an Internet bank, or extort money from victims by threatening electronic sabotage.

Potential Threat

To understand the potential threat of cyberterrorism, two factors must be considered: first, whether there are targets that are vulnerable to attack that could lead to violence or severe harm, and second, whether there are actors with the capability and motivation to carry them out.

Looking first at vulnerabilities, several studies have shown that critical infrastructures are potentially vulnerable to cyberterrorist attack. Eligible Receiver, a Ano notice@ exercise conducted by the Department of Defence in 1997 with support from National Security Agency penetration testing teams, found the power grid and emergency 911 systems had weaknesses that could be exploited by an adversary using only publicly available tools on the Internet. Although neither of these systems were actually attacked, study members concluded that service on these systems could be disrupted. Also in 1997, the President=s Commission on Critical Infrastructure Protection issued its report warning that through mutual dependencies and interconnectedness, critical infrastructures could be vulnerable in new ways, and that vulnerabilities were steadily increasing, while the costs of attack were decreasing.

Although many of the weaknesses in computerized systems can be corrected, it is effectively impossible to eliminate all of them. Even if the technology itself offers good security, it is frequently configured or used in ways that make it open to attack. In addition, there is always the possibility of insiders, acting alone or in concert with other terrorists, misusing their access capabilities. According to Russia=s Interior Ministry Col. Konstantin Machabeli, the state-run gas monopoly, Gazprom, was hit by hackers in 1999 who collaborated with a Gazprom insider. The hackers were said to have used a Trojan horse to gain control of the central switchboard which controls gas flows in pipelines, although Gazprom, the world=s largest natural gas producer and the largest gas supplier to Western Europe, refuted the report.

Consultants and contractors are frequently in a position where they could cause grave harm. This past March, Japan=s Metropolitan Police Department reported that a software system they had procured to track 150 police vehicles, including unmarked cars, had been developed by the Aum Shinryko cult. At the time of the discovery, the cult had received classified tracking data on 115 vehicles. Further, the cult had developed software for at least 80 Japanese firms and 10 government agencies.

They had worked as subcontractors to other firms, making it almost impossible for the organizations to know who was developing the software. As subcontractors, the cult could have installed Trojan horses to launch or facilitate cyberterrorist attacks at a later date. Fearing a Trojan horse of their own, last February, the U.S. State Department sent an urgent cable to about 170 embassies asking them to remove software, which they belatedly realized had been written by citizens of the former Soviet Union. If we take as given that critical infrastructures are vulnerable to a cyberterrorist attack, then the question becomes whether there are actors with the capability and motivation to carry out such an operation. While many hackers have the knowledge, skills, and tools to attack computer systems, they generally lack the motivation to cause violence or severe economic or social harm. Conversely, terrorists who are motivated to cause violence seem to lack the capability or motivation to cause that degree of damage in cyberspace.

Future Prospects

In August 1999, the Centre for the Study of Terrorism and Irregular Warfare at the Naval Postgraduate School in Monterey, California, issued a report titled "Cyberterror: Prospects and Implications."

Their objective was to articulate the demand side of terrorism. Specifically, they assessed the prospects of terrorist organizations pursuing cyberterrorism. They concluded that the barrier to entry for anything beyond annoying hacks is quite high, and that terrorists generally lack the wherewithal and human capital needed to mount a meaningful operation. Cyberterrorism, they argued, was a thing of the future, although it might be pursued as an ancillary tool.

The Monterey team defined three levels of cyberterror capability. First is simple-unstructured: the capability to conduct basic hacks against individual systems using tools created by someone else. The organization possesses little target analysis, command and control, or learning capability.

Second is advanced-structured: the capability to conduct more sophisticated attacks against multiple systems or networks and possibly, to modify or create basic hacking tools. The organization possesses an elementary target analysis, command and control, and learning capability.

Third is complex-coordinated: the capability for a coordinated attacks capable of causing mass-disruption against integrated, heterogeneous defenses (including cryptography). The organization has the ability to create sophisticated hacking tools. They possess a highly capable target analysis, command and control, and organization learning capability.

The Monterey team estimated that it would take a group starting from scratch 2-4 years to reach the advanced-structured level and 6-10 years to reach the complex-coordinated level, although some groups might get there in just a few years or turn to outsourcing or sponsorship to extend their capability.

The study examined five terrorist group types: religious, New Age, ethno-nationalist separatist, revolutionary, and far-right extremists. They determined that only the religious groups are likely to seek the most damaging capability level, as it is consistent with their indiscriminate application of violence. New Age or single issue terrorists, such as the Animal Liberation Front, pose the most immediate threat, however, such groups are likely to accept disruption as a substitute for destruction. Both the revolutionary and ethno-nationalist separatists are likely to seek an advanced-structured capability.

The far-right extremists are likely to settle for a simple-unstructured capability, as cyberterror offers neither the intimacy nor cathartic effects that are central to the psychology of far-right terror. The study also determined that hacker groups are psychologically and organizationally ill-suited to cyberterrorism, and that it would be against their interests to cause mass disruption of the information infrastructure.

Thus, at this time, cyberterrorism does not seem to pose an imminent threat. This could change. For a terrorist, it would have some advantages over physical methods. It could be conducted remotely and anonymously, and it would not require the handling of explosives or a suicide mission. It would likely garner extensive media coverage, as journalists and the public alike are fascinated by practically any kind of computer attack. Indeed cyberterrorism could be immensely appealing precisely because of the tremendous attention given to it by the government and media. Cyberterrorism also has its drawbacks. Systems are complex, so it may be harder to control an attack and achieve a desired level of damage than using physical weapons. Unless people are injured, there is also less drama and emotional appeal. Further, terrorists may be disinclined to try new methods unless they see their old ones as inadequate, particularly when the new methods require considerable knowledge and skill to use effectively.

Terrorists generally stick with tired and true methods. Novelty and sophistication of attack may be much less important than assurance that a mission will be operationally successful. Indeed, the risk of operational failure could be a deterrent to terrorists. For now, the truck bomb poses a much greater threat than the logic bomb.

The next generation of terrorists will grow up in a digital world, with ever more powerful and easy-to-use hacking tools at their disposal. They might see greater potential for cyberterrorism than the terrorists of today, and their level of knowledge and skill relating to hacking will be greater.

Hackers and insiders might be recruited by terrorists or become self-recruiting cyberterrorists, the Timothy McVeigh=s of cyberspace. Some might be moved to action by cyber policy issues, making cyberspace an attractive venue for carrying out an attack.

Cyberterrorism could also become more attractive as the real and virtual worlds become more closely coupled, with a greater number of physical devices attached to the Internet. Some of these may be remotely controlled. Terrorists, for example, might target robots used in telesurgery. Unless these systems are carefully secured, conducting an operation that physically harms someone may be easy as penetrating a Web site is today.

Although the violent pursuit of political goals using exclusively electronic methods is likely to be at least a few years into the future, the more general threat of cybercrime is very much a part of the digital landscape today. In addition to cyberattacks against digital data and systems, many people are being terrorized on the Internet today with threats of physical violence. On-line stalking, death threats, and hate messages are abundant. These crimes are serious and must be addressed. In so doing, we will be in a better position to prevent and respond to cyberterrorism if and when the threat becomes more serious.

CYBERTERRORISM TODAY AND TOMORROW

It seems fair to say that the current threat posed by cyberterrorism has been exaggerated. No single instance of cyberterrorism has yet been recorded; U.S. defence and intelligence computer systems are air-gapped and thus isolated from the Internet; the systems run by private companies are more vulnerable to attack but also more resilient than is often supposed; the vast majority of cyberattacks are launched by hackers with few, if any, political goals and no desire to cause the mayhem and carnage of which terrorists dream. So, then, why has so much concern been expressed over a relatively minor threat?

The reasons are many. First, as Denning has observed, "cyberterrorism and cyberattacks are sexy right now.... [Cyberterrorism is] novel, original, it captures people's imagination." Second, the mass media frequently fail to distinguish between hacking and cyberterrorism and exaggerate the threat of the latter by reasoning from false analogies such as the following: "If a sixteen-year-old could do this, then what could a well-funded terrorist group do?" Ignorance is a third factor. Green argues that cyberterrorism merges two spheres—terrorism and technology—that many people, including most lawmakers and senior administration officials, do not fully understand and therefore tend to fear. Moreover, some groups are eager to exploit this ignorance. Numerous technology companies, still reeling from the collapse of the high-tech bubble, have sought to attract federal research grants by recasting themselves as innovators in computer security and thus vital contributors to national security. Law enforcement and security consultants are likewise highly motivated to have us believe that the threat to our nation's security is severe. A fourth reason is that some politicians, whether out of genuine conviction or out of a desire to stoke public anxiety about terrorism in order to advance their own agendas, have played the role of prophets of doom. And a fifth factor is ambiguity about the very meaning of "cyberterrorism," which has confused the public and given rise to countless myths.

Verton argues that "al Qaeda [has] shown itself to have an incessant appetite for modern technology" and provides numerous citations from bin Laden and other al Qaeda leaders to show their recognition of this new cyberweapon. In the wake of the 9/11 attacks, bin Laden reportedly gave a statement to an editor of an Arab newspaper claiming that "hundreds of Muslim scientists were with him who would use their knowledge... ranging from computers to electronics against the infidels." Sheikh Omar Bakri Muhammad, a supporter of bin Laden and often the conduit for his messages to the Western world, declared in an interview with Verton, "I would advise those who doubt al Qaeda's interest in cyber-weapons to take Osama bin Laden very seriously. The third letter from Osama bin Laden... was clearly addressing using the technology in order to destroy the economy of the capitalist states."

"While bin Laden may have his finger on the trigger, his grandchildren may have their fingers on the computer mouse," remarked Frank Cilluffo of the Office of Homeland Security in a statement that has been widely cited. Future terrorists may indeed see greater potential for cyberterrorism than do the terrorists of today. Furthermore, as Denning argues, the next generation of terrorists is now growing up in a digital world, one in which hacking tools are sure to become more powerful, simpler to use, and easier to access. Cyberterrorism may also become more attractive as the real and virtual worlds become more closely coupled. For instance, a terrorist group might simultaneously explode a bomb at a train station and launch a cyberattack on the communications infrastructure, thus magnifying the impact of the event. Unless these systems are carefully secured, conducting an online operation that physically harms someone may be as easy tomorrow as penetrating a website is today.

Paradoxically, success in the "war on terror" is likely to make terrorists turn increasingly to unconventional weapons such as cyberterrorism. The challenge before us is to assess what needs to be done to address this ambiguous but potential threat of cyberterrorism—but to do so without inflating its real significance and manipulating the fear it inspires. Denning and other terrorism experts conclude that, at least for now, hijacked vehicles, truck bombs, and biological weapons seem to pose a greater threat than does cyberterrorism. However, just as the events of 9/11 caught the world by surprise, so could a major cyberassault. The threat of cyberterrorism may be exaggerated and manipulated, but we can neither deny it nor dare to ignore it.

THE CONCEPT OF CYBER TERRORISM

Cyber crime and cyber terrorism are both crimes of the cyber world. The difference between the two however is with regard to the motive and the intention of the perpetrator.

While a cyber crime can be described simply as an unlawful act wherein the computer is either a tool or a target or both, cyber terrorism deserves a more detailed definition.

One can define cyber terrorism as a premeditated use of disruptive activities or the threat thereof, in cyber space, with the intention to further social, ideological, religious, political or similar objectives, or to intimidate any person in furtherance of such objectives.

Cyber Criminals

Any person who commits an illegal act with a guilty intention or commits a crime is called an offender or a criminal. In this context, any person who commits a Cyber Crime is known as a Cyber Criminal. The Cyber Criminals may be children and adolescents aged b/w 6-18 years, they may be organized hackers, may be professional hackers or crackers, discontented employees, cheaters or even psychic persons.

Kids & Teenagers (age group 9-16 etc.)

This is really difficult to believe but it is true. Most amateur hackers and cyber criminals are teenagers. To them, who have just begun to understand what appears to be a lot about computers, it is a matter of pride to have hacked into a computer system or a website. There is also that little issue of appearing really smart among friends. These young rebels may also commit cyber crimes without really knowing that they are doing anything wrong. According to the BBC, Teen hackers have gone from simply trying to make a name for them selves to actually working their way into a life of crime from the computer angle. According to Kevin Hogan, One of the biggest changes of 2004 was the waning influence of the boy hackers keen to make a name by writing a fast-spreading virus. Although teenage virus writers will still play around with malicious code, 2004 saw a significant rise in criminal use of malicious programs. The financial incentives were driving criminal use of technology.

Another reason for the increase in number of teenage offenders in cyber crimes are that many of the offenders who are mainly young college students are unaware of its seriousness. Recently the Chennai city police have arrested an engineering college student from Tamil Nadu for sending unsolicited message to a chartered accountant. The boy is now released on bail. So counseling session for college students has to be launched to educate them on the gravity and consequences emanating from such crimes.

In September, 2005, A Massachusetts teenager pleaded guilty in federal court in Boston for a string of hacking crimes reported to include the February compromise of online information broker Lexis Nexis and socialite Paris Hilton's T-Mobile cellular phone account. The US Court noted that the number of teenage hackers is on the rise and only the lowest 1 percent of hackers is caught.

In the above instance, the judge imposed a sentence of 11 months' detention in a juvenile facility. If he had been an adult, he would have faced charges of three counts of making bomb threats against a person or property, three counts of causing damage to a protected computer system, two counts of wire fraud, one count of aggravated identity theft and one count of obtaining information from a protected computer in furtherance of a criminal act. This is clearly a deviation from the traditional principles of criminal law.

Organized Hacktivists

Hacktivists are hackers with a particular (mostly political) motive. In other cases this reason can be social activism, religious activism, etc. The attacks on approximately 200 prominent Indian websites by a group of hackers known as Pakistani Cyber Warriors are a good example of political hacktivists at work.

Disgruntled Employees

One can hardly believe how spiteful displeased employees can become. Till now they had the option of going on strike against their bosses. Now, with the increase independence on computers and the automation of processes, it is easier for disgruntled employees to do more harm to their employers by committing computer related crimes, which can bring entire systems down.

Professional Hackers (Corporate espionage)

Extensive computerization has resulted in business organizations storing all their information in electronic form. Rival organizations employ hackers to steal industrial secrets and other information that could be beneficial to them. The temptation to use professional hackers for industrial espionage also stems from the fact that physical presence required to gain access to important documents is rendered needless if hacking can retrieve those.

FORMS OF CYBER TERRORISM

It is very difficult to exhaustively specify the forms of cyber terrorism. In fact, it would not be a fruitful exercise to do the same. The nature of cyber terrorism requires it to remain inclusive and open ended in nature, so that new variations and forms of it can be accommodated in the future. The following can be safely regarded as the forms of cyber terrorism applying the definition and the concepts discussed above:

Privacy Violation

The law of privacy is the recognition of the individual's right to be let alone and to have his personal space inviolate. The right to privacy as an independent and distinctive concept originated in the field of Tort law, under which a new cause of action for damages resulting from unlawful invasion of privacy was recognised. *In recent times, however, this right has acquired a constitutional status, the violation of which attracts both civil as well as criminal consequences under the respective laws.* The intensity and complexity of life have rendered necessary some retreat from the world.

Man under the refining influence of culture, has become sensitive to publicity, so that solitude and privacy have become essential to the individual. *Modern enterprise and invention have, through invasions upon his privacy, subjected him to mental pain and distress, far greater than could be inflicted by mere bodily injury.*

Right to privacy is a part of the right to life and personal liberty enshrined under Article 21 of the Constitution of India. With the advent of information technology the traditional concept of right to privacy has taken new dimensions, which require a different legal outlook. To meet this challenge recourse of Information Technology Act, 2000 can be taken.

The various provisions of the Act aptly protect the online privacy rights of the netizens. Certain acts have been categorised as offences and contraventions, which have tendency to intrude with the privacy rights of the netizens. These rights are available against private individuals as well as against cyber terrorists. Section 1 (2) read with Section 75 of the Act provides for an extra-territorial application of the provisions of the Act. Thus, if a person (including a foreign national) contravenes the privacy of an individual by means of computer, computer system or computer network located in India, he would be liable under the provisions of the Act. This makes it clear that the long arm jurisdiction is equally available against a cyber terrorist, whose act has resulted in the damage of the property, whether tangible or intangible.

Secret Information Appropriation and Data Theft

The information technology can be misused for appropriating the valuable Government secrets and data of private individuals and the Government and its agencies. A computer network owned by the Government may contain valuable information concerning defence and other top secrets, which the Government will not wish to share otherwise. The same can be targeted by the terrorists to facilitate their activities, including destruction of property. It must be noted that the definition of property is not restricted to moveables or immoveables alone. In R.K. Dalmia v Delhi Administration the Supreme Court held that the word "property" is used in the I.P.C in a much wider sense than the expression "movable property".

There is no good reason to restrict the meaning of the word "property" to moveable property only, when it is used without any qualification. Whether the offence defined in a particular section of IPC can be committed in respect of any particular kind of property, will depend not on the interpretation of the word "property" but on the fact whether that particular kind of property can be subject to the acts covered by that section. Thus, if any person without permission of the owner or any other person who is incharge of a computer, computer system or computer network -

(a) accesses or secures access to such computer, computer system or computer network.

(b) downloads, copies or extracts any data, computer data base or information from such computer, computer system or computer network including information or data held or stored in any removable storage medium;

(c) damages or causes to be damaged any computer, computer system or computer network, data, computer data base or any other programmes residing in such computer, computer system or computer network;

he shall be liable to pay damages by way of compensation not exceeding one crore rupees to the person so affected. The expression "Computer Database" means a representation of information, knowledge, facts, concepts or instructions in text, image, audio, video that are being prepared or have been prepared in a formalised manner or have been produced by a computer, computer system or computer network and are intended for use in a computer, computer system or computer network.

The expression "Damage" means to destroy, alter, delete, add, modify or re-arrange any computer resource by any means. These provisions make it clear that secret information appropriation and data theft by the cyber terrorists will be dealt with punitive sting and monetary impositions.

Demolition of e-governance Base

The aim of e-governance is to make the interaction of the citizens with the government offices hassle free and to share information in a free and transparent manner. It further makes the right to information a meaningful reality. In a democracy, people govern themselves and they cannot govern themselves properly unless they are aware of social, political, economic and other issues confronting them. To enable them to make a proper judgment on those issues, they must have the benefit of a range of opinions on those issues. Right to receive and impart information is implicit in free speech. This, right to receive information is, however, not absolute but is subject to reasonable restrictions which may be imposed by the Government in public interest. In P.U.C.L. V U.O.I the Supreme Court specified the grounds on which the government can withhold information relating to various matters, including trade secrets. The Supreme Court observed: " Every right- legal or moral- carries with it a corresponding objection. It is subject to several exemptions/ exceptions indicated in broad terms. Generally, the exemptions/ exceptions under those laws entitle the Govt to with hold information relating to the following matters:

(1) International relations;

(2) National security (including defiance) and public safety;

(3) Investigation, detection and prevention of crime;

(4) Internal deliberations of the Govt;

(5) Information received in confidence from a source outside the Govt;

(6) Information, which, if disclosed, would violate the privacy of the individual;

(7) Information of an economic nature (including Trade Secrets) which, if disclosed, would confer an unfair advantage on some person or concern, or, subject some person or Govt, to an unfair disadvantage;

(8) Information, which is subject to a claim of legal professional privilege, e.g. communication between a legal adviser and the client; between a physician and the patient;

(9) Information about scientific discoveries".

It must be noted that the primary aim of all cyber terrorist activities is to collapse a sound communication system, which includes an e-governance base.

Thus, by a combination of virus attacks and hacking techniques, the e-governance base of the government can be caused to be collapsed. This would be more deleterious and disastrous as compared to other tangible damages, which were caused by the traditional terrorist activities. Similarly, the terrorists to the common detriment of the nation at large can illegally obtain information legitimately protected from public scrutiny by the government in the interest of security of the nation. Thus, a strong e-governance base with the latest security methods and systems is the need of the hour.

Distributed denial of services Attack

The cyber terrorists may also use the method of distributed denial of services (DDOS) to overburden the Government and its agencies electronic bases. This is made possible by first infecting several unprotected computers by way of virus attacks and then taking control of them. Once control is obtained, they can be manipulated from any locality by the terrorists. These infected computers are then made to send information or demand in such a large number that the server of the victim collapses.

Further, due to this unnecessary Internet traffic the legitimate traffic is prohibited from reaching the Government or its agencies computers. This results in immense pecuniary and strategic loss to the government and its agencies.

It must be noted that thousands of compromised computers can be used to simultaneously attack a single host, thus making its electronic existence invisible to the genuine and legitimate netizens and end users. The law in this regard is crystal clear. If any person without permission of the owner or any other person who is incharge of a computer, computer system or computer network :

(a) introduces or causes to be introduced any computer contaminant or computer virus into any computer, computer system or computer network;

(b) disrupts or causes disruption of any computer, computer system or computer network;

(c) denies or causes the denial of access to any person authorised to access any computer, computer system or computer network by any means;

The shall be liable to pay damages by way of compensation not exceeding one crore rupees to the person so affected. The expression "Computer Contaminant" means any set of computer instructions that are designed -

(a) to modify, destroy, record, transmit data or programme residing within a computer, computer system or computer network; or

(b) by any means to usurp the normal operation of the computer, computer system, or computer network. Thus, distribute denial of services by the cyber terrorists will be tackled by invoking the provisions of sections 43,65 and 66 collectively.

Network damage and Disruptions

The main aim of cyber terrorist activities is to cause networks damage and their disruptions. This activity may divert the attention of the security agencies for the time being thus giving the terrorists extra time and makes their task comparatively easier. This process may involve a combination of computer tampering, virus attacks, hacking, etc. The law in this regard provides that if any person without permission of the owner or any other person who is incharge of a computer, computer system or computer network-

(a) accesses or secures access to such computer, computer system or computer network

(b) introduces or causes to be introduced any computer contaminant or computer virus into any computer, computer system or computer network;

(c) damages or causes to be damaged any computer, computer system or computer network, data, computer data base or any other programmes residing in such computer, computer system or computer network;

(d) disrupts or causes disruption of any computer, computer system or computer network;

(e) denies or causes the denial of access to any person authorised to access any computer, computer system or computer network by any means;

The shall be liable to pay damages by way of compensation not exceeding one crore rupees to the person so affected. The expression "Computer Virus" means any computer instruction, information, data or programme that destroys, damages, degrades or adversely affects the performance of a computer resource or attaches itself to another computer resource and operates when a programme, data or instruction is executed or some other event takes place in that computer resource. The person tampering with such computer source documents shall be punishable with imprisonment up to 3 years or with fine, which may extend up to Rs.2 lakhs, or with both. Further, if a person causes wrongful loss or damage to any person, by destroying, deleting or altering any information residing in his (owner's) compute resource or diminishes its value or utility or affects it injuriously by any means, he commits hacking and thus, violates the privacy of the owner. The person hacking shall be punishable with imprisonment up to 3 years or with fine, which may extend up to Rs.2 lakhs, or with both. However, an innocent infringer will not be liable if he proves that he committed the act without any intention or knowledge. A network service provider will be liable for various violations and contraventions mentioned under the Act if he makes available any third party information or data to a person for the commission of an offence or contravention. However, a network service provider will not be liable if he proves that the offence or contravention was committed without his knowledge or he had exercised all due diligence to prevent such commission. Thus, these provisions can be safely invoked for meeting challenges posed by network damage and disruptions caused by cyber terrorists.

The Roads Ahead

The menace of cyber terrorism can be effectively curbed, if not completely eliminated, if the three sovereign organs of the Constitution work collectively and in harmony with each other. Further, a vigilant citizenry can supplement the commitment of elimination of cyber terrorism.

Legislative commitment

The legislature can provide its assistance to the benign objective of elimination of cyber terrorism by enacting appropriate statutes dealing with cyber terrorism. It must be noted that to give effect to the provisions of Information Technology Act, 2000 appropriate amendments have been made in the I.P.C, 1860, the Indian Evidence Act, 1872, the Bankers' Books Evidence Act, 1891 and the Reserve Bank of India Act, 1934. On the same lines a new chapter dealing with "Cyber terrorism" can be added to the already existing criminal statues to make them compatible with modern forms of terrorisms. Similarly, a new chapter dealing with cyber terrorism can be incorporated in the Information Technology Act, 2000 by way of its amendment to bring harmonization among various laws. The repealment of POTA and its likely replacement with a new ordinance is an opportunity for the legislature to make the terrorist law effective to deal with cyber terrorism.

Executives concern

The Central Government and the State Governments can play their role effectively by making various rules and regulations dealing with cyber terrorism and its facets from time to time. The Central Government can, by notification in the Official Gazette and in the Electronic Gazette, makes rules to carry out the provisions of the Information Technology Act. Similarly, the State Government can, by notification in Official Gazette, makes rules to carry out the provisions of the Act. In exercise of the powers conferred by section 90 of the Information Technology Act, 2000 (Central Act 21 of 2000), the Government of Karnataka has made the Information Technology (Karnataka) Rules 2004. The Rules define "Cyber Café" as premises where the Cyber Café Owner/Network Service Provider provides the computer services including Internet access to the public. Rule 3 (1) provides that the owner of the Cyber Café shall take sufficient precautions so that computers and computer systems in the Cyber Café are not used for any illegal or criminal activity. Rule 3 (2) mandates that the Cyber Café Owner/ Network Service Provider shall not allow any User to use his Computer, Computer System and/or Computer Network without the identity of the User being established before him before use.

The Rule provides that the intending User may establish his Identity by producing any Photo Identity Card issued by any School or College or a Photo Credit Card of any Bank or Passport or Voters Identity Card or PAN Number Card issued by Income-Tax authorities or Photo Identity Card issued by the Employer or Driving License to the satisfaction of Cyber Café Owner. Rule 4(1) provides that after the identity of the User is established, the owner of the Cyber Café or the manager or the attendant or on his behalf any authorised person managing the Cyber Café shall obtain and maintain the following information in the Log Register for each user: (i) Name of the User, (ii) Age and Sex of the User, (iii) Present residential address of the User, (iv) Log in time, and (v) Log out time. Rule 4 (2) provides that if a User cannot produce any Photo Identity

Card to establish his identity to the satisfaction of the Cyber Café Owner/Network Service Provider, he may be photographed by the Cyber Café Owner/Network Service Provider after obtaining his consent using a 'Web Camera' hooked onto one of the computers or computer systems in the Cyber Café and the User shall be explained that his photograph will be taken and stored in the hard disk of the computer, for verification by Law enforcement authorities, whenever required.

This is in addition to the entries made in the log register. The Rule further provides that in case the User does not agree for storing his photograph he shall not be allowed to use any computer, computer system and /or computer network or access to the Internet in the Cyber Café. Rule 4(3) provides that all time clocks in Cyber Cafes must be regularly checked and synchronized with Indian Standard Time (IST). Rule 4(4) provides that maintaining proper account of the User as explained shall be the responsibility of the Cyber Café Owner/ Network Service provider.

Rule 5(5) provides that the Log Register and the Photograph of the User shall be maintained by the Cyber Café Owner/ Network Service Provider for a minimum period of ONE YEAR and the same shall be provided to Law enforcement agencies as and when required. Rule 4(6) provides that the Cyber Police authorities may on complaint inspect Cyber Cafes at all reasonable time to ensure compliance of these rules.

If any Cyber Café Owner/Network Service Provider fails to maintain Log Register and records he shall be liable for penalties as provided in the Act or any other Law, for the time being in force. These provisions are sufficient to take care of illegal use of cyber café for terrorist activities. Further, the government can also block web sites propagating cyber terrorism.

It must be noted that the Indian Computer Emergency Response Team (CERT-In) has been designated as the single authority for issuing of instructions in the context of blocking of web sites. CERT-In has to instruct the Department of Telecommunications to block the web sites after verifying the authenticity of the complaint and satisfying that action of blocking of website is absolutely essential. There is no explicit provision in the IT Act, 2000 for blocking of websites.

In fact, blocking is considered to be censorship; hence it can be challenged if it restricts the freedom of speech and expression. But websites promoting hate, contempt, slander or defamation of others, promoting gambling, promoting racism, *violence and terrorism*, pornography and violent sex can reasonably be blocked since all such websites cannot claim the Fundamental Right of free speech and expression.

The blocking of such website may be equated to "balanced flow of information" and not censorship. If the blocking of a website is arbitrary, unreasonable and unfair and is based on extraneous and irrelevant materials and reasons, then it would be vulnerable to the attack of unconstitutionality, being in violation of Articles 14, 19 and 21 of the Constitution of India.

Judicial response

The judiciary can play its role by adopting a stringent approach towards the menace of cyber terrorism. It must, however, first tackle the jurisdiction problem because before invoking its judicial powers the courts are required to satisfy themselves that they possess the requisite jurisdiction to deal with the situation. Since the Internet "is a cooperative venture not owned by a single entity or government, there are no centralized rules or laws governing its use. The absence of geographical boundaries may give rise to a situation where the act legal in one country where it is done may violate the laws of another country. This process further made complicated due to the absence of a uniform and harmonised law governing the jurisdictional aspects of disputes arising by the use of Internet. It must be noted that, generally, the scholars point towards the following "theories" under which a country may claim prescriptive jurisdiction:

(a) a country may claim jurisdiction based on "objective territoriality" when an activity takes place within the country,

(b) a "subjective territoriality" may attach when an activity takes place outside a nation's borders but the "primary effect" of the action is within the nation's borders,

(c) a country may assert jurisdiction based on the nationality of either the actor or the victim,

(d) in exceptional circumstances, providing the right to protect the nation's sovereignty when faced with threats recognised as particularly serious in the international community.

In addition to establishing a connecting nexus, traditional international doctrine also calls for a "reasonable" connection between the offender and the forum.

Depending on the factual context, courts look to such factors, as whether the activity of individual has a "substantial and foreseeable effect" on the territory, whether a "genuine link" exists between the actor and the forum, the character of the activity and the importance of the regulation giving rise to the controversy, the extent to which exceptions are harmed by the regulation, and the importance of the regulation in the international community. The traditional jurisdictional paradigms may provide a framework to guide analysis for cases arising in cyberspace. It must be noted that by virtue of section 1(2) read with section 75 of the Information Technology Act, 2000 the courts in India have "long arm jurisdiction" to deal with cyber terrorism.

Vigilant citizenry

The menace of cyber terrorism is not the sole responsibility of State and its instrumentalities. The citizens as well as the netizens are equally under a solemn obligation to fight against the cyber terrorism. In fact, they are the most important and effective cyber terrorism eradication and elimination mechanism. The only requirement is to encourage them to come forward for the support of fighting against cyber terrorism. The government can give suitable incentives to them in the form of monetary awards. It must, however, be noted that their anonymity and security must be ensured before seeking their help. The courts are also empowered to maintain their anonymity if they provide any information and evidence to fight against cyber terrorism.

TYPES OF CYBERTERROR CAPABILITY

The following three levels of cyberterror capability is defined by Monterey group

- Simple-Unstructured: The capability to conduct basic hacks against individual systems using tools created by someone else. The organization possesses little target analysis, command and control, or learning capability.
- Advanced-Structured: The capability to conduct more sophisticated attacks against multiple systems or networks and possibly, to modify or create basic hacking tools. The organization possesses an elementary target analysis, command and control, and learning capability.
- Complex-Coordinated: The capability for a coordinated attack capable of causing mass-disruption against integrated, heterogeneous defenses (including cryptography). Ability to create sophisticated hacking tools. Highly capable target analysis, command and control, and organization learning capability.

Concerns

As the Internet becomes more pervasive in all areas of human endeavor, individuals or groups can use the anonymity afforded by cyberspace to threaten citizens, specific groups (i.e. with membership based on ethnicity or belief), communities and entire countries, without the inherent threat of capture, injury, or death to the attacker that being physically present would bring. Many groups such as Anonymous, use tools such as Denial-of-service attack to attack and censor groups who oppose them, creating many concerns for freedom and respect for differences of thought.

Many believe that cyberterrorism is an extreme threat to our economy, and fear an attack could potentially lead to another Great Depression. Several leaders agree that cyberterrorism has the highest percentage of threat over other possible attacks on U.S. territory. Although natural disasters are considered a top threat and have proven to be devastating to people and land, there is ultimately little that can be done to prevent such events from happening. Thus, the expectation is to focus more on preventative measures that will make Internet attacks impossible for execution.

As the Internet continues to expand, and computer systems continue to be assigned increased responsibility while becoming more complex and interdependent, sabotage or terrorism via the Internet may become a more serious threat and is possibly one of the top 10 events to "end the human race."

Dependence on the internet is rapidly increasing on a worldwide scale, creating a platform for international cyber terror plots to be formulated and executed as a direct threat to national security. For terrorists, cyber-based attacks have distinct advantages over physical attacks. They can be conducted remotely, anonymously, and relatively cheaply, and they do not require significant investment in weapons, explosive and personnel. The effects can be widespread and profound. Incidents of cyberterrorism are likely to increase. They will be conducted through denial of service attacks, malware, and other methods that are difficult to envision today.

In an article about cyber attacks by Iran and North Korea, the New York Times observes, "The appeal of digital weapons is similar to that of nuclear capability: it is a way for an outgunned, outfinanced nation to even the playing field. 'These countries are pursuing cyberweapons the same way they are pursuing nuclear weapons,' said James A. Lewis, a computer security expert at the Center for Strategic and International Studies in Washington. 'It's primitive; it's not top of the line, but it's good enough and they are committed to getting it.'"

History

Public interest in cyberterrorism began in the late 1980s. As 2000 approached, the fear and uncertainty about the millennium bug heightened, as did the potential for attacks by cyber terrorists. Although the millennium bug was by no means a terrorist attack or plot against the world or the United States, it did act as a catalyst in sparking the fears of a possibly large-scale devastating cyber-attack. Commentators noted that many of the facts of such incidents seemed to change, often with exaggerated media reports.

The high profile terrorist attacks in the United States on September 11, 2001 and the ensuing War on Terror by the US led to further media coverage of the potential threats of cyberterrorism in the years following. Mainstream media coverage often discusses the possibility of a large attack making use of computer networks to sabotage critical infrastructures with the aim of putting human lives in jeopardy or causing disruption on a national scale either directly or by disruption of the national economy.

Authors such as Winn Schwartau and John Arquilla are reported to have had considerable financial success selling books which described what were purported to be plausible scenarios of mayhem caused by cyberterrorism. Many critics claim that these books were unrealistic in their assessments of whether the attacks described (such as nuclear meltdowns and chemical plant explosions) were possible. A common thread throughout what critics perceive as cyberterror-hype is that of non-falsifiability; that is, when the predicted disasters fail to occur, it only goes to show how lucky we've been so far, rather than impugning the theory.

U.S. military

The US Department of Defense (DoD) charged the United States Strategic Command with the duty of combating cyberterrorism. This is accomplished through the Joint Task Force-Global Network Operations, which is the operational component supporting USSTRATCOM in defense of the DoD's Global Information Grid. This is done by integratingGNO capabilities into the operations of all DoD computers, networks, and systems used by DoD combatant commands, services and agencies.

On November 2, 2006, the Secretary of the Air Force announced the creation of the Air Force's newest MAJCOM, the Air Force Cyber Command, which would be tasked to monitor and defend American interest in cyberspace. The plan was however replaced by the creation of Twenty-Fourth Air Force which became active in August 2009 and would be a component of the planned United States Cyber Command.

On December 22, 2009, the White House named its head of Computer security as Howard Schmidt to coordinate U.S Government, military and intelligence efforts to repel hackers. He left the position in May, 2012. Michael Daniel was appointed to the position of White House Coordinator of Cyber Security the same week and continues in the position during the second term of the Obama administration.

Estonia and NATO

The Baltic state of Estonia was target to a massive denial-of-service attack that ultimately rendered the country offline and shut out from services dependent on Internet connectivity for three weeks in the spring of 2007. The infrastructure of Estonia including everything from online banking and mobile phone networks to government services and access to health care information was disabled for a time. The tech-dependent state was in severe problem and there was a great deal of concern over the nature and intent of the attack.

The cyber attack corresponded to an Estonian-Russian dispute over the removal of a bronze statue depicting a World War II-era Soviet soldier from the center of the capital, Tallinn. In the midst of the armed conflict with Russia, Georgia likewise was subject to sustanined and coordinated attacks on its electronic infrastructure in August 2008. In both of these cases, circumstantial evidence point to coordinated Russian attacks, but attribution of the attacks is difficult; though both the countries point the finger at Moscow, proof establishing legal culpability is lacking.

Estonia joined NATO in 2004, therefore NATO carefully monitored its member state's response to the attack and worried both about escalation and the possibility of cascading effects beyond Estonia's border to other NATO members. In 2008, directly as a result of the attacks, NATO opened a new center of excellence on cyberdefense to conduct research and training on cyber warfare in Tallinn.

China

The Chinese Defense Ministry confirmed the existence of an online defense unit in May 2011. Composed of about thirty elite internet specialists, the so-called "Cyber Blue Team," or "Blue Army," is officially claimed to be engaged in cyber-defense operations, though there are fears the unit has been used to penetrate secure online systems of foreign governments.

Israel

May 2011 Israeli Prime Minister Benjamin Netanyahu announced the establishment of the National Internet Defense Taskforce, charged with developing tools to secure vital Israeli online infrastructure. "The main responsibility of the taskforce will be to expand the state's ability to defend vital infrastructure networks against cybernetic terrorist attacks perpetrated by foreign countries and terrorist elements."

Examples

An operation can be done by anyone anywhere in the world, for it can be performed thousands of miles away from a target. An attack can cause serious damage to a critical infrastructure which may result in casualties. Attacking an infrastructure can be power grids, monetary systems, dams, media, and personal information.

Some attacks are conducted in furtherance of political and social objectives, as the following examples illustrate:

- In 1996, a computer hacker allegedly associated with the White Supremacist movement temporarily disabled a Massachusetts ISP and damaged part of the ISP's record keeping system. The ISP had attempted to stop the hacker from sending out worldwide racist messages under the ISP's name. The hacker signed off with the threat, "you have yet to see true electronic terrorism. This is a promise."

- In 1998, Spanish protesters bombarded the Institute for Global Communications (IGC) with thousands of bogus e-mail messages. E-mail was tied up and undeliverable to the ISP's users, and support lines were tied up with people who couldn't get their mail. The protestors also spammed IGC staff and member accounts, clogged their Web page with bogus credit card orders, and threatened to employ the same tactics against organizations using IGC services. They demanded that IGC stop hosting the Web site for the Euskal Herria Journal, a New York-based publication supporting Basque independence. Protestors said IGC supported terrorism because a section on the Web pages contained materials on the terrorist group ETA, which claimed responsibility for assassinations of Spanish political and security officials, and attacks on military installations. IGC finally relented and pulled the site because of the "mail bombings."
- In 1998, ethnic Tamil guerrillas attempted to disrupt Sri Lankan embassies by sending large volumes of e-mail. The embassies received 800 e-mails a day over a two-week period. The messages read "We are the Internet Black Tigers and we're doing this to disrupt your communications." Intelligence authorities characterized it as the first known attack by terrorists against a country's computer systems.
- During the Kosovo conflict in 1999, NATO computers were blasted with e-mail bombs and hit with denial-of-service attacks by hacktivists protesting the NATO bombings. In addition, businesses, public organizations, and academic institutes received highly politicized virus-laden e-mails from a range of Eastern European countries, according to reports. Web defacements were also common. After the Chinese Embassy was accidentally bombed in Belgrade, Chinese hacktivists

posted messages such as "We won't stop attacking until the war stops!" on U.S. government Web sites.

- Since December 1997, the Electronic Disturbance Theater (EDT) has been conducting Web sit-ins against various sites in support of the Mexican Zapatistas. At a designated time, thousands of protestors point their browsers to a target site using software that floods the target with rapid and repeated download requests. EDT's software has also been used by animal rights groups against organizations said to abuse animals. Electrohippies, another group of hacktivists, conducted Web sit-ins against the WTO when they met in Seattle in late 1999. These sit-ins all require mass participation to have much effect, and thus are more suited to use by activists than by terrorists.
- In 2000, a Japanese Investigation revealed that the government was using software developed by computer companies affiliated with Aum Shirinkyo, the doomsday sect responsible for the sarin gas attack on the Tokyo subway system in 1995. "The government found 100 types of software programs used by at least 10 Japanese government agencies, including the Defense Ministry, and more than 80 major Japanese companies, including Nippon Telegraph and Telephone." Following the discovery, the Japanese government suspended use of Aum-developed programs out of concern that Aum-related companies may have compromised security by breaching firewalls. gaining access to sensitive systems or information, allowing invasion by outsiders, planting viruses that could be set off later, or planting malicious code that could cripple computer systems and key data system.
- In March 2013, the New York Times reported on a pattern of cyber attacks against U.S. financial institutions believed to be instigated by Iran as well as incidents affecting South Korean financial institutions that originate with the North Korean government.

- In August 2013, media companies including the New York Times, Twitter and the Huffington Post lost control of some of their websites Tuesday after hackers supporting the Syrian government breached the Australian Internet company that manages many major site addresses. The Syrian Electronic Army, a hacker group that has previously attacked media organisations that it considers hostile to the regime of Syrian president Bashar al-Assad, claimed credit for the Twitter and Huffington Post hacks in a series of Twitter messages. Electronic records showed that NYTimes.com, the only site with an hours-long outage, redirected visitors to a server controlled by the Syrian group before it went dark.

Sabotage

Non-political acts of sabotage have caused financial and other damage, as in a case where a disgruntled employee, Vitek Boden (aka Peter Markan) caused the release of 800,000 litres of untreated sewage into waterways in Maroochy Shire, Australia.

More recently, in May 2007 Estonia was subjected to a mass cyber-attack in the wake of the removal of a Russian World War II war memorial from downtown Tallinn. The attack was a distributed denial-of-service attack in which selected sites were bombarded with traffic to force them offline; nearly all Estonian government ministry networks as well as two major Estonian bank networks were knocked offline; in addition, the political party website of Estonia's current Prime Minister Andrus Ansip featured a counterfeit letter of apology from Ansip for removing the memorial statue.

Despite speculation that the attack had been coordinated by the Russian government, Estonia's defense minister admitted he had no conclusive evidence linking cyber attacks to Russian authorities. Russia called accusations of its involvement "unfounded," and neither NATO nor European Commission experts were able to find any conclusive proof of official Russian government participation. In January 2008 a man from Estonia was convicted for launching the attacks against the Estonian Reform Party website and fined.

During the Russia-Georgia War, on 5 August 2008, three days before Georgia launched its invasion of South Ossetia, the websites for OSInform News Agency and OSRadiowere hacked. The OSinform website at osinform.ru kept its header and logo, but its content was replaced by a feed to the Alania TV website content.

Alania TV, a Georgian government supported television station aimed at audiences in South Ossetia, denied any involvement in the hacking of the websites. Dmitry Medoyev, at the time the South Ossetian envoy to Moscow, claimed that Georgia was attempting to cover up information on events which occurred in the lead up to the war.

One such cyber attack caused the Parliament of Georgia and Georgian Ministry of Foreign Affairs websites to be replaced by images comparing Georgian president Mikheil Saakashvili to Adolf Hitler. Other attacks involved denials of service to numerous Georgian and Azerbaijani websites, such as when Russian hackers allegedly disabled the servers of the Azerbaijani Day.Az news agency.

Website defacement and denial of service

Even more recently, in October 2007, the website of Ukrainian president Viktor Yushchenko was attacked by hackers. A radical Russian nationalist youth group, the Eurasian Youth Movement, claimed responsibility. In 1999 hackers attacked NATO computers. The computers flooded them with email and hit them with a denial of service (DoS). The hackers were protesting against the NATO bombings of the Chinese embassy in Belgrade. Businesses, public organizations and academic institutions were bombarded with highly politicized emails containing viruses from other European countries.

In fiction

- The Japanese cyberpunk manga, *Ghost in the Shell* (as well as its popular movie and TV adaptations) centers around an anti-cyberterrorism and cybercrime unit. In its mid-21st century Japan setting such attacks are made all the more threatening by an even more widespread use of technology including cybernetic enhancements to the human body allowing people themselves to be direct targets of cyberterrorist attacks.

- Dan Brown's *Digital Fortress*.
- Amy Eastlake's *Private Lies*.
- In the movie *Live Free or Die Hard*, John McClane (Bruce Willis) takes on a group of cyberterrorists intent on shutting down the entire computer network of the United States.
- The movie *Eagle Eye* involves a super computer controlling everything electrical and networked to accomplish the goal.
- The plots of *24* Day 4 and Day 7 include plans to breach the nation's nuclear plant grid and then to seize control of the entire critical infrastructure protocol.
- The Tom Clancy created series Netforce was about a FBI/Military team dedicated to combating cyberterrorists.
- Much of the plot of *Mega Man Battle Network* is centered around cyberterrorism.
- In the 2009 Japanese animated film *Summer Wars*, an artificial intelligence cyber-terrorist attempts to take control over the world's missiles in order to "win" against the main characters that attempted to keep it from manipulating the world's electronic devices.
- In the 2012 film Skyfall, part of the James Bond franchise, main villain Raoul Silva (Javier Bardem) is an expert cyberterrorist who is responsible for various cyberterrorist incidents in the past.
- Cyberterrorism plays a role in the 2012 video game Call of Duty: Black Ops II, first when main antagonist Raul Menendez cripples the Chinese economy with a cyberattack and frames the United States for it, starting a new Cold War between the two powers. Later, another

cyberattack with a computer worm leads to Menendez seizing control of the entire U.S drone fleet. Finally, one of the game's endings leads to another attack similar to the latter, this time crippling the U.S' electrical and water distribution grids. An alternate ending depicts the cyberattack failing after it is stopped by one of the game's characters pivotal to the storyline.

- The plot of the 2013 video game Watch Dogs is heavily influenced by cyber-terrorism. In which players take control of the game's protagonist, Aiden Pierce, an accused murder suspect, who hacks into a ctOS (Central Operating System), giving him complete control of Chicago's mainframe in order to hunt down his accusers.
- The video game *Metal Slug 4* focuses on Marco and Fio, joined by newcomers Nadia and Trevor, to battle a terrorist organization known as Amadeus that is threatening the world with a computer virus.
- The visual novel *Baldr Force* has the main character Tooru Souma joining a military organization to fight cyberterrorism to avenge the death of his friend.
- The Japanese Manga and Live Action *Bloody Monday* is Highly influenced with Hacking and Cracking, the main character Takagi Fujimaru is a Super Elite hacker which use his hacking knowledge to fight against his enemies.

STATISTICS ON CYBER-TERRORISM

Who is at risk of an attack?

Most feel that military installations, power plants, air traffic control centers, banks and telecommunication networks themselves are the most likely targets. Other targets include police, medical, fire and rescue systems, which could be hurt, along with Wall Street, water systems, etc.

Who are the terrorists?

Cyber terrorism does not have to come from the average

hacker or even online terrorists. The Govt. carried out a series of its own attacks on itself, in order to test its own defenses against online-based attacks. The Defence Information Security Agency (DISA) found that 88% of the 3000 defence computer systems that were attacked were "easily penetrable". Of the systems that were illegally entered, 96% of the entries were not detected. Of the 4% that were detected, only 5% of them were reported or investigated.

How common is unauthorized system entry?

A survey conducted by the Science Applications International Corp. in 1996 found that 40 major corporations reported losing over $800 million to computer break-ins. An FBI survey of 428 government, corporate and university sites found that over 40% reported having been broken into at least once in the last year. One third said that they had been broken into over the Internet. Another survey found that the Pentagon's systems that contain sensitive, but unclassified information, had been accessed via networks illegally 250,000 times and only 150 of the intrusions were detected. The FBI estimates that U.S. businesses loose $138 million every year to hackers. According to the CIA in the past three years government systems have been illegally entered 250,000.

Costs of cyber-terrorism

According to a source in Great Britain, terrorists have gained at least up to 400 million pounds from 1993 to 1995 by threatening institutions. Over the three years, there were 40 reported threats made to banks in the U.S. and Britain. In January of 1993, three separate incidents took place in London. During the sixth, a brokerage house paid out 10 million pounds after receiving a threat and one of their machines crashed. On the fourteenth incident, a blue-chip bank paid blackmailers 12.5 million pounds after receiving threats. Another brokerage house paid out 10 million pounds on the twenty-ninth incident. Some terrorists just take money, rather than resorting to blackmail. A Russian hacker, for example, tapped into Citibank's funds transfer system and took $10 million.

HACKING AND TERROR

Much of the early work on the 'cyber threat' depicted hackers, terrorists, foreign spies and criminal gangs who, by typing a few commands into a computer, can take over or disrupt the critical infrastructure of entire nations. This frightening scenario is not supported by any evidence. Terrorist groups like Al Qaeda do make significant use of the Internet, but as a tool for intra-group communications, fund-raising and public relations. Cyber terrorist could also take advantage of the Internet to steal credit card numbers or valuable data to provide financial support for their operations. Cyber-terrorism has attracted considerable attention, but to date, it has meant little more than propaganda, intelligence collection or the digital equivalent of graffiti, with groups defacing each other's websites. No critical infrastructures have been shut down by cyber attacks.

Terrorists seek to make a political statement and to inflict psychological and physical damage on their targets. If terrorism is an act of violence to achieve political objects, how useful will terrorists find an economic weapon whose effects are gradual and cumulative? One of Al Qaeda's training manuals, "Military Studies in the Jihad Against the Tyrants" notes that explosives are the preferred weapon of terrorist because "explosives strike the enemy with sheer terror and fright." Explosions are dramatic, strike fear into the hearts of opponents and do lasting damage. Cyber attacks would not have the same dramatic and political effect that terrorists seek. A cyber attack, which might not even be noticed by its victims, or attributed to routine delays or outages, will not be their preferred weapon. If terrorism is an act of violence to create shock and achieve political objects, how useful will terrorists find an economic tool whose effects are at best gradual and cumulative?

An analysis of the risk of cyber terrorism is also complicated by the tendency to initially attribute cyber events to military or terrorist efforts when their actual source is civilian recreational hackers. When DOD computer networks were penetrated in an attack that occurred in the late 1990s, the U.S. was quick to suspect potential opponents, particularly

Iraq or China, as the culprit. U.S. officials debated the merits of an active defence and whether this was an act of war, justifying a counter-attack. As tension mounted, the U.S. discovered that far from being a hostile power, the source of the attack was two high school students in southern California. It is difficult, especially in the early stages of an incident, to determine if the attacker is a, terrorist, group, foreign state, criminals, or a teenager in California. However, a quick survey of incidents over the last four years suggests that criminals and bored teenagers are the most likely sources of attack. To this day, the vast majority of hacking incidents result from the actions of recreational hackers.

While the press has reported that government officials are concerned over Al Qaeda plans to use the Internet to wage cyber-terrorism, these stories often recycle the same hypothetical scenarios previously attributed to foreign governments' cyber-warfare efforts. The risk remains hypothetical but the antagonist has changed from hostile states to groups like Al Qaeda. The only new element attributed to Al Qaeda is that the group might use cyber attacks to disrupt emergency services in order to reinforce and multiply the effect of a physical attack. If cyber-attacks were feasible, the greatest risk they might pose to national security is as corollaries to more traditional modes of attacks.

Espionage opportunities created by a greater reliance on internet-accessible computer networks will create greater risk for national security than cyber attacks. Terrorist groups are likely to use the Internet to collect information on potential targets, and intelligence services can not only benefit from information openly available on the web but, more importantly, can benefit from the ability to clandestinely penetrate computer networks and collect information that is not publicly available. This is very different from hacking, in that in the event of a successful penetration of a hostile network, a terrorist group or an intelligence service will want to be as unobtrusive as possible. A sophisticated opponent might hack into a system and sit there, collecting intelligence and working to remain unnoticed. It will not disrupt essential services or leave embarrassing messages on websites, but remain quietly in the background collecting information. Collection techniques for the Internet differ significantly from earlier signals and communications intercept techniques, and while different kinds of data will be collected, the overall effect may be to make some espionage activities much more rewarding. This topic, the implications for espionage of the greater use of computer networks and Internet protocols, deserves further study.

ACCESSING SYSTEMS

The first type of attacks is aimed at enabling access to protected data and computer systems. This can be achieved if the victim computer is vulnerable to a security weakness that can be exploited by the attacker. Software and techniques for this purpose can be acquired through different channels: many specialized security forums discuss the known weaknesses of different operating systems and other software. If the designated victim computer is not immune against all current (and known) software flaws (socalled "patching"), this information can be used to gain access to it. However, even if all known patches have been applied to a computer system, this does not mean that the system is protected against all possible attacks. So-called "Zero-Day-Exploits", i.e. software flaws that have not yet been disclosed to the manufacturer (and therefore not yet been patched), can be acquired via the black market. Such software enables access to a system even though the system administrators have followed all publicly known security measures.

Once an attacker has gained access to a computer system, several possibilities lie ahead. First, the system can simply be shut down, thereby making it unavailable to legitimate users. However, the system can be restarted by administrators immediately, giving the attackers only a very short moment of success. Nevertheless, even a very short interruption can be hazardous for some systems, such as control systems for power plants or in medical environments. Furthermore, an outage can be combined with a conventional attack, e.g. to handicap rescue workers after a bomb attack.

Furthermore, the information on a system can be altered, thereby giving it a new meaning, e.g. to mislead people relying on that information, or destroyed. Finally, some attacks can be conducted without anybody noticing, making countermeasures extremely difficult.

Large-Scale Attacks

If the information inside a computer is not of essence, but the aim is simply to make its services unavailable, the use of large-scale attacks might be preferred over a hacking attack. Large-scale attacks are often committed with the help of hundreds or thousands of other computers (so-called Distributed-Denial-of-Service-Attacks or DDoS-Attacks). In these cases, viruses and Trojan horses are used to control other computers.

These computers are turned into so-called "zombies" that are forced to report to a botnet on a regular basis. These zombies are, in turn, controlled by a bot-master that instructs them, for instance, to forward thousands of requests to a particular site in order to make it inaccessible to its users. In 2006, more than 60,000 active bot-infected computers were observed per day. Furthermore, over 6 million distinct bot-infected computers were detected in 6 months. These "zombies" were controlled by less than 5,000 command-and-control-servers. It can therefore be safely assumed that the persons in control of these bot-nets are not hobby hackers, but well experienced and organized groups.

For terrorist groups, however, it is not necessary to acquire these skills or to organize bot-nets by themselves as bot-nets can also be rented. Prices for attacks range from about 150 to 400 US-dollars, depending on the target and the duration of the attack. Some bot-net-operators even offer discounts for multiple orders. Also – as a nontechnical alternative – the same effect as that achieved with a bot-net attack can be obtained if enough human supporters are available who can take over the part of will-less "zombies" in bot-net attacks. This can be observed in an online demonstration that was launched against the German airline "Lufthansa" in 2001. In order to call attention to the involvement of the company in the deportation of illegal alien residents, supporters were asked to open the web page of the company at the same date and time. Over 13,000 people followed the call. The Lufthansa server was unable to reply to the sudden peak of requests so that the web page became unavailable to customers during this time frame. This technique is also known as "swarming", "virtual blockade", or "virtual sit-in" and it shows that even technically non-adept organizations can use the power of distributed attacks against targets in the Internet.

However, for a terrorist organization, the operation of a bot-net could also be an interesting option, since it can be used in a variety of ways. Two main options seem to be realistic: the use of bot-nets for email campaigns and for aggressive attacks on other Internet sites. In the first option, the "zombie" computers can be used to send out massmailings with terrorist content (e.g. propaganda). These mails are difficult to trace back since they do not originate from the computer of the terrorist organization, but from thousands of computers linked to the bot-net. Furthermore, this service can also be rented out to other companies wishing to cover their tracks in order to forward spamemails and willing to pay for this service. Therefore, by using this first option, the botnet can also be used as a source of income for the organization. When using a bot-net for the second option, i.e. utilization for attacks on other targets in the Internet, a terrorist organization can benefit from the large diversification of attackers in a bot-net. Such aggressions can hardly be traced back and, in addition, the defence against such attacks is often not possible.

Manifold examples of the use of bot-nets to bring down other services in the Internet can be found. Among them are actions that can be classified as terrorist or part of a cyber war. For example, six different Hizbollah sites, the Hamas site, and other Palestinian information sites were brought down by a so-called "FloodNet" attack of pro- Israeli hackers. The service virtually "flooded" the respective servers with pings resulting in the unavailability of the servers for all other requests. Even after a relaunch with a slightly different spelling, the sites were still unreachable as the hackers immediately adjusted the attack to the new name. The targets of such attacks can be chosen freely, i.e. any system that is reachable over the Internet can be the victim of a (distributed or simple) denial-of-service-attack. Therefore, the internal and external communication systems of NATO troops were the victim of an attack during the allied air strikes on Kosovo and Serbia as well as the thirteen root servers for the Internet domain name systems (DNS).

Hybrid Attacks

Many of the attacks described above can result in violence against persons or property and they can generate fear within a population. However, this depends largely on the chosen target and the actual effect that the attack was able to accomplish. Therefore, some authors claim that a conventional bomb attack is – in many ways – easier to plan and conduct and that the results can be better foreseen. However, even in cases of conventional bomb attacks, the losses can be increased if hybrid attacks are launched, i.e. an attack that is aimed at a physical target is combined with one or both of the abovementioned electronic forms of attack.

The bomb attack can be aimed at any given target. For example, it is often chosen to bring forth a high number of casualties. In this case, a supplementary digital attack could be launched that is aimed at the communication devices of police or ambulances in order to hinder an effective coordination of rescue teams,. Another possibility would be for attackers to choose to launch an assault on the economic stability of a country.

In this case, a hybrid attack against national financial networks (such as Fedwire or Fednet) or against transfer networks (such as SWIFT) could be launched. It is estimated that such an attack could wreak havoc on the entire global economy. Another possibility would be to directly attack the infrastructure that forms the basis of the Internet. To achieve this, offenders could assault any system whose operation is of the essence for the functioning of the Internet. One example would be the domain name service (DNS). The DNS is responsible for the translation of domain names (such as www.mpicc.de) into IP-numbers (such as 194.94.219.193). This task is necessary for many transactions, e.g. the opening of a web page or the sending of an email. If an attacker was able to disturb this service, large parts of Internet-based services would be inaccessible. Therefore, a DDoS attack on the thirteen root servers of the DNS in October 2002 was described as an attack against the "heart of the Internet network." However, due to built-in safeguards, no slowdowns or even outages were caused. The same is true for a recent attack which took place in February 2007: even though the aggression lasted for almost twelve hours, the influence was hardly noticeable.

Such attacks against the infrastructure are possible not only by digital, but also by conventional means. For example, many transcontinental data connections rely on transatlantic cable connections between Europe and the United States. Whereas European cable ends are widely spread between many different countries, they are often bundled on the American side (e.g. in New Jersey and Rhode Island). An attack on one or two of these connections could have a serious impact on Internet connections in general. In the past, this was observed when cables were damaged accidentally. For example, after an underground cable between China and the USA was severely damaged, according to a survey, 97% of Chinese users reported problems of accessing foreign web pages and 57% claimed that their life and work was being affected by the damage. Another focus of a conventional attack against IT infrastructures could be to target one or more of the central so-called peeringpoints that interconnect different networks in the Internet.

The German peeringpoint DE-CIX in Frankfurt, for example, is said to handle 80% of German and 35% of European Internet traffic. The London Internet Exchange LINX is the world's largest Internet peeringpoint. In 2006, it was at the centre of a planned assault. However, Scotland Yard arrested suspects beforehand. An MI5-website is reported to have said that "without these services, the UK could suffer serious consequences, including severe economic damage, grave social disruption, or even large-scale loss of life." Since this report is focused on the use of the Internet by terrorists, there will be no further analysis of possible targets for conventional attacks. The examples above show, however, that terrorists can severely damage targets in the Internet even without any technical knowledge.

Altering Information

The second possibility is to change information that is being stored on the computer system. This can lead to so-called "defacements" that often take place after a web server has been compromised,. In the case of a defacement, a web page (usually an entry page) is replaced with another page that informs the visiting user that this particular web server has been hacked (and most likely also provides information about who has done it). In doing so, the attackers can easily demonstrate their capabilities and the weakness of the victim. In addition, the impression is created that the attacker will be able repeat his action at any given point in time and even with other, even more highly protected systems. Therefore, defacements of web servers that belong to security agencies, the military, or other important services are popular targets for attackers. The group "Pentaguard", for example, demonstrated its capabilities in 2001 when it simultaneously defaced a multitude of government and military websites in the U.K, Australia, and the United States. This attack was later evaluated as one of "the largest, most systematic defacements of worldwide government servers on the Web". Terrorist organizations had also already used this technique in the past. Al-Qaeda, for example, hacked the website of Silicon Valley Landsurveying Inc. in order to deposit a video file showing the hijacked (and later beheaded) Paul Marshal Johnson. By publishing the link to the stored video, the organization could simultaneously demonstrate its technical as well as conventional dangerousness. In another case, pro-Palestinian hackers used a coordinated attack to break into 80 Israel-related sites and deface them. Instead of defacing a web server, all other information stored on a computer system can also be affected, i.e. deleted or altered. If, for example, vital data, such as the U.S. Social Security database, financial institutions' records, or secret military documents, were able to be irreversibly damaged, grave social disorder and a long-lasting lack of trust in all government institutions could be the consequence. Studies, such as the exercise "Eligible Receiver", and recent attacks have shown that even top-secret military computers and sensitive nuclear research centers are not immune against all attacks.

Silent Operations

The shutting down of a computer or the defacement of a web page each have the advantage that the success of the attack becomes immediately known to both operators and users of the affected system. However, if an attacker does not aim at a demonstration of his powers, but rather tries to gather information, secrecy is of essence.

Therefore, the third possibility for an attacker to proceed after gaining access to a computer is simply to search for useful information and try to leave few or no traces at all. This form of action also has another advantage: whereas a security flaw that has been detected can be fixed after an intruder has been detected, an unknown security weakness allows the attacker to use it not only once but for a longer period of time. Hence, apart from the above-mentioned "Zero-Day-Exploits", other forms of custommade software are of also interest.

A mode of operation that could also be put to use by a terrorist organization can be observed in a case that a security company has tested. The company prepared USB sticks with a custom-designed, newly developed Trojan horse program that could not be detected by virus scanners. Twenty of these sticks were "lost" on the premises of a credit union. Of these, 15 sticks were found by employees – and promptly connected to the company network where the Trojan started to collect passwords and other valuable information and e-mailed this data back to the offenders. Such an attack would be a powerful way for a terrorist organization to initiate counterespionage.

Another way to introduce such software could be through legal channels. This was observed in the year 2000, when Japan's Metropolitan Police Department used a software system to track 150 police vehicles, including unmarked cars. It turned out that this software had been developed by the Aum Shinrikyo cult – the same group that gassed the Tokyo subway in 1995. It turned out that members of the cult had developed software for at least eighty firms and ten government agencies. The cult had been able to work largely undetected because the software developers were engaged as subcontractors, thus enabling personnel clearance to be easily circumvented.

COUNTER-ATTACKS

As mentioned, the jihad relies heavily on the web for the dissemination of information from the upper echelons, as well as for discussion at all levels. Statements by the leaders of the movement should be considered a useful input for intelligence analysis. Content analysis of such statements may give some hint of intentions, although there is a significant amount of bluster, hype, and misdirection present in much of these statements. Context analysis may therefore be of greater utility. This kind of analysis can determine what the person making the statement *thinks that his followers want to hear*. Thus, context analysis can provide some measure of the "temperature" of the "street." This is a useful input to foundation intelligence, as well as an aid to determining the focus of tactical intelligence gathering. Special attention should be given to the language, focus, and design of jihadi websites. The languages used can tell us who the jihadis see as their primary audience for recruits. In some cases, this points to perceived vulnerabilities among the targeted group. But it can also tell us who the jihadis *would like to have* as recruits—who can be of most use to them. For example, European Muslim converts are increasingly the focus of "narrow casting" on jihadi websites. Another point of consideration is the imagery and design of the sites. These sites are frequently the work of some of the best and brightest of the new generation jihadi recruits. They know their audience, and they know what techniques are likely to be effective. With this in mind, we can say that imitation is the sincerest form of counterterrorism! But it isn't only the style of outreach that can be copied. Here too, a bottom-up approach can yield benefits that would be unthinkable for top-down institutionalized responses. Web designers from the jihadis' own target audience can be recruited by the counter-terrorism community to build a counter-offensive. The success of this kind of campaign depends on working at the "grass roots" community level. The main allies of the counter-terrorism community will be those singled out for recruitment by the jihadis themselves. Terrorists and counter-terrorists are competing for the same audience. The techniques used successfully by both sides will reflect this. Psychological Operations

Analyst Stephen Ulph of the Jamestown Foundation has been monitoring jihadi forums, with a special emphasis on those dealing with the situation in Iraq, the new training ground for the jihadi movement. In July 2005, Ulph noted how news of ongoing discussions between the US military and the Iraqi insurgents was affecting traffic and commentary on jihadi forums: The news evoked considerable notes of distress on the jihadi forums. On the al- Qal'a forum one signing himself al-Sharif al-Idrisi, noted, on June 28, the similarity of this potential development with the situation in Afghanistan, "when those fleeing the Tora Bora caves were met by the Pakistanis not intent on helping them but in selling them to the Americans. We pray God that this doesn't happen to our brothers in Iraq." This kind of commentary highlights a key weakness as perceived by the jihadi militants themselves—their vulnerability to betrayal by the wider society in which they operate. Such fears are, of course, easily played on. One obvious stratagem for exploiting this sense of paranoia would be to "feed" news of betrayals to local news media, then cast blame in the relevant forums upon elements within the organization, or in rival organizations.

Ulph also noted that the news of meetings between coalition leaders and insurgents was met with denial by many: At the same time strenuous denials were being posted on the internet forums that any such meeting took place, including from groups said to have participated in the talks. One posting on June 30 appeared on the al-Qal'a forum signed by The Islamic Army in Iraq, the Army of the Mujahideen and the Army of Ansar al-Sunna. It expressed exasperation at Ayham al-Samarrai's "lies and America's games" and swiftly pointed to the impending peril for the Islamist mujahideen in Iraq: "its intentions are to split the ranks of the mujahideen ... to divide the Iraqis from non-Iraqis... to pull the rug from under the mujahideen ... How can a heroic mujahid Muslim brother in any country be a foreigner?"

What is significant here is the perceived motive of these "American games," namely, "to split the ranks of the mujahideen ... to divide the Iraqis from non-Iraqis... to pull the rug from under the mujahideen." One can gain a good deal of insight into the state of insecurity of the opponent from this sort of posting. Obviously, one forum posting or internet statement does not give an indication of the psychology of a whole organization. However, if monitored on an ongoing basis, the total compendium of such statements can provide a real "feel" for the psychological state of the opponent.

And if "being sold out" is what they fear, then by all means, one should play up any and every possible case of such a sell-out, and milk it for all it's worth. The potential of such suspicions to turn the opponents' forces against his own is indicated by the continuation of the same statement quoted by Ulph above: With America's designs being "to return the Baathists to power, in the name of the resistance" the statement accused Iyad Allawi of "giving orders to the Baathist Ayham al-Samarrai to intrigue against the mujahideen and the resistance ... So we proscribe the life of Ayham al-Samarrai, and declare him to be a target of the mujahideen in general and in particular of all members of the three groups (The Islamic Army in Iraq, the Army of the Mujahideen and the Army of Ansar al-Sunna). … Anyone who allows himself to be seduced into doing what the fantasist Ayham is doing will share the same fate." In other words, whether correct or not, the suspicions served to drive a wedge between the organization and its perceived enemies. Ulph points out that if the same suspicion can be cast upon elements within the organization, instances of "red on red" firing between opponent groups will be seen to increase.

Countering Recruitment and Propaganda

The global jihad movement, like any other major social movement, depends on a broad base of support. Positive public opinion from within its constituencies is a must, not only for bringing new recruits into its cadres, but also for garnering support for its less obviously goal-driven activities. As has been pointed out by Yoav Mimran, one of the key values of Muslim societies is social unity and harmony. Anyone seen as sowing discord or endangering public order is likely to be seen as an enemy of the public good, no matter how otherwise worthy are his goals. Brachman and McCants have noted that the movement "declines in popularity when it is perceived to be attacking fellow Muslims, causing public disorder, damaging critical national industries, or engaging in sectarianism." They point out that one effective point of counter-attack would be to "harness the power of the 'Shayma Effect' [referring to an incident where an Egyptian schoolgirl was killed in a jihadi attack], broadcasting images of jihadi attacks that have killed Muslim children.

The authors point out, however, that any such campaign must be managed very much "from the rear" and by proxy. To this we may add that an institutionalized campaign can never have the same power or reach as a genuine "grass roots" campaign among the potential constituency of the opponent. Only when we are able to inspire local actors to join the fray will such a media counter-offensive really be effective. A government-sponsored campaign, no matter how skillfully managed, is no substitute for the participation of local bloggers, media people, and commentators.

CYBERTERROR THREAT EXAGGERATED

Amid all the dire warnings and alarming statistics that the subject of cyberterrorism generates, it is important to remember one simple statistic: so far, there has been no recorded instance of a terrorist cyberattack on U.S. public facilities, transportation systems, nuclear power plants, power grids, or other key components of the national infrastructure. Cyberattacks are common, but they have not been conducted by terrorists and they have not sought to inflict the kind of damage that would qualify them as cyberterrorism.

When U.S. troops recovered al Qaeda laptops in Afghanistan, officials were surprised to find its members more technologically adept than previously believed. They discovered structural and engineering software, electronic models of a dam, and information on computerized water systems, nuclear power plants, and U.S. and European stadiums. But the evidence did *not* suggest that al Qaeda operatives were planning cyberattacks, only that they were using the Internet to communicate and coordinate physical attacks. Neither al Qaeda nor any other terrorist organization appears to have tried to stage a serious cyberattack. For now, the most damaging attacks and intrusions, experts say, are typically carried out either by disgruntled corporate insiders intent on embezzlement or sabotage or by individual hackers—typically young and male—seeking thrills and notoriety. According to a report issued in 2002 by IBM Global Security Analysis Lab, 90 percent of hackers are amateurs with limited technical proficiency, 9 percent are more skilled at gaining unauthorized access but do not damage the files they read, and only 1 percent are highly skilled and intent on copying files or damaging programs and systems. Most hackers, it should be noted, concentrate on writing programs that expose security flaws in computer software, mainly in the operating systems produced by Microsoft. Their efforts in this direction have sometimes embarrassed corporations but have also been responsible for alerting the public and security professionals to major security flaws in software.

Moreover, although there are hackers with the ability to damage systems, disrupt e-commerce, and force websites offline, the vast majority of hackers do not have the necessary skills and knowledge. The ones who do, generally do not seek to wreak havoc. Douglas Thomas, a professor at the University of Southern California, spent seven years studying computer hackers in an effort to understand better who they are and what motivates them. Thomas interviewed hundreds of hackers and explored their "literature." In testimony on July 24, 2002, before the House Subcommittee on Government Efficiency, Financial Management and Intergovernmental Relations, Thomas argued that "with the vast majority of hackers, I would say 99 percent of them, the risk [of cyberterrorism] is negligible for the simple reason that those hackers do not have the skill or ability to organize or execute an attack that would be anything more than a minor inconvenience." His judgment was echoed in *Assessing the Risks of Cyberterrorism, Cyber War, and Other Cyber Threats*, a 2002 report for the Centre for Strategic and International Studies, written by Jim Lewis, a sixteen-year veteran of the State and Commerce Departments. "The idea that hackers are going to bring the nation to its knees is too far-fetched a scenario to be taken seriously," Lewis argued. "Nations are more robust than the early analysts of cyberterrorism and cyberwarfare give them credit for. Infastructure systems [are] more flexible and responsive in restoring service than the early analysts realized, in part because they have to deal with failure on a routine basis."

Many computer security specialists believe it is virtually impossible to use the Internet to inflict death on a large scale and scoff at the notion that terrorists would bother trying. The resilience of computer systems to attack, they point out, is no accident but rather the result of significant investments of time, money, and expertise. Nuclear weapons and other sensitive military systems enjoy the most basic form of Internet security. They are "air-gapped," meaning that they are not physically connected to the Internet and are therefore inaccessible to outside hackers. The Defence Department has been particularly vigilant in protecting key systems by isolating them from the Internet and even from the Pentagon's internal computer network. All new software must be submitted to the National Security Agency for security testing.

The 9/11 hijackings understandably led to an outcry that airliners are particularly susceptible to cyberterrorist attacks. In 2002, for instance, Senator Charles Schumer (D-N.Y.) described "the absolute havoc and devastation that would result if cyberterrorists suddenly shut down our air traffic control system, with thousands of planes in mid-flight."

In fact, cybersecurity experts give some of their highest marks to the Federal Aviation Authority, which separates its administrative and air traffic control systems. And there is a reason the 9/11 hijackers used box-cutters instead of keyboards: it is impossible to hijack a plane remotely, which eliminates the possibility of a high-tech 9/11 scenario in which planes are used as weapons. Another source of concern is terrorist infiltration of the intelligence agencies. But here, too, the risk is described by Internet experts as slim. The CIA's classified computers are also air-gapped, as is the FBI's entire computer system.

That leaves less-well-protected secondary targets such as power grids, oil pipelines, and dams that do not present opportunities as nightmarish as do nuclear weapons systems but that nonetheless might be used to inflict other forms of mass destruction. Because most of these systems are in the private sector, they tend to be less secure than government systems. In addition, as noted above, companies increasingly use the Internet to manage SCADA systems that control such processes as regulating the flow of oil in pipelines and the level of water in dams. To illustrate the supposed ease with which terrorists could seize control of a dam, a story in the *Washington Post* in June 2003 on al Qaeda cyberterrorism related an anecdote about a twelve-year-old who hacked into the SCADA system at Arizona's Theodore Roosevelt Dam in 1998 and was, according to the article, within mere keystrokes of unleashing millions of gallons of water upon helpless downstream communities. However, a subsequent investigation by the tech-news site CNet.com revealed the tale to be largely apocryphal; investigators concluded that the hacker could not have gained control of the dam and that no lives or property were ever at risk.

To assess the potential threat of cyberterrorism, experts such as Denning suggest that two questions be asked: Are there targets that are vulnerable to cyberattacks? And are there actors with the capability and motivation to carry out such attacks? The answer to the first question is yes: critical infrastructure systems are complex and therefore bound to contain weaknesses that might be exploited, and even systems that seem "hardened" to outside manipulation might be accessed by insiders, acting alone or in concert with terrorists, to cause considerable harm. But what of the second question?

Few people besides a company's own employees possess the specific technical know-how required to run a specialized SCADA system. The most commonly cited example of SCADA exploitation bears this out.

In April 2002, an Australian man used an Internet connection to release a million gallons of raw sewage along Queensland's Sunshine Coast after being turned down for a government job. When police arrested him, they discovered that he had worked for the company that designed the sewage treatment plant's control software.

It is possible, of course, that such disgruntled employees might be recruited by terrorist groups, but even if the terrorists did enlist inside help, the degree of damage they could cause would still be limited. As Joshua Green argues in "The Myth of Cyberterrorism" (which appeared in the *Washington Monthly* in November 2002), the employees of companies that handle power grids, oil and gas utilities, and communications are well rehearsed in dealing with the fallout from hurricanes, floods, tornadoes, and other natural disasters. They are also equally adept at containing and remedying problems that stem from human action.

In August 1999, the Centre for the Study of Terrorism and Irregular Warfare at the Naval Postgraduate School (NPS) in Monterey, California, issued a report titled *Cyber-terror: Prospects and Implications*.

The report concluded that terrorists generally lack the wherewithal and human capital needed to mount attacks that involve more than annoying but relatively harmless hacks. The study examined five types of terrorist groups: religious, New Age, ethnonationalist separatist, revolutionary, and far-right extremists.

Of these, only the religious groups were adjudged likely to seek the capacity to inflict massive damage. Hacker groups, the study determined, are psychologically and organizationally ill suited to cyberterrorism, and any massive disruption of the information infrastructure would run counter to their self-interest.

In October 2000, the NPS group issued a second report, this one examining the decision-making process by which substate groups engaged in armed resistance develop new operational methods, including cyberterrorism. The report concluded that while substate groups may find cyberterror attractive as a nonlethal weapon, terrorists have not yet integrated information technology into their strategy and tactics and that significant barriers between hackers and terrorists may prevent their integration into one group.

Another illustration of the limited likelihood of terrorists launching a highly damaging cyberattack comes from a simulation sponsored by the U.S. Naval War College. The college contracted with a research group to simulate a massive cyberattack on the nation's information infrastructure.

Government hackers and security analysts gathered in July 2002 in Newport, R.I., for a war game dubbed "Digital Pearl Harbor." The results were far from devastating: the hackers failed to crash the Internet, although they did cause serious sporadic damage. According to a CNet.com report on the exercise published in August 2002, officials concluded that terrorists hoping to stage such an attack "would require a syndicate with significant resources, including $200 million, country-level intelligence and five years of preparation time."

SECURITY RISKS

As a result of the Internet and e-mail, there has been a sharp increase in security incidents involving the accidental disclosure of classified and other sensitive information. One common problem occurs when individuals download a seemingly unclassified file from a classified system, and then fail to carefully review this file before sending it as an attachment to an e-mail message. Too often, the seemingly unclassified file actually has some classified material or classification markings that are not readily apparent when the file is viewed on line. Sending such material by e-mail is a security violation even if the recipient has an appropriate security clearance, as e-mail can easily be monitored by unauthorized persons.

More important, even if the downloaded file really is unclassified, the electronic version of that file may have recoverable traces of classified information. This happens because data is stored in "blocks." If a file does not take up an entire block, the remainder of that block may have recoverable traces of data from other files. Your system administrator must follow an approved technical procedure for removing these traces before the file is treated as unclassified.

Some organizations have found it necessary to lock their computer drives to prevent any downloading of files from the classified system. If an individual wishes to download and retransmit an unclassified file from a classified system, the file must be downloaded and processed by the system administrator to remove electronic traces of other files before it is retransmitted.

Inappropriate Materials

Sending e-mail is like sending a postcard through the mail. Just as the mailman and others have an opportunity to read a postcard, network eavesdroppers can read your e-mail as it passes through the Internet from computer to computer. E-mail is not like a telephone call, where your privacy rights are protected by law.

The courts have repeatedly sided with employers who monitor their employees' e-mail or Internet use. In an American Management Association poll, 47% of major companies reported that they store and review their employees' e-mail. Organizations do this to protect themselves against lawsuits, because the organization can be held liable for abusive, harassing, or otherwise inappropriate messages sent over its computer network. In the same poll, 25% of companies reported that they have fired employees for misuse of the Internet or office e-mail.

In the past couple years, *The New York Times* fired 23 employees for exchanging off-colour e-mail. Xerox fired 40 people for inappropriate Internet use. Dow Chemical fired 24 employees and disciplined another 230 for sending or storing pornographic or violent material by e-mail. Several years ago, Chevron Corp. had to pay $2.2 million to plaintiffs who successfully brought a suit of sexual harassment, in part because an employee sent an e-mail to coworkers listing the reasons why beer is better than women.

Security of Tools

Secrets in the computer require the same protection as secrets on paper. This is because information can be recovered from a computer hard drive even after the file has been deleted or erased by the computer user. It is estimated that about a third of the average hard drive contains information that has been "deleted" but is still recoverable.

Computers on which classified information is prepared must be kept in facilities that meet specified physical security requirements for processing classified information. If necessary to prepare classified information on a computer in a non-secure environment, use a removable hard drive or laptop that is secured in an approved safe when not in use. Alternatively, use a typewriter. Check with your security office concerning rules for traveling with a laptop on which classified or other sensitive information has been prepared. Laptop computers are a particular concern owing to their vulnerability to theft.

Computer Passwords

Passwords are used to authenticate an individual's right to have access to certain information. Your password is for your use only. Lending it to someone else is a security violation and may result in disciplinary action against both parties. Never disclose your password to anyone. Memorize it – do not put it in writing. If you leave your terminal unattended for any reason, log off or use a screen lock. Otherwise, someone else could use your computer to access information they are not authorized to have. You will be held responsible if someone else uses your password in connection with a system transaction.

Do change your password regularly. Use a password with at least six and preferably eight characters and consisting of a mix of upper and lower case letters, numbers, and special characters such as punctuation marks This mix of various types of characters makes it more difficult for a hacker to use an automated tool called a "password cracker" to discover your password. Cracking passwords is a common means by which hackers gain unauthorized access to protected systems.

Social Engineering

"Social engineering" is hacker-speak for conning legitimate computer users into providing useful information that helps the hacker gain unauthorized access to their computer system. The hacker using social engineering usually poses as a legitimate person in the organization (maintenance technician, security officer, inexperienced computer user, VIP, etc.) and employs a plausible cover story to trick computer users into giving useful information. This is usually done by telephone, but it may also be done by forged e-mail messages or even in-person visits.

Most people have an incorrect impression of computer break-ins. They think they are purely technical, the result of technical flaws in computer systems which the intruders are able to exploit.

The truth is, however, that social engineering often plays a big part in helping an attacker slip through security barriers. Lack of security awareness or gullibility of computer users often provides an easy stepping stone into the protected system if the attacker has no authorized access to the system at all.

Computer Applications in Business

Computer Applications in Business provides an overview of the integrated software packages most often used in the workplace. By the end of this course, you will have a sound understanding of the basic features and business applications for the word processor, spreadsheet, database, and presentation software in your choice of either Microsoft Works Suite or Microsoft Office Professional packages. This process of completing this course, you will also learn how to problem solve and use the Help function and online tutorial assistance for your software. Finally, as this is an online course, you will learn about using the Internet and e-mail.

Delivery Method

There is continuous enrolment for this course. Delivery is self-paced, allowing you the flexibility to proceed through the course according to your own schedule.

Prerequisites

None. Students will need access to a PC with full internet access and MS Office Professional (XP preferred) including Access database software or MS Works (the 2002 or newer Works 'Suite' with Word included is preferred). This course is not ideal for those using the MS Office 2007 version.

Exclusions

Students with credit for CMPT 109, 150 or a similar course may not take CMPT 119 for further credit.

Objectives

- Answer questions regarding your computer's hardware, software, and basic operations.

- Set up your computer for World Wide Web connection.
- Use e-mail to send messages and file attachments.
- Participate in on-line discussion groups.
- Describe the types of documents created with a word processing programme.
- List the principal features of a word processing programme.
- Create and format a business letter.
- Create and format a schedule containing a table.
- Design either a textual or a visual message for a public audience.
- Select and use style features to create new documents.
- Use the Help system to answer questions and troubleshoot problems.
- Describe the purposes of a spreadsheet and define its vocabulary.
- Set up and analyse itemized lists of numbers, such as the various types of budgets or financial statements.
- Perform and manipulate the calculations to achieve meaningful information.
- Present the numerical data in the spreadsheet in a graphical format.
- Conduct "what if" simulations of the numerical statements.
- Import spreadsheet reports and charts into word processing and/or database documents.
- Define the purpose of a database programme.
- Describe the components of a database.
- Plan a simple two-table database.
- Use wizards to enter and to search data, and to create a report.
- Enter data in a form.
- Merge data with a document.
- Create mailing labels.

- Analyse data in a database.
- Privacy issues related to databases.
- Plan a presentation.
- Apply good design principles to a presentation.
- Examine examples of a presentation.
- Describe the purpose of presentation software.
- Describe the components of a presentation.
- Create a presentation outline.
- Apply and modify a design template.
- Add clip art and charts to a presentation.
- Run a slide show.

Small, rural high schools are constantly trying to determine what type of computer training should be provided to students to meet the needs of business in the surrounding area. Many students in high schools today are not college bound and attempt to find local employment after graduation. Leaders in the community are also interested in retaining as many young people as possible in the area by helping them find local jobs through adequate high school training.

Changing Face of Business

Reports of shipments of personal computers to small businesses and home offices are growing at a 16% annual rate.(1) The power of the computer, the fax machine and voice mail allow a small company to do almost anything a larger corporation does. New technology has streamlined every part of our business lives.

The challenge for small firms is to apply these technologies appropriately. After investing in a computer, for example, most discover other peripherals they want to incorporate into their office systems. The bottom line is that even small businesses can, and do, utilize computers and related technologies in their day-to-day operations. This means that even a high school graduate who does not plan to further his or her formal education should have some knowledge of computers. In addition, it is important to bridge the gap between basic theory and computer applications.2 There is a strong correlation between high anxiety and reduced computer competence. Experience with computers in school tends to reduce anxiety on the job and leads to more productive workers. A good computer course also shows students how the computer can be utilized in many diverse fields.

Identifying Skills

Businesses must be periodically surveyed for information on the type of skills needed by their workers. In today's evolving world of work, required skills change as fast as the available technologies.

In Nebraska, for example, the Manpower company surveyed offices from Lincoln west to the Colorado border by sending a questionnaire on office automation topics to over 2,500 businesses.

The results indicated that word processing was the number one activity, using a spreadsheet was number two, and manipulating a database was number three. Lotus 1-23 was the most widely installed software. WordPerfect was the most popular word processing package, capturing 40% of those responding to their survey. Service companies were the largest number of respondents, with government second and retail/ wholesale businesses third.

Previous to its decisions on what type of computers to purchase and which software packages to teach, Auburn High School needed to know similar information. They wanted to provide their students specific experience with the computers and applications being utilized by business and industry in the local geographic area. This would reassure their students that they would be employable after graduation. It would also assist the local communities by keeping young people in the area and not have them travel to find jobs elsewhere. Upon the suggestion of Auburn's computer programming teacher, Claudette Stevens, a comprehensive survey of local area businesses was conducted in southeast Nebraska in two rural counties, Richardson and Nemaha. All of both counties' businesses were identified from the telephone book and local Chamber of Commerces, totalling 627. A random sample of 150 (approximately 25%) of these firms were contacted by telephone. All companies that were contacted agreed to answer the questions on the survey. Table 1 contains the exact numbers and results of the survey.

Examining the Survey Results

Almost half of the small, rural businesses contacted (46%) are still not using computers. Of those using computers, over 68% said they purchased them mainly for accounting. However, most companies indicated they use computers for a variety of functions. Surveyed companies reported using a total of 38 different software packages. The most common type of programme used was for accounting, the second most common was word processing, and the third most common software produced customer receipts.

The questionnaire also dealt with the amount of knowledge new employees were expected to possess. Only one employer expected to hire a person with a bachelor's degree in computer science, and that job also required a four month period of intense training. A majority of companies expected to hire employees with basic knowledge on how to use the type of computer the firm owned. Some companies wanted potential employees to have an amount of keyboarding skills; other firms wanted general computer ability.

ASSESSING THE RISKS OF CYBER TERRORISM, CYBER WAR AND OTHER CYBER THREATS

Cyber-warfare conjures up images of information warriors unleashing vicious attacks against an unsuspecting opponent's computer networks, wreaking havoc and paralyzing nations. This a frightening scenario, but how likely is it to occur? What would the effects of a cyber attack be on a potential opponent?

Cyber attacks, network security and information pose complex problems that reach into new areas for national security and public policy. This paper looks at one set of issues – those related to cyber-terrorism and cyber attacks on critical infrastructure and their implications for national security. Cyber-terrorism is "the use of computer network tools to shut down critical national infrastructures (such as energy, transportation, government operations) or to coerce or intimidate a government or civilian population."

The premise of cyber terrorism is that as nations and critical infrastructure became more dependent on computer networks for their operation, new vulnerabilities are created – "a massive electronic Achilles' heel." A hostile nation or group could exploit these vulnerabilities to penetrate a poorly secured computer network and disrupt or even shut down critical functions.

Much of the literature on cyber-terrorism assumes that the vulnerability of computer networks and the vulnerability of critical infrastructures are the same, and that these vulnerabilities put national security at a significant risk. Given the newness of computer network technology and the rapidity with which it spread into economic activity, these assumptions are not surprising. A closer look at the relationships between computer networks and critical infrastructures, their vulnerability to attack, and the effect on national security, suggests that the assumption of vulnerability is wrong. A full reassessment is outside the scope of this paper, but a brief review suggests that while many computer networks remain very vulnerable to attack, few critical infrastructures are equally vulnerable.

A reassessment of the cyber threat has four elements. First, we need to put cyber-warfare and cyber-terrorism in the historical context of attacks against infrastructure. Strategies that emphasize attacks on critical civil infrastructures have discussed for more than eighty years. Second, we need to examine cyber attacks against a backdrop of routine infrastructure failures.

There is extensive data on power outages, flight delays and communications disruptions that occur normally and the consequences of these routine failures can be used to gage the effect cyber-warfare and cyber-terrorism. Third, we need to measure the dependence of infrastructure on computer networks and the redundancy already present in these systems.

Finally, for the case of cyber-terrorism, we must consider the use of cyber-weapons in the context of the political goals and motivations of terrorists, and whether cyber-weapons are likely to achieve these goals. A preliminary review of these factors suggests that computer network vulnerabilities are an increasingly serious business problem but that their threat to national security is overstated. Modern industrial societies are more robust than they appear at first glance. Critical infrastructures, especially in large market economies, are more distributed, diverse, redundant and self-healing than a cursory assessment may suggest, rendering them less vulnerable to attack. In all cases, cyber attacks are less effective and less disruptive than physical attacks. Their only advantage is that they are cheaper and easier to carry out than a physical attack.

Infrastructure as Target

Cyber-terrorism is not the first time a new technology has been seized upon as creating a strategic vulnerability. While the match between theories of cyber-warfare and air power is not precise, a comparison of the two is useful. In reaction to the First World War, European strategists like Douhet and Trenchard argued that aerial bombing attacks against critical infrastructure well behind the front lines would disrupt and cripple an enemies' capacity to wage war. Their theories were put to the test by the U.S. Army and Royal Air Forces during World War II in strategic bombing campaigns aimed at destroying electrical power, transportation and manufacturing facilities. Much of the first tranche of literature on cyber attacks resembles in many ways (and owes an unspoken debt to) the early literature on strategic bombing.

A key document for understanding how attacks on infrastructure affect societies is the Strategic Bombing Survey conducted by the United State during and after World War II. During the war, Britain and America launched thousands of heavy bombers that dropped millions of tons of high explosives on Germany, seeking to cripple its infrastructure, destroy its industrial base and break the will of the population to continue the war. Early theorists of air warfare had predicted that such an onslaught would paralyze or cripple the target. What the survey found, however, is that industrial societies are impressively resilient. Industrial production actually increased for two years under the bombing and it was not until ground forces occupied Germany that resistance ceased:

As the air offensive gained in tempo, the Germans were unable to prevent the decline and eventual collapse of their economy. Nevertheless, the recuperative and defensive powers of Germany were immense; the speed and ingenuity with which they rebuilt and maintained essential war industries in operation clearly surpassed Allied expectations. Germany resorted to almost every means an ingenious people could devise to avoid the attacks upon her economy and to minimize their effects....

The mental reaction of the German people to air attack is significant. Under ruthless Nazi control, they showed surprising resistance to the terror and hardships of repeated air attack, to the destruction of their homes and belongings, and to the conditions under which they were reduced to live. Their morale, their belief in ultimate victory or satisfactory compromise, and their confidence in their leaders declined, but they continued to work efficiently as long as the physical means of production remained.... The U.S. found similar results from aerial bombardment during the Vietnam War.

Counter-intuitively, the effect of aerial attack was often to harden and increase popular support for continued resistance. The advent of nuclear weapons (and perhaps large precision-guided munitions) gave air power the ability to disrupt civil infrastructures needed to achieve the visions of Douhet, Trenchard or Mitchell, but cyber attacks do not pose the same level of lethality.

One of the Strategic Bombing Survey's conclusions was that "The German experience showed that, whatever the target system, no indispensable industry was permanently put out of commission by a single attack. Persistent re-attack was necessary." However, cyber attacks are likely to be single attacks.

Once a hacker has gained access and the damage done, the target usually responds quickly to close off the vulnerability that allowed that line of attack and to bring systems back on line. Cyber attackers would continually need to exploit new vulnerabilities and new tactics to ensure sustained disruption. Cyber attacks also seldom if ever produce physical damage that requires time-consuming repairs.

'Routine' Failure versus Cyber Attack

Critical infrastructure protection creates a new set of problems for national security. Different actors are involved. The focus is on civilian and commercial systems and services. Military force is less important. The scope of these new problems depends on how we define national security and how we set thresholds for acceptable damage. From a legal or public safety perspective, no country will accept even a single attack on infrastructure or interruption of services. If the goal is to prevent cyber-attacks from costing a single day of electric power or water service, we have set a very high standard for security. However, from a strategic military perspective, attacks that do not degrade national capabilities are not significant. From this perspective, if a cyber-attack does not cause damage that rises above the threshold of the routine disruptions that every economy experiences, it does not pose an immediate or significant risk to national security.

It is particularly important to consider that in the larger context of economic activity, water system failures, power outages, air traffic disruptions and other cyber-terror scenarios are routine events that do not affect national security. On a national level, where dozens or even hundreds of different systems provide critical infrastructure services, failure is a routine occurrence at the system or regional level, with service denied to customers for hours or days. Cyber-terrorists would need to attack multiple targets simultaneously for long periods of time to create terror, achieve strategic goals or to have any noticeable effect. For most of the critical infrastructure, multiple sustained attacks are not a feasible scenario for hackers, terrorist groups or nation states (particularly for nation states, where the risk of discovery of what would be universally seen as an act of war far outweigh the limited advantages gained from cyber attacks on infrastructure).

Weapons of Mass Annoyance

A detailed examination of some of the scenarios for attacks on critical infrastructures helps place cyber-attacks more accurately in a strategic or national security context. For example, dams used for water storage and for power generation are often cited as a likely target for cyber attack. The Washington Post recently wrote that unnamed "U.S. analysts" believe that "by disabling or taking command of the floodgates in a dam, for example, or of substations handling 300,000 volts of electric power, an intruder could use virtual tools to destroy real-world lives and property."

In the United States, the water supply infrastructure would be an elusive target for cyber attack. There are 54,064 separate water systems in the U.S. Of these, 3,769 water systems serve eighty one percent of the population and 353 systems served forty-four percent of the population. However, the uneven spread of diverse network technologies complicates the terrorists' task. Many of these water supply systems in the U.S., even in large cities, continue to rely on technologies not easily disrupted by network attacks. There have been cases in the U.S. when a community's water supply has been knocked out for days at a time (usually as a result of flooding), but these have produced neither terror nor paralysis. A cyber terrorist or cyber warrior would need to carry out a sustained attack that would simultaneously disrupt several hundred of these systems to gain any strategic benefit.

Assuming that a terrorist could find a vulnerability in a water supply system that would allow him to shut down one city's water for a brief period, this vulnerability could be exploited to increase the damage of a physical attack (by denying fire fighters access to water). In general, a cyber attack that alone might pass unnoticed in the normal clutter of daily life could have useful multiplier effects if undertaken simultaneously with a physical attack. This sort of simultaneous combination of physical and cyber attacks might be the only way in which cyber weapons could be attractive to terrorists. The American Waterworks Association assessment of the terrorist threat to water supplies placed "physical destruction of the system's components to disrupt the supply of water" as the most likely source of infrastructure attack.

Comparing aerial and cyber attacks on hydroelectric dams helps provide a measure for cyber-threats. Early in World War II, the Royal Air Force mounted a daring attack on dams in the Ruhr, a chief source of electrical power for German industry. The raid was a success, the dams breached by bombs and, for a period of time, the electrical supply in the region was disrupted.

A comparable cyber attack occurred when a young hacker reportedly gained access to the computer controls for a dam in the U.S. Southwest, but did not disrupt service or cause physical damage.

In neither attack was the damage or the reduction in electrical power paralyzing. Of the two, the cyber attack was less effective in that it caused no physical damage and could be classed more as an annoyance than a threat. The aerial attack resulted in physical damage that needed to be repaired. The only advantage of a cyber attack is that it is less expensive - a teen-ager and a desktop computer rather than valuable aircrews and expensive aircraft.

Many analyses have cyber-terrorists shutting down the electrical power system. One of the better cyber security surveys found that power companies are a primary target for cyber attacks and that seventy percent of these companies had "suffered a severe attack" in the first six months of 2002. The U.S. electrical power grid is a desirable target, but it is a network of multiple, redundant systems that are used to routine system failure and disruption. The national electrical grid is a highly interconnected system of over 3,000 public and private utilities and cooperatives. These 3,000 electrical power providers use a variety of different information technologies to operate their controls for power generation and transmission. A hacker or even a large group of hackers would need to find vulnerabilities in multiple systems to significantly disrupt the power supply and even then, an attack might only disrupt service for a few hours.

The North American Electric Reliability Council, an industry group formed after the 1965 New York blackout, has been working with the Federal government since the 1980s to improve the security of the electrical system and to develop rapid responses to large outages. In Congressional testimony, NERC officials have said that in the last few years, neither viruses nor Distributed Denial of Service attacks against the U.S. electrical system have interrupted service. While industry sources can paint an over-optimistic picture at times, it remains true that falling trees have caused many electric system disruptions while cyber attacks have caused none.

A risk assessment by the Information Assurance Task Force of the National Security Telecommunications Advisory Committee concluded "Physical destruction is still the greatest threat facing the electric power infrastructure. Compared to this, electronic intrusion represents an emerging, but still relatively minor, threat." The U.S. has already run a large-scale experiment on the effects of disrupting electrical power supplies, thanks to California's experience with 'deregulation' last year.

California's efforts to de-regulate the electrical power market resulted in months of blackouts and rolling brownouts across the state. Deregulation was a more powerful 'attack' on the electrical infrastructure than anything a cyber-terrorist could mount.

There was clearly economic cost to the California regulatory event, but it was not crippling nor did it strike terror into the hearts of Americans. Similarly, power outages across the country in 1999 affected millions of people and cost electrical power customers millions of dollars in lost business and productivity. These outages were the result of increased electricity use prompted by sustained high summer temperatures. In contrast to California's State government or hot weather, the number of blackouts in U.S. caused by hackers or cyber-terrorists remains zero.

Interference with national air traffic systems to disrupt flights, shut down air transport and endanger passenger and crews is another frequently cited cyber-threat. We are not yet at a stage where computer networks operate aircraft remotely, so it is not possible for a cyber-attacker to take over an aircraft. Aircraft still carry pilots who are trained to operate the plane in an emergency.

Similarly, the Federal Aviation Authority does not depend solely on computer networks to manage air traffic, nor are its communications dependent on the Internet. The high level of human involvement in the control and decision making process for air traffic reduces the risk of any cyber attack.

In a normal month storms, electrical failures and programming glitches all ensure a consistently high level of disruption in air traffic. Pilots and air traffic controllers are accustomed to unexpected disruptions and have adapted their practices to minimize the effect. Airlines and travelers are also accustomed to and expect a high degree of disruption in the system. In the United States, it is normal for 15,000 to 20,000 flights to be delayed or cancelled every month. A cyber attack that degraded the air traffic system would create delays and annoyance, but it would not pose a risk to national security.

The FAA has 90 major computer systems and nine different communications networks. These networks rely on elderly equipment and use proprietary software that make them difficult for outsiders to hack.

This may explain why the few reported attacks have not affected air traffic. In one reported incident, a young hacker interrupting local phone service in a New England, cutting off a regional airport's control tower and the ability to turn on runway lights. Although the interruption lasted six hours, there were no accidents at the airport. In other cases, FAA headquarters computer networks have been penetrated, allowing hackers to make public unpublished information on airport passenger screening activities, and in another case, a hacker was able to enter an FAA mail server. None of these cases resulted in any disruption to flight. Ironically, modernization could actually increase FAA vulnerability if greater attention is not given to security.

A recent attack on the Internet illustrates the nature of vulnerabilities from cyber attack. For a one-hour period in October 2002, unknown parties launched a Distributed Denial of Service attack on the thirteen 'root servers' that form the basis of the domain names system that governs Internet addresses.

Eight of the thirteen servers were forced off-line because of the attacks. The attack itself was invisible and without effect on Internet users. The attack on the DNS system did not noticeably degrade Internet performance. Most DNS data needed for the daily operation of the Internet is stored locally and updated daily.

Very few requests require assistance from the root servers. Additionally, the presence of thirteen servers (of which five were not affected by the attack) gives a degree of redundancy that suggests that if there are vulnerabilities to the Internet, the DNS servers are not one of them. In contrast to the DNS attack, shortly after it occurred thousands of Internet customers in the western United States experienced serious delays when their service provider had routing problems due to programming errors. Unlike the attack, this DNS failure actually disrupted service, but it had no effect on national security.

While the Internet may have a few points of failure that offer the possibility for system-wide disruption, it was designed to be a robust, distributed communications network capable of continuing operations after a strategic nuclear exchange. Packet switching and Internet protocols were developed to allow communications to be maintained even when some nodes in the network were eliminated and the Internet itself was designed to automatically route around damage to allow for continued communications. Additionally, computer networks rely on a backbone of high capacity telecommunications systems that are relatively secure from cyber-attack. The introduction of new communications technologies also enhances survivability. Wireless and satellite communications also provide some redundancy for landline systems.

Most industrial countries now have access to three or four different modes of communications, making the system considerably more robust than it was a decade ago. Increased use of ultra wideband and mesh radio networks will also increase redundancy and survivability against cyber attack in communications networks.

The 911 emergency response system, a specialized communications network that relies on local telephone service, is also a favorite target for theorists of cyber-terrorism, but like other infrastructures, it is a robust target. The U.S. for example, does not use a single 911 system in but instead has several thousand local systems using different technologies and procedures. No 911 system in a major city has been hacked. It might be possible to send a flood of email messages instructing people to call 911 for important information and thus overload the system (this was the technique used in the 1997 U.S. cyber exercise "Eligible Receiver"). This sort of technique usually works only once - but made in conjunction with a bombing or other physical attack they could act as a 'force multiplier' for a terrorist event.

Manufacturing and economic activity are increasingly dependent on computer networks, and cyber crime and industrial espionage are new dangers for economic activity. However, the evidence is mixed as to the vulnerability of manufacturing to cyber attack. A virus in 2000 infected 1,000 computers at Ford Motor Company. Ford received 140,000 contaminated e-mail messages in three hours before it shut down its network. E-mail service was disrupted for almost a week within the company. Yet, Ford reported, "the rogue program appears to have caused only limited permanent damage. None of its 114 factories stopped, according to the automaker. Computerized engineering blueprints and other technical data were unaffected. Ford was still able to post information for dealers and auto parts suppliers on Web sites that it uses for that purpose." Companies now report that the defensive measures they have taken meant that viruses that were exceptionally damaging when they first appeared are now only "nuisances."

Cyber attacks are often presented as a threat to military forces and the Internet has major implications for espionage and warfare.

Information warfare covers a range of activities of which cyber attacks may be the least important. While information operations and information superiority have become critical elements in successful military operations, no nation has placed its military forces in a position where they are dependent on computer networks that are vulnerable to outside attack. This greatly limits the effectiveness of cyber weapons (code sent over computer networks).

The many reports of military computer networks being hacked usually do not explain whether these networks are used for critical military functions. It is indicative, however, that despite regular reports of tens of thousands of network attacks every year on the Department of Defence, there has been no degradation of U.S. military capabilities.

For example, while there were many attack against U.S. military computer networks during operations in Kosovo, these attacks did not result in sorties being cancelled or in a single casualty. Similarly, a foreign power that used cyber-weapons to try to prevent a carrier battle group from leaving the U.S. would be unlikely to succeed.

A recent attack by a British hacker neither compromised classified information nor disrupted military operations. A Rand study conducted for the U.S. Air Force on military operations and information vulnerabilities noted "while most of the current topical interests has focused on the newer, trendier threats to information systems, particularly computer hacking and associated disruption and manipulation...our analysis showed that some of the "old-fashioned" threats pose a greater danger...."

TODAY'S HACKERS - TOMORROWS SECURITY ANALYSTS

Frank William Abagnale, Jr. is a former check con artist, forger and imposter who, for five years in the 1960s, passed bad checks worth more than $2.5 million in 26 countries. During this time, he used eight aliases — even more to cash bad checks. Currently he runs Abagnale and Associates, a financial fraud consultancy company. His life story provided the inspiration for the feature film Catch Me if You Can.

An Indian teenage hacking expert who has helped global think-tanks and police officials combat computer attackers and digital swindlers is spurning job offers to pursue a degree at the prestigious Stanford University. Ankit Fadia, 18 has crisscrossed India, giving lectures to police departments, software companies, educational institutions and government agencies on how to fight "cyber criminals" and deal with computer viruses.

Fadia, developed his computer skills after spending long hours on the Internet, breaking into Web sites as an "ethical hacker" and then informing companies about their sites' vulnerability. Also, he wants to start his own computer security firm.

Also, Not all hackers are bad. There are certain hackers whose job is to intrude into a software system by evading or disabling security measures and checks how vulnerable the system is to the bad hackers. Ethical computer hacking has come of age in order to stop or pre-empt intruders from messing around with a computer programme. "Financial transactions are the mainstay of banking operations. Banks and other such institutions need to be extra careful of the bad hackers. Ethical hackers do what a hacker does but only to identify the loopholes in software programmes.

Cyber Ethics

Ethics and morality in different circumstances connotes varied and complex meanings. Each and everything which is opposed to public policy, against public welfare and which may disturb public tranquility may be termed to be immoral and unethical.

In the past terms such as imperialism, colonialism, apartheid, which were burning issues have given way to cyber crime, hacking, 'cyber-ethics' etc. Today in the present era there is a need to evolve a 'cyber-jurisprudence' based on which 'cyber-ethics' can be evaluated and criticized. Further there is a dire need for evolving a code of Ethics on the Cyber-Space and discipline.

7

An International Convention on Cyberspace Security

Cyber security is becoming an indispensable dimension of information security. The rapid growth of ICTs has contributed immensely to human welfare but has also created risks in cyberspace, which can destabilise international and national security. Global and national critical infrastructure is extremely vulnerable to threats emanating in cyberspace. Additionally, the growth of social media (Twitter, Facebook, etc.) has created a new medium for strategic communication that bypasses national boundaries and national authorities. The global data transmission infrastructure also depends critically on the NW of undersea cables, which is highly vulnerable to accidents and motivated disruptions.

The UNGA resolution of 8 December 2010 (A/RES/65/41) deals with the impact of ICT on international security. The underlying concern is that ICT should not be used to destabilise international peace and stability.

Given the positive as well as negative potential of cyberspace, there has been talk of devising an international convention on cyber security which would ensure that states behave responsibly in cyberspace. There already exist several international conventions (chemical weapons convention, biological toxins and weapons convention, NPT, etc.) and a body of international humanitarian law (Geneva and Hague conventions) from which inspiration to draw up a cyber warfare convention can be drawn.

A pressing question to be considered in the current unpredictable cyber scenario is the following. Should India actively engage itself in international efforts in framing a treaty or drawing up a framework of coherent cyber laws? Or, alternatively, should it wait till its own cyber capabilities mature to a level that they are beyond the ambit of control regimes that may evolve as subsidiaries of a proposed cyberspace treaty?

Such a question has faced decision-makers right from the missile to nuclear technology control regime eras.

Opponents of a cyberspace-related treaty argue that even though the international efforts for harmonisation of international legal frameworks for cyberspace do not refer to technology control regimes in their current manifestations, it would be just a matter of time before ancillaries/corollaries of such a treaty may emerge which would be based on technology control regimes; and signing such a treaty would result in undermining national sovereign interests. Similar arguments are brought up in respect of the European Convention on Cyber crime, specifically Article 32, which, countries like Russia maintain, undermines their sovereignty.

The argument is that such treaties are biased in favour of the requirements of the major international players/powers and that India should stay aloof from such exercises till its own cyber capabilities mature to a level that they are beyond the ambit of control regimes. But this type of isolationist approach is extensively dependent on capability maturity model; and derives little or no benefit of the opportunities that can be capitalised by following an engagement model towards these treaties and conventions.

On the other hand, most of these cyber treaties are currently in their infancy and are undergoing development at various tier 2 and tier 1 forums. If at this stage India proactively engages with the international community in drafting these cyber treaties and conventions, and capitalises on this opportunity by moulding these cyber treaties and conventions to suit its sovereign interests, then the benefits achieved by the engagement approach would, without doubt, outweigh the potential outcomes of an isolationist approach.

Can there be a convention to govern cyber warfare, cyber weapons, use of force in cyber warfare, prevent cyber crime, etc.? As debate on these issues goes on, there is as yet no convention governing cyberspace. One idea that has been mooted is that critical systems like those of schools and hospitals should be protected from attacks in cyberspace, as attacking them would be tantamount to violating international humanitarian law. It is a separate matter whether such information systems can be marked for protection and whatever source of attack can be identified and sanctioned.

A cyber convention would be unlike existing conventions in many ways. This is because in cyberspace attribution and identification is extremely difficult and identities can be easily masked. Cyber attacks also typically involve systems located in many countries. Often, cyber attacks are silent and go unnoticed for long periods.

UNGA has regularly passed resolutions on information security. Information security summits have been held in which cyber security has also been discussed. Several regional initiatives like the European Convention on Cyber crime have been in existence for decades. These efforts can be consolidated in the form of a cyberspace convention. The key issues for consideration for a possible cyberspace convention would be:

- National critical infrastructures should not be harmed.
- Secure, stable and reliable functioning of the Internet should be ensured.
- A common understanding of Internet security issues should be evolved.
- National governments should have the sovereign right to make national policies on ICT consistent with international norms.
- A global culture of cyber security based on trust and security should be encouraged.

- The digital divide should be overcome.
- International cooperation should be strengthened.
- PPP should be encouraged.
- CIA of information systems should be ensured.
- Balance between the need to maintain law and order and fundamental human rights should be maintained.

Such a convention would also define more precisely what constitutes threat in cyberspace and what would be the basic principles of information security. It would have many don'ts, as for instance the obligations on states not to take any overt or clandestine measures which would result in cyber warfare. It would also need to define what the use of force in cyberspace would mean and in what circumstances such force can be used, if at all. How would a state react if it is subjected to cyber attacks by a state, or a non-state actor, or by a combination of the two? Given the nature of cyberspace, where attribution is difficult, these prohibitions will be hard to define and even harder to agree upon.

Arriving at a cyberspace convention would prove highly contentious. Yet, in India we need to debate openly the merits and demerits of the international law on cyberspace. Is such a convention possible at all? An Indian view needs to be evolved.

THE UNITED STATES' SPACE SECURITY POLICY: CYBER SECURITY VULNERABILITIES

The United States has the largest number of satellites in orbit, arguably the most technically advanced assets in orbit and ostensibly garners the most from these assets in terms of military advantages and civilian applications. It is also the country that relies most on these systems. Thus, although space assets are a valuable enabler of the information age and a powerful force-enhancement tool, the United States' dependence on these assets has also created a potential Achilles heel, making the country vulnerable to asymmetric attacks. Both the private sector and the public sector must therefore be proactive in protecting these assets. The question is how.

Cyberdefence of satellites

As bright objects in predictable orbits against a dark sky, satellites are vulnerable to kinetic attack. Moreover, several countries have demonstrated the capability to reach these satellites for potentially hostile purposes. The idea of protecting space hardware, especially satellites, with hardware has elicited much support in recent years in the United States. But the technological difficulties involved have shown that defensive options are limited. Offence is easier and cheaper than defence, as is demonstrated by countermeasures that can be used to thwart missile defence. Furthermore, the potential for debris created by kinetic impacts in space, including defensive ones, would have harmful consequences for all countries with activities in space. As a result, countries are growing increasingly concerned over cyber attacks on satellites and are attaching greater importance to cyberdefence.

Cyber attacks on satellites are on the rise. The US-China Economic and Security Review Commission alleged in 2011 that cyber attacks on US satellites had taken place, citing incidents in 2007 and 2008. According to its report, hackers had achieved 'all steps required to command' a NASA satellite and had interfered with other satellites too. More recently, the military is recognizing the vulnerability of military satellite communications terminals and very small aperture terminals (VSATs) used by military units. US vulnerability is considered high owing to heavy reliance on satellites by both the civilian and military sectors. Both sectors are actively involved in addressing these vulnerabilities.

Civilian/private sector activities. Private companies provide cyber protection for ground stations, satellite testing equipment and satellite operations. Hacking can include industrial espionage, stealing trade secrets and general economic espionage. The US charged five Chinese military officers with such crimes in May 2014. Private companies are working to thwart these attacks by countering not only known issues but also 'zero-day' exploits. These exploits make use of 'zero-day' vulnerabilities, which are vulnerabilities that have not yet been identified, so no patches or defences exist against them. The most effective way to combat threats from both inside and outside the network is by 'tamper-proofing' the algorithms, an approach that the military is increasingly using as well.

Military/public sector activities. Military officials have emphasized that building defences into space systems is the preferred way to approach the problem, rather than trying to retrofit or to react after the fact. But acquisition regulations are cumbersome and have already proven a hindrance, at times impeding the maximization of design choices. Officials have complained that the acquisition process for military satellites is not sufficiently responsive to keep up with the latest threats. Many cyber analysts believe that the US civilian/private sector can innovate more quickly to response to the cyber threat.

Blurring of the distinction between offensive and defensive cyber capabilities

The United States' policy is to employ 'active cyber defence' capabilities to defend military networks and systems and to conduct 'full-spectrum military cyberspace operations' when directed to assist in this regard. The term 'active cyber defence' is commonly understood to include offensive actions in cyberspace taken with defensive purposes in mind. These actions are tactical operations with the limited goal of mitigating an immediate hostile act. The US Cyber Command, the military's combatant command tasked with cyber operations, announced an increase in personnel from 900 to more than 4,000 in 2013.40 One of its tasks is to protect the computer systems undergirding 'electrical grids, power plants and other infrastructure deemed critical to national and economic security'.

Recognition of the widening reach of cyber threats across the public and private spectrum has led to several governmental initiatives to address the threats. The National Defence Authorization Act for Fiscal Year 2014 called for 'control of the proliferation of cyber weapons'. According to the Act, 'The President shall establish an interagency process to provide for the establishment of an integrated policy to control the proliferation of cyber weapons through unilateral and cooperative law enforcement activities, financial means, diplomatic engagement, and such other means as the President considers appropriate.' This followed the Comprehensive National Security Initiative, signed into law by President George W. Bush in 2008, to defend proactively against network intrusion, guard against the full spectrum of threats through counterintelligence and strengthen the future cyber security environment through education, coordination and research. The National Security Agency has begun to build data centres pursuant to the programme, including a $1.5 billion centre in Utah.

Conclusions

The rising profile of cyber activities related to space hardware, threats to those activities and consequent countering efforts guarantees increased attention to these topics in the US. The first step for both government agencies and the private sector is to sort through the complex problems involved and to identify and implement an approach that balances security with revenue, as the most secure networks can be extremely expensive. The government will probably be hindered by interagency turf battles and intra-agency allocation of resources; while in the private sector, security requirements can slow down operations, costing money and generating resistance.

There is no choice regarding whether to deal with these issues; it is merely a matter of how to do so. As Mark Maybury, Chief Technology Officer at MITRE Corporation and a former US Air Force Chief Scientist, said in January 2014, 'The single largest vulnerability of space systems today is cyber.' If cyber is indeed the Achilles heel of space systems security, then it is ignored at peril.

JAPAN'S CYBER AND SPACE SECURITY POLICIES

Cyber security policy

A major strength of Japan's cyber security policy is its public-private partnerships. Japan views cyber security not only as important for defence but also as an opportunity for its industry to improve its international competitiveness. The Japanese electronics industry, which has faced strong foreign competition, has found that it needs to develop more advanced security technologies and products in order to compete in the international market. With the emergence of the 'internet of things', it predicts an explosive growth in the necessity of incorporating cyber security protection into everyday physical objects as they become increasingly internet-connected over the coming years. The Japanese government also understands the industrial implications of cyber security: its latest Cyber security Strategy, adopted in June 2013, emphasizes the country's goal of becoming the world's most advanced IT country. Its aim is to construct a 'world-leading', 'resilient' and 'vigorous' cyberspace that leads to a cyber society that is 'full of innovations.' It also underlines the importance of a risk- based approach, developing capabilities to meet various kinds of risk by partnering with other stakeholders to share responsibilities.

A weakness of Japan's cyber security policy is its lack of focus on national security risks. Its Cyber security Strategy underscores commercial and industrial aspects but the national security implications remain vague and undefined. The document defines 'cyber attacks' in a narrow sense, viewing them as attacks on commercial or government IT infrastructure. However, it does not emphasize the potential consequences of such attacks. In other words, Japan views cyber security as an issue that concerns primarily the security of IT systems but not the underlying critical infrastructure such as power plants and the electricity grid, telecommunications, railway systems and so forth, which depend on those IT systems. Although the Cyber security Strategy addressed the importance of protecting critical infrastructure, it provides guidelines and action plans only for governmental agencies, not for the operators of that critical infrastructure.

Space security policy

The strengths of Japan's space policy include a combination of high technological standards and political commitment. For many years, Japan's space policy focused on technological development, on catching up with other advanced countries. Japanese launchers are, technologically, more sophisticated than those of Europe and the United States. Japanese satellites provide high-quality services with complex technologies. But this technological sophistication has not made Japanese industry competitive because market demand is for cheaper spacecraft that have a proven track record. Because the high cost of R&D makes Japanese spacecraft so expensive, they have not been proven to be reliable owing to a lack of launching opportunities. To address this and other challenges, the Diet passed the Basic Space Law in 2008, which established the Office of National Space Policy in the Cabinet Office, tasked with coordinating Japan's overall space policy, and created a ministerial portfolio in the cabinet to oversee it. (Previously, various government ministries had developed elements of space policy independently.) This aims to make Japanese space policy and industry more competitive and reliable.

A weakness of Japan's space policy is its lack of focus on security and defence aspects. Japan abided by a self-imposed a restriction on the use of space for military purposes for many years. Conforming to Article 9 of its Constitution (renouncing war as a means of settling international disputes), it limited the military applications of space technology from the onset. The country's space programme is centred on the principle of 'peaceful' use, which it considered to mean 'non-military' use until recently.

However, the 2008 Basic Space Law stated that one objective of Japan's space activities is to contribute to the country's national security. It also reinterpreted 'peaceful' use to mean 'non-aggressive' use, which is more closely in line with international community norms. This has opened the way for the possible use of space for defensive purposes. Indeed, the Ministry of Defence is gradually recognizing the importance of having space assets. This is particularly true in view of the nuclear and missile threat from North Korea as well as recent disputes with China'. Moreover, the country is increasingly taking part in international peacekeeping operations worldwide, and the United States is applying political pressure on Japan to contribute to space situational awareness activities as part of these operations. But as the defence ministry does not have the technical capability to engage in space programmes, space at present has a limited role in defence policy.

Cyber security and space security

The Japanese public and private sectors have a limited capability for dealing with cyber security challenges to space-based platforms. There is no institutional linkage between the cyber and space communities, and key decision-makers in each community do not realize that they need to communicate with one another. In most cases, the cyber security threat to space-based assets is thought to be preventable if the system is robust enough. The Japanese Aerospace Exploration Agency requires all spacecraft to incorporate cyberdefence systems into their hardware, but this is the extent of its efforts to promote cyber security. There is some security awareness of the need to protect ground stations but this is not focused on defence against cyber attack. Thus awareness of cyber and space security risks and the capability to handle them are quite primitive at this time.

RUSSIA'S INFORMATION SECURITY POLICY

Russia's information security concept

Russia's cyber security policies have several specific features that constitute both its key advantages and its weak points. Its whole approach, especially its foreign policy dimension, is built on the concept of information security. This encompasses a broad range of content issues, including propaganda and psychological operations conducted through information networks. In fact, the term 'cyber security' does not exist in Russian legislation or in any adopted doctrines. The Russian government used the term for the first time in a draft document, the Concept of Russia's Cyber Security Strategy, which was circulated in January 2014.

Impact on Russia's organizational structure

Russia's focus on information security has far-reaching consequences not only at the doctrinal level but also for the policy-making process and the distribution of powers within the government. Owing to information security's broad scope, responsibility for these issues is divided among a number of government agencies and ministries. The major ones are the Federal Security Service (FSB) and the Federal Protective Service (FSO), other civil regulators (the Ministry of the Interior, the Ministry of Communications and Mass Media, the Ministry of Energy and the Federal Service for Technical and Export Control) and the military (the Ministry of Defence and the General Staff of the Armed Forces' Main Intelligence Directorate). In addition, the Security Council and the Ministry of Foreign Affairs are responsible for the development and promotion of international information security, i.e. for the national approach to global legal regulation of the information space.

The variety of government bodies involved in regulation allows Russia to distribute competencies and to allocate specialized resources to achieve its information security goals. A drawback of this organizational framework is that Russia lacks a single coordinating body that oversees all major information security issues. This can result in ambiguity and an overlap of responsibilities. For example, Russia is currently establishing an information operations force ('information troops') and capabilities under the command of the General Staff of the Armed Forces in the Ministry of Defence. But other bodies, such as the FSB or the FSO, may believe that the troops should come under their authority.

A more general implication of the diversified structure of policy-making bodies in charge of information security affairs is the lack of single, comprehensive legal policies in some segments of information security. Thus far, this has not resulted in any serious failures of foreign policy issues and initiatives. On the other hand, it has at times introduced non-compliance and contradictions among domestic laws, orders, strategies and other forms of regulation. One example is Russia's legislation on critical information infrastructure (CII). At least three pieces of legislation have been proposed and debated by different bodies since 2006,29, 30 including the recently proposed legislation of 2014,31 but there is still neither a single set of legal definitions nor a comprehensive legal regime to protect CII from information and other threats. And the Conception of Russia's National Cyber security Strategy, drafted in 2013, has also introduced some new definitions for CII and measures for its protection.

Moreover, the list of federal bodies in charge of protecting CII is broad and not always definitive; this can lead to clashes of jurisdiction and the duplication of functions.

Cyberdefence capabilities

One of the strengths of Russia's information security policy is the greater protection of a broader range of critical infrastructure from cyber threats than in other countries. In particular, it is well guarded against internet-enabled attacks on critical infrastructure pertaining to information systems and industrial facilities: only 3–5 per cent of Supervisory Control and Data Acquisition (SCADA) systems in Russia can be accessed through the internet; and even then, the majority of these systems are air- gapped, or completely isolated from the public internet.

This is a direct result of a general regulation policy that follows a conservative approach to connecting SCADA systems and other information systems of industrial facilitates to the internet. By contrast, the share of SCADA connected to the internet in the United States, South Korea, the United Kingdom and a number of other developed countries may reach 35–40 per cent, resulting in a corresponding increase in the number of vulnerabilities and the level of risk.

Russia is still significantly behind the US in terms of its cyber-attack capabilities. But the situation is changing rapidly: Russia announced in May 2014 the creation of its 'information troops', which will become operational in the coming months.

Although this force, which will consist of several hundred troops, cannot rival the size of the US Cyber Command – which has more than 3,000 operatives – it nonetheless creates and provides proactive potential in the information space that is new to the Russian military.

The armed forces also have a clear advantage over most of their Western counterparts, such as those in the United States, the United Kingdom and France in terms of dependence on information systems. In the longer term, Russia's development of its information operations force may reduce the gap between it and other major 'cyber powers' such as the United States in offensive capabilities.

GLONASS satellite navigation system

Russia's national assets in outer space, including its global navigation satellite system (GNSS), are more vulnerable. Russia owns one of the two major GNSS services in the world, GLONASS (Globalnaya Navigatsionnaya Sputnikovaya Sistema). The other, GPS (Global Positioning System), is owned by the United States. GLONASS includes a group of 24 satellites that transmit two types of signals: an open signal for civilian use, which is less precise and a protected signal for military use, which has increased precision. The protected signal can contain up to 36 kilobytes of data and require up to 12 minutes for transmission. As with GPS, GLONASS is vulnerable to jamming, which is a major information security risk to Russia's global navigation system.

Moreover, the Russian armed forces' increasing reliance on GLONASS-enabled systems may partially erode the advantage that a lower dependency on information systems currently gives them over the West. In 2010, the Russian armed forces introduced GALS-M1 equipment, which are navigation devices that use GLONASS technology and can be operated on numerous models of military vehicle and weapon system. This increases the armed forces' combat potential but also brings vulnerabilities from jamming and other electromagnetic countermeasures to these vehicles and systems.

Geographic reach

The biggest obstacle to the further development of GLONASS is not its cyber vulnerabilities but its geographic reach. GLONASS itself is global but it still does not provide adequate precision (especially for military purposes) in a number of geographic locations (near the equator etc.) owing to an insufficient quantity of Earth monitoring and augmentation stations outside Russia. At present, there are 46 GLONASS ground stations on Russian territory, eight in neighbouring countries, three in Antarctica and one in Brazil. This is not sufficient for a global network and cannot compete with GPS, which has more than 100 stations around the world. Russia plans to build seven more stations abroad in 2014. But in order to provide a uniform global signal quality, it also needs stations in North America, South Asia, Africa and beyond.

This is becoming more difficult to achieve today given the continuing deterioration of Russia's relations with the West. As a result, the industry that produces combined GPS/GLONASS devices may fall victim to diplomatic battles and 'sanction wars'. This industry is led by IT giants such as Explay and Lenovo and is aimed primarily at end-user dual-system devices for civilian users. The combination of these two systems makes sense, as each system has different 'strong points' in terms of coverage and quality of signal (e.g. GLONASS is better than GPS near the poles). If Russia and the United States continue to clash, and perhaps more intensely still, and to apply sanctions to each other's satellite navigation infrastructure, the industry based on combined GPS/GLONASS devices may stagnate or eventually disappear – a disadvantage for civilian Russian users as well as for users in many other countries.

Russia–West relations

The impact of increasing tensions between Russia and the West is also being felt in the information security sector. In March 2014 the United States suspended the work of the 21st Working Group on Threats to and in the Use of ICTs in the Context of International Security, established under the US-

Russia Bilateral Presidential Commission. The Working Group was established in 2013 as a step in implementing a series of bilateral agreements with Russia that had been signed in June 2013 by President Obama and President Putin. The agreements involved the implementation of confidence-building measures in cyberspace and promoted an unprecedented level of active collaboration between the two Cold War-era rivals. Concretely these agreements would have put in place an information exchange hotline between the Kremlin and the White House, a bilateral group of experts to discuss cyber security issues, a mechanism for direct communication and cooperation between national Computer Emergency Response Teams (CERTs) and Computer Security Incident Response Teams (CSIRTs), and direct communication links between the national Nuclear Risk Reduction Centers.

The general freezing of these agreements, which might follow from a further deterioration of US– Russia bilateral relations, would show how the general political environment imperils encouraging prospects for collaboration. This is to be avoided if we want to build a global framework to counter threats in cyberspace and to overcome security challenges in outer space.

Conclusions

In a broader perspective, one of the major challenges facing Russia is the effective synchronization and integration of its efforts in information security on the levels of domestic regulation and global initiatives. Owing to the transborder nature of the ICT and global connectivity of the internet, any specific model of domestic IT regulation would be genuinely efficient and advantageous only if it were incorporated into global practices and approaches. This is why the foreign policy dimension, its future now highly controversial, remains vitally important for Russia's information security policy.

On the one hand, political clashes with the West and continuing contradictions over legal regulation concepts and governance practices in the IT sector threaten to undermine global perspectives of Russia's ICT-security paradigms. On the other hand, Russia's leadership among the countries calling for more responsible internet governance (i.e. its internationalization) raises its chance to seize the post-Snowden moment and finally promote many of the initiatives that it has been proposing since 1998. Joining forces in this effort with the BRIC states (Brazil, Russia, India, and China) and other countries and stakeholders irritated and spurred to action by the Snowden case might bring it strong support.

Changing the rules of the game globally would also enable the realization of nationwide projects such as the hybrid digital sovereignty model (from hardware to software applications level), the localization of data and content regulation. In the move towards these goals, the win-lose confrontation logic with the West and other stakeholders must be avoided, as must a digital arms race, which might result in cyber conflicts.

CHINA'S INFORMATION AND SPACE

Security Policies

China has not published a *cyber security strategy* to date. However, it has issued a number of *information security policies.* The Chinese approach goes beyond cyber security to encompass the broader concept of information security, which China defines as the 'protect[ion of] information, information systems and internet security from any unauthorized access, usage, leak, damage, modification and destruction in order to assure the[ir] integrity, confidentiality and availability'. A strategy document would need to be issued at the national level, either by President Xi Jinping or by the National Congress of the Communist Party, while policy documents are issued at the ministry level. To this end, the relevant statements of President Xi have been taken as guidance in the formulation of ministry-level policies. The present lead document is the Ministry of Industry and Information Technology's 12th Five-Year Development Plan of the Information Security Industry (2011–15), which sets forth objectives and targets and guides the development of the country's information security industry. However, the document is more of an *industry development* policy than a comprehensive *information security* policy.

The policies set out in the Five-Year Development Plans governing the information security industry have promoted China's economic growth, proving especially conducive to the rapid development of the information security industry. The issuance of a more comprehensive information security policy (or of a strategy) could therefore provide even more benefits. First, it would allow China to engage in international cooperation more effectively. For example, a more comprehensive policy could clarify the connections between information security and cyber security, contributing to greater international understanding.

Second, it could better highlight the relevance of information security to national security, thereby increasing public and industry awareness. While China's current information security policy focuses on industrial development, a more comprehensive policy should encompass national security as well, emphasizing it as a key goal. Third, it would 'enable a more proactive rather than reactive foreign policy'. For instance, although China's Ministry of Foreign Affairs created an office to deal with cyber security issues in 2013, the absence of specific policies guiding how it might respond to international situations impedes long-term planning.

Fourth, it could also form an important part of the country's declaratory policy. More specifically, by outlining what China would consider a cyber attack, and how it would respond, a more comprehensive policy could have a deterrent effect.

In a promising recent development, China may be preparing to issue a more comprehensive information security policy or a strategy. In February 2014 the Chinese government established the Central Internet Security and Informatization Leading Group. Headed by President Xi, the group is tasked with 'lead[ing] and coordinat[ing] internet security and informatization work among different sectors, as well as draft[ing] national strategies, development plans and major policies in this field'.

Space policy

China has issued neither a national space *strategy* nor a national space *policy*. The Information Office of the State Council has released three white papers on China's space activities, in 2000, 2006 and 2011, which were presented to the press by the China National Space Administration. They play an irreplaceable role in guiding the development of the space industry and achieving economic development goals, and many commentators have taken them to constitute the country's national space policy.

However, they are primarily programme documents on China's space activities issued at five-year intervals. Thus, as in the information security domain, they represent a space *industry development* policy rather than a dedicated space policy. The development of an official space policy (or strategy) would bring China many advantages. First, as in the information security sphere, a space policy would enable China to take part in international cooperation more effectively. Increasing China's transparency in this regard would bolster the country's international reputation and increase other countries' willingness to collaborate with it.

Second, in another parallel with the information security domain, a space policy could further emphasize the importance of space to national security, particularly among the public and industry in China. For example, a better understanding of space's national security role would contribute to the greater political legitimacy of space activities relevant to national security. Third, it would further spur the economic growth of China's space sector, as China's information security policies have done in the information security sector. For example, by providing more clarity on the country's security priorities, a space policy would help to further delineate the respective roles of various space actors and would help industry to better prioritize the allocation of resources.

The Chinese government has recently taken steps that may contribute to the development of such a space policy. In April, President Xi underscored the national security importance of space, citing the need 'to speed up air and space integration and sharpen their offensive and defensive capabilities'. This might be an ideal time for China to consider advancing its national security and other relevant interests in outer space through an official space policy.

Conclusions

Issuing policy (or strategy) documents at the national level brings a host of benefits ranging from greater prospects for international cooperation to an opportunity to better highlight the national security relevance of certain sectors. The Chinese government appears to have recognized this, and may be considering developing a more comprehensive information security policy and issuing a space security policy. Moreover, it seems to be preparing to issue an overall national security strategy as well that would include both information security and space security. In 2013 China established the Central National Security Commission, a high-level interagency coordination group for security, headed by President Xi, in which cyber security, space security and other relevant issues can be addressed as part of an overarching national security policy or strategy.

Bibliography

Abbate, Janet: *Inventing the Internet.* Cambridge: MIT Press, 1999

Amoroso, E. : *Fundamentals of Computer Security Technology*, Prentice Hall, Englewood Cliffs, 1994.

Augastine, Paul T : *Cyber Security*, Crescent Pub, Delhi, 2007.

Bajpai, G.S. : *On Cyber Crime and Cyber Law*, Serials Publications, Delhi, 2011.

Charlotte Waelde, *Law and the Internet: Regulating Cyberspace.* Hart Pub, 1997.

Clark, R. M. : *Intelligence analysis a target-centric approach*, Washington D.C: CQ Press, 2004.

Dartnell, M. Y. : *Insurgency online, Web activism and global conflict*, Toronto, University Toronto Press, 2006.

David Post : *The Rise of Law in Cyberspace*, 48 Stan, L. Rev. 1367, 1996.

David R. Johnson & David Post : *The Rise of Law in Cyberspace*, 48 Stan, L. Rev. 1367, 1996.

Dresher, M. : *The mathematics of games of strategy, Theory and applications*, New York, Dover, 1981.

Dunnigan, J. F. : *Wargames handbook, How to play and design commercial and professional wargames,* New York, Writers Club Press, 2000.

Erbschloe, Michael: *Information Warfare : How to Survive Cyber Attack.* New York: Osborne/ McGraw-Hill, 2001.

Fellbaum C.: *WordNet: An Electronic Lexical Database*, MIT Press, Delhi, 1998.

Frederick B.: *Protection and Security on the Information Superhighway.* John Wiley & Sons, Inc.: New York, 1995.

Froomkin, Michael : *The Essential Role of Trusted Third Parties in Electronic Commerce*, 75 Ore. L. Rev. 49, 1996.

Gast, A. P. : *The impact of restricting information access on science and technology* Retrieved October 1, 2008.

Hahn, Harley: *Harley Hahn's Internet InSecurity.* Prentice Hall: Upper Saddle River, 2002.

Joel Moses: *The Computer Age, A Twenty-Year View.*Cambridge, MA, The MIT Press, 1979.

Laliberte, S. : *Security by Example Defend I.T.* New York, Addison Wesley, 2004.

Laquer, Walter: *Terrorism Attack from Computer Hacking,* Oxford: Oxford University Press, 1999.

Moteff, J. : *Critical infrastructure, The national asset database* Congressional Research Service, Library of Congress, 2006.

Rizvi, Askari : *Nuclear Terrorism and South Asia,* Albuquerque, NM: Sandia National Laboratories, February 2003.

Robert L.: *Software Creativity,* Prentice Hall PTR, 1995.

Rosen, P.: *Policy of Cyber Laws,* Ithaca, Cornell University Press, 1996.

Sharma, Vakul *: Handbook of Cyber Laws,* Macmillan Publishers India, Delhi, 2002.

Thom, M. C. : *Information warfare arms control, Risks and costs* Colorado Springs Colorado, USAF Institute for National Security Studies, 2006.

Uday O. and Vijay K. Gurbani: *Internet & TCP/IP Network Security.* McGraw-Hill: New York, 1996.

Williams, J. D. : *The complete strategyst, Being a primer on the theory of games of strategy,* New York, Dover, 1986.

Wilson, C. : *Information Operations and Cyberwar, Capabilities and related Policy Issues,* In C. R. Service, Congressional Research Service, The Library of Congress, 2006.

Zanini, M.: *Countering the New Terrorism,* Santa Monica, CA: RAND, 1999.

Index

N

P

S

T

V

❑❑❑